Montaigne & Melancholy

Montaigne & Melancholy

The Wisdom of the *Essays*

NEW EDITION

M.A. Screech

Foreword by Marc Fumaroli

ROWMAN & LITTLEFIELD PUBLISHERS, INC.
Lanham • Boulder • New York

ROWMAN & LITTLEFIELD PUBLISHERS, INC.

Published in the United States of America
by Rowman & Littlefield Publishers, Inc.
4720 Boston Way, Lanham, Maryland 20706
http://www.rowmanlittlefield.com

ISBN 0-7425-0863-3 (pbk: alk. Paper)

Printed in Great Britain

For

Professor

Araki Shôtarô

the wise authority on

Montaigne

in the University of

Tokyo

When Thales reckons that a knowledge of man is very hard for man to acquire, he is telling him that knowledge of anything else is impossible.

(Montaigne, *Essays* II.12).

Montaigne – the 'French Thales'.

(Justus Lipsius).

Contents

Contents

A Spirituality for Gentlemen

by Marc Fumaroli

A pre-established harmony could be said to exist between M. A. Screech and the subject of his latest book. Such a precondition is rare, and even less often is it evoked at conferences on methodology in the humanities – out of modesty I would like to think. The fact is that such fortunate encounters, between the right man and the right subject, are as hard to define as the friendship between Montaigne and La Boétie: '*Parce que c'étoit luy, parce que c'étoit moy.*' Like divine grace, it is either there or it isn't, and if it isn't there, then all the epistemological scholasticism in the world cannot prevent a work born under an evil star from being grace-less. To take just one, uncontroversial example: if Sainte-Beuve's *Port-Royal* is such a triumph that is because everything had conspired to make him the right man at that moment for that subject. The great critic had just recovered from his Romantic fervour and the exacting niceness of his taste meant that he was the first to grasp the atticism implicit in Jansenist spirituality. His experience as a poet and an autobiographer (in *Volupté*), nurtured on Augustine's *Confessions*, enabled him to interpret correctly, from within, the exquisite individual nuances which characterize the doctrine and the sensibilities of each member of the Port-Royal group. Compared with that masterpiece of historical and literary *Einfühlung,* the conceptual apparatus and ambitious methodology of Lucien Goldman, in his *Dieu caché,* crush the subject rather than elucidate it. In this sense, and to this extent, any successful work of criticism is autobiographical.

Professor Screech's book is as brief as it is dense. It is written with the warm simplicity of speech, of maturity addressing youth, of one friend addressing another in evocation of a friend in common. We are here *'en mesnage'* with Montaigne. Screech's aim is not to say everything about Montaigne, and in this respect the book may seem less ambitious than the same author's epochal *Rabelais* (1979), but this implicit *'figure de modestie'* is not to be taken literally. The whole of Screech's earlier work had predisposed him, once he turned to Montaigne, to go straight to the heart of the *Essays,* and that he has done. The rest, as the Gospel has it, shall be added unto us.

What we discover here for the first time, and what Screech alone could have made us discover, is quite simply the religious dimension of the *Essays,* the spirituality contained within Montaigne's wisdom. Hitherto, and largely under the secretly determinant influence of Pascal, Montaigne's religious attitude has been studied negatively, as it were. It is a subject that has been thrust into the margins of the best books devoted to the *Essays.* Whether Montaigne has been adjudged an agnostic, or a pre-libertine or even a good Catholic for political reasons, he has passed as the very type of the secular humanist, untouched by the religious experience and *a fortiori* by that refinement of it by culture and psychological tact which we call spirituality. More recently, the tendency has been to see in him the pure writer achieving a 'secular salvation' through 'writing'. In vain did St François de Sales declare his debt to Montaigne, while a whole current of Christian humanism which dominated France in the seventeenth century was fed by the *Essays*; in vain did Henri Busson, in his *Littérature et religion* (1948), insist on the close friendship between Montaigne and the great Jesuit theologian Juan Maldonado. Pascal has always had the last word, as if he alone epitomized authentic religious experience. He had the last word similarly over Descartes, who was for a long time cast out from the religious sphere by Pascal's remark: *'Descartes inutile et incertain'.* It took the work of Ferdinand Alquié and his follower, Jean-Luc Marion, to get people to notice, in France at least, the religious and spiritual dimension of Descartes's philosophy, by distinguishing this carefully from the posthumous developments of Cartesianism. In the world of spirituality, as in that of art, the Father's house has many mansions. Questions of style, and of adaptation to social conditions, to individual temperament, to a profession, to the historical and cultural moment, all modify the *'données immédiates'* of religious experience.

As a layman and a member of the gentry, free from all vows or constraints, Montaigne was certainly no *moine manqué*. But must we conclude necessarily, from his liberated 'air', his ingenuity in sexual matters, his style and his manners, which were deliberately other than those of the academics and the clerics, that he was not, at bottom, a Christian? On the contrary, it could well be that his greatest originality, and his powerful and lasting influence in classical France, rests on his successful attempt to work out a perfectly orthodox form of spirituality for the use of laymen and of the gentry, a *liberal* spirituality quite distinct from the models traditionally conceived for clerics bound by constraining vows, inscribed within a narrow hierarchical discipline and thus ill suited to the specificity of an independent lay existence. Everything seems to show that such a need was keenly felt in the last third of the sixteenth century in Catholic circles, as an answer to the solution which the Protestants of the Reformation had proposed to this old malaise in Christendom. Granted which hypothesis, St François de Sales's *Introduction à la vie dévote* appears as one panel, conceived by a bishop for the use of noblewomen living 'in the world', of a diptych of Christian *'honnesteté'* whose masculine panel is the *Essays*. The difference between the two is that Montaigne's *moy*, which is at once the director of his conscience and the directed, takes more risks than would be allowed to a woman. This is proper for a gentleman, but it does not imply that he was unable, within these margins of extreme risk, to find the right path, in accordance with the traditional teachings of the Church.

Screech does not formulate the hypothesis in these terms, but his book provides a cluster of proofs which from now on it will be hard to disregard. By taking it upon himself to confront, for the first time in its full extent, the religious dimension of the *Essays,* Screech is in fact tackling the major difficulty. Unlike those critics who have broached the question before him, his starting-point is not the essay on the *Apologie de Raimond de*

Sebonde, although he naturally takes it fully into account elsewhere. However important this particular essay may be, it is only one chapter among many in the work, and there is a strong temptation for the interpreter of Montaigne to lodge the few religious 'ideas' attributed to him in this one place. We know however, since Popkin's fundamental *History of Scepticism from Erasmus to Descartes* (1964), that even the radical scepticism to be found in that essay is in the mainstream of the most vigorous Catholic apologetics after the Council of Trent. Screech is elegant enough not to insist on this established fact in the history of ideas: it is not his starting-point either.

He starts by addressing not Montaigne's ideas, but the roots of those ideas in Montaigne's 'experience'. Now the root of his ideas is also the origin of the literary undertaking of the *Essays* and remains the horizon of the entire work: an attack of melancholy, with all that that term implies of threats of insanity as well as the promise of ecstasy or the temptation to heresy. Screech is not the only one to draw attention to the insistent presence of the topos of melancholy in the *Essays*; it is excellently developed by Jean Starobinski in his fine study, *Montaigne en mouvement.* As well as being a great literary critic, Starobinski is also a doctor, a historian of medicine and a philosopher. Screech does not neglect the therapeutic aspects of the *Essays,* which are brought out by Starobinski, but he puts the accent on the other side of the topos: the one involving enthusiasm, inspiration, ecstasy and the *furor poeticus*; in short, the experience of the dionysiac and the perils as well as the exaltations of the soul. He shows that this zone of *véhémentes agitations* is constantly present, not only at the origin but throughout the writing of the *Essays.*

In his books on Rabelais, and especially in his superb *Ecstasy and the Praise of Folly* (1980), Screech has analysed meticulously the scholarly fascination which these extreme states of religious experience, pagan as well as Christian, exercised on the best minds of the sixteenth century: Ficino, Erasmus, Rabelais, Cardano. He has done more than Bakhtin to uncover for us the Dostoevskyan side of the sixteenth century, and who better to draw attention now to the experience and consciousness of this 'Dostoevskyanism' in Montaigne, who is in this the creature of his age? By the same token Screech is able to show the perseverance and faultless sense of spiritual *good taste* with which Montaigne broke with the fascinations of his predecessors. By channelling and controlling the disruptive energies that threatened his equilibrium, he gave to them the form of a 'civil' Christian wisdom, nurtured no doubt by the wisdom of antiquity, but softened and pacified by faith, hope and charity. Having started from a solitary *moy*, grieving and endangered, he is reunited with the universal form of man, the image of God, accepting the grace of being that image, however imperfect, but an image just the same, of divine perfection and plenitude. Montaigne appears here as the Loyola of a religious order without either vows or ecclesiastical discipline, and the *Essays* as the *Spiritual Exercises* of the modern Christian gentleman. This was to be the sentiment of the next century in France, though not that of Pascal and most modern commentators. In 1668, *Le gentilhomme chrétien,* the work of the capuchin Yves de Paris, offered, in a version different from Charron's *Sagesse*, a compendium of Montaignian spirituality for the use of the nobility.

I wish I had the space to deal with every point raised by Screech's demonstration which, in its sober way, covers the themes of the *Essays* as a whole – his setting-right of the traditional misinterpretation of the *'entre-nous'* in the essay 'On Experience' is particularly enjoyable. Suffice it to say that the book has, aside from its author's masterly scholarship, the two distinguishing marks of the truth: coherence and simplicity. There are, thank heaven, other ways in which Montaigne can and will be read, but from now on this book will be the key to any reading of him in his context, by the light of history and philology. It opens a fresh chapter in the critical 'fortune' of the *Essays*. It offers a sure foundation of the reinterpretation of classical French humanism, and among other things, of its supposed 'libertine' element, which is perhaps less 'libertine' or, at least, libertine in another way from what is currently believed.

Screech's book may also have other, broader repercussions. The founder of a spirituality for the lay gentry in France is also the founder of French literature. Starting from Screech, it is not now excessive to see taking shape the singular authority which that spirituality was to acquire in French culture, from La Rochefoucauld to Joubert, and Maine de Biran to Marcel Jouhandeau: that of a direction of conscience for laymen, more sinuous than that of the casuists, but aiming always to keep the individual *moi* within the limits – which are also an assumption – of a simple, noble *humanitas*, itself inseparable from *sanitas*.

Preface to the 1983 edition

This book has been simmering for over a quarter of a century. It embodies an approach to the wisdom of Montaigne which I have developed when reading the *Essays* with university students in England, Canada and the United States – especially in the University of Birmingham in the 1950s and, since 1961, at University College London.

Madness, good, bad or merely medical, underlies a great deal of Renaissance thought, worship, morals, literature and humour. When I was studying ecstasy and folly in Erasmus and Rabelais, I was led to find out how Montaigne came to terms with them. The case made out in this book can be resumed succinctly: the melancholy element in Montaigne's complexion encouraged him to take all forms of ecstasy and mania very seriously indeed.

If we follow the ins and outs of Montaigne's thought we can see the reasons for his preoccupation. Virtually unshaken authority took his complexion to be the essential foundation for genius. Aristotle believed that many madmen, and all geniuses, were melancholic, an assertion he explained with the help of Plato: he took the inspiration of the true genius to be one of the good 'manias' which Socrates praised in the *Phaedrus* – a form of ecstatic madness closely allied to the raptures experienced by seers, prophets, poets and lovers. No essential distinction could be made between the mania which led Hercules, say, to kill his children and the mania which inspired Plato or made Socrates the wisest of men. Melancholy was behind them all.

These doctrines were adopted and expounded in the late fifteenth century by Marsiglio Ficino (1433-1499), a learned priest who dominated the Florentine Academy. Ficino had been brought up in the court of Cosimo de' Medici, where he fell under the influence of the movement started by the Greek scholar Gemistus Pletho, who had visited Italy to attend the Council of Florence (1438-9). Pletho encouraged Cosimo to have Plato and Plotinus, as well as the works of Hermes Trismegistus, translated into Latin.

Ficino did not produce Renaissance Platonism single-handed, but most Renaissance readers knew their Plato in his Christianised version. Even scholars like Erasmus who rejected his Platonising magic were influenced by the exciting leaven of Platonism and Neoplatonism with which he enlivened traditional scholastic philosophy and Christian theology.

Ficino's world was marked by magic, by spirits and daemons, by talismans and by all the charismatic manias of Plato – which he also found in Aristotle, as he interpreted him. This was the foundation of so much that strikes us as irrational in the Renaissance – including the widespread belief in witchcraft and in revelations, raptures and ecstasies of many different kinds.

Montaigne is the heir to the best part of a century of criticism of such doctrines. The *Essays* show that he rejected a great deal of what Ficino and others stood for; what he kept he hedged about with caveats and provisos. The *Essays* wander in and out of the problems posed by Ficino's reading of the ancient philosophers and the Christian authorities. In the course of writing them, Montaigne came to terms with Renaissance irrationality and Renaissance magic, and with widespread claims to inspiration.

The *Essays* do not treat such matters systematically. The pleasure to be found in them depends partly on their apparent lack of order – a feature sometimes artistically contrived but also attributable to the various layers of text with which the reader is confronted. Montaigne may return to the same topic in widely different places or, more confusingly, on the same page at widely different dates. That is because the *Essays* are not a work expounding an established doctrine; they lead us along the criss-cross paths of a journey of discovery. Montaigne set out to discover himself. What he discovered was the human race. He came to see that local labourers dying of the plague were a match for the Roman Stoics; that Socrates, Seneca or Cato may be better than we are, but are not different in kind; that Socrates,

Plato or anybody else may teach us something as men, but nothing at all infallibly, so that we must not take them for God's mouthpiece. If we are to find infallible guidance, we have to turn away from Man to God or his Church.

In this book I have tried not to impose an order or system on Montaigne, but to tease out these ideas in a way that will, I hope, make Montaigne more widely enjoyable, as well as more understandable. The *Essays* are cited in English. So are all other works. An appendix gives a concordance of references to the original texts in modern editions.

Whenever it helps to do so, I have followed the standard practice of indicating the main layers of Montaigne's text by means of (A), (B) and (C). What comes after (A) represents the text of the earliest editions – those before 1587 and mainly, in fact, the text of 1580 and 1582. What comes after (B) is the text of 1588, which was Montaigne's first major revision and expansion of his existing chapters as well as the whole of Book III, newly conceived. Everything after (C) derives mainly from the manuscript notes and variants written by Montaigne for the printer in the copy of his works which he was preparing for the press when he died. Partly in the interest of simplicity, other variants are not given, fascinating though they are. In all cases the translations are based on the *Edition Municipale*.

I am most grateful to the Provost of University College London who, despite the current economies, found means of granting me a term's paid leave, thus enabling me to spend nearly four months (September to December 1981) at All Souls College, Oxford, where I was a visiting fellow and where this book was mainly written. These months form a period of pure delight, of uninterrupted reading and writing in the best of company, in that most delightful of libraries, the Codrington. To the Warden and Fellows I owe a debt which I can scarcely begin to repay.

Many people have helped me, not least those students who have discussed Montaigne with me in tutorial and seminar. As always, D.P. Walker and the other members of the annual University College London Renaissance Colloquy (now well into its second decade) have provided help, advice, stimulus and challenge. A special word of thanks is due to Mrs Ruth Calder who collaborates closely with me in the teaching of the Renaissance. Another is due to the scholarship of my wife, Anne

Reeve, who works so selflessly as my research assistant. The last
is due to Mrs Pamela King, who can type with speed, accuracy
and intelligence from the most daunting of manuscripts.[1]

University College London, 1982   M.A.S.

Preface to the new edition

Montaigne and Melancholy was given a warm reception when it
first appeared. It has stood the test of time. A handful of slips and
misprints have been corrected for this new edition. The Concordance at the end has been expanded to include references to my
translation of the *Essays*.[2]

Meanwhile an exciting discovery has been made. The most
quoted poem in the *Essays* is *On the Nature of Things* by Lucretius,
the Roman poet who thought like a Greek. Montaigne's own copy
has turned up in England covered with his copious notes. They
have now been studied and transcribed.[3] Lucretius is a major
source of our knowledge of Epicureanism. He was convinced that
the senses form our only gateway to knowledge. He loathed super-
stition – and all the religions he knew were superstitions for him.
His outlook was intuitively akin to that of many a nineteenth-
century natural scientist. He was also a very great poet. Montaigne's first copious notes – in Latin – were made before 16 October
1564. Many more, in French, were added later. Montaigne's learned
leisure in retirement brought to a head his attack of melancholy.
Did long studying of Lucretius contribute to the build up of that
melancholy humour? Probably. It certainly influenced his life.

Montaigne's *Lucretius* helps to deepen our appreciation of his
masterpiece. Nothing in it entails any modification to the themes
of this book.

Wolfson College, Oxford   M.A.S.
The Feast of Lancelot Andrewes, 1999

[1] This book has been so written that the footnotes can be entirely ignored by
those who do not want to go into technicalities.

[2] The hardback edition is published by Allen Lane, the Penguin Press; the
paperback edition by the Penguin Classics. The pagination is the same for both.

[3] M.A.S., *Montaigne's Annotated Copy of Lucretius. A transcription and study
of the manuscript, notes and pen-marks. With a Foreword by Gilbert de Botton.*
Droz, Geneva, 1998.

CHAPTER ONE

Originality

1. Curiosity

Montaigne was a man of rare originality – the kind of man who, if he had been a professional philosopher, could have turned the philosophy schools upside down. He stands astride the gap separating Rabelais and Shakespeare, but, while Rabelais and Shakespeare partly share a common view of the universe now long discarded, he seems to inhabit a world whose intellectual assumptions are close to our own. Indeed the way Montaigne thought has profoundly influenced ways of thinking right up to the present – both directly and through thinkers as diverse as Pascal and Francis Bacon. But this very 'modernity' can be misleading: for all his originality, Montaigne was very much a man of his time.

Montaigne's family was noble, though not venerably so. He was a Macmillan among Douglas Homes. As Michel Eyquem he was born on the family estates at Montaigne near Bordeaux on 28 February 1533. Rabelais was then probably in his fifties, with *Pantagruel* published and *Gargantua* on the stocks. Michel Eyquem, sieur de Montaigne, died – still at Montaigne – on 13 September 1592, some five months before his sixtieth birthday; the youthful Shakespeare then had nearly all his plays still to write. Rabelais's *Chronicles*, like Shakespeare's plays, mirroring the convictions of many of the best thinkers of their age, found room for witches with real powers, for enigmatic prophecies, for portents, for impressive magic, good or bad, for spirits and daemons who guided wise men, for inspired charismatic fools, for a constant overlapping of the human, the superhuman and the

divine. At one extreme man might rise above humanity to
angelic heights; at the other, he might open the way to the devil
or sink below humanity to the level of the beast. Neither
Rabelais nor Shakespeare sensed the natural limits of humanity
as sharply as Montaigne came to do. In the end Montaigne
discarded absolutely the notion that natural man, in his wisdom,
can or should aspire to rise above humanity. On the other hand
there is no room in Montaigne for naturally brutish Calibans, or
for Othello's

> ... Cannibals that each other eat,
> The Anthropophagi and men whose heads
> Do grow beneath their shoulders.

Montaigne, especially when it suited him in a sceptical mood,
was prepared to put other people's credulity to good use. This is
particularly true of his delightfully paradoxical 'Apologia for
Raimond Sebond'. Pliny and Herodotus were notoriously
gullible; Montaigne cited them – 'if you will believe them' – for
tall stories (which even Pliny doubted) about 'species of men in
some places which have very little similarity to our own', and for
'half-breed, ambiguous forms between human nature and beasts'
(II. 12, p.259). In fact the world as Montaigne conceived it
contained no strange savages remotely like that. On the
contrary, he came to insist on the unity of the species 'Man', and
on the 'humanity' of every single human creature.

Montaigne took little on trust, whether in book, legend or
traveller's tale. He wanted to find things out for himself. He
would visit men and women with strange deformities; he did not
find them to be 'monsters' – miraculously 'demonstrative' signs
from God, that is – but human beings of interest to doctors (not
soothsayers) and within the infinitely varied orders of creation,
even if they did seem to have something wrong with them. He
went to see self-confessed witches in their prison-cells and found
them to be silly old women, deluded but not diabolical; it was
more likely, he thought, that an old woman should be mad, than
that she should be able to ride about on a broomstick (III. 11,
p. 316). In the same spirit he was not put off by the horror evoked
by the name of Cannibal. Many thought of these creatures
(whom Cardano for example dubbed the 'Anthropophagi, whom
we now call Cannibals') as uncouth, barely human savages who

farmed children for food on slave-women. (They were, Cardano thought, rather like Scottish highlanders.) Montaigne did not accept such notions. He did his best to find out what Cannibals were really like by reading and inquiry. (As for Scotsmen, he had been taught by one of the best of their humanists, George Buchanan.) Montaigne found that Cannibals were not sub-human beasts, wallowing in the forbidden delights of human flesh; they were warriors performing a liturgy of ritual vengeance – an act humanly understandable and far less bestial than French cruelties in the Wars of Religion or Spanish barbarity in the New World. He was more inclined to idealise the savages than to condemn them. He saw Cannibals as men and women closer than moderns were to the simple goodness of the Golden Age of the poets. Give Montaigne the chance to question through an interpreter a couple of Cannibals brought to France from the Americas, and he soon has them showing the beauty of their poetry – and making criticisms of the French monarchy so devastating that Gallic insularity was reduced to impotent sneers: 'Not bad; but they don't wear breeches' ...

2.   Doubt

Montaigne throve on doubt, on uncertainty, on an endless search for truth. He was not alone in his grasp of scepticism as an intellectual tool; scepticism was in vogue among Roman Catholics as a defence against Protestants who sought to subvert them with arguments they could not answer. In such cases, the only safe reaction was to demolish reason and scholarship entirely – both theirs and yours, while clinging, by faith, to the Church alone. Christian scepticism was Catholic scepticism.

The fifteenth and sixteenth centuries experienced assault after assault on inherited certainties – assaults from classical literature made widely available; from Church Fathers edited and translated; from original texts of the Scriptures, translated, glossed and preached upon; from rival schools and methodologies within every university discipline, not least philosophy; from New Worlds discovered and from the Old Worlds of China and Japan, with all the troubling impact of their venerable cultures based on premises other than those of Jerusalem, Athens and Rome.

Montaigne was not a pure sceptic – he found too much to

admire in Stoicism and Epicureanism for that – but he also found scepticism a good prop to his faith in the Old Religion as taught by 'the Catholic, Apostolic and Roman Church'. He also found scepticism a stimulus. He delighted in the ancient sceptical authors – in Sextus Empiricus (whose writings had finally been printed and translated in the 1560s), in that most sceptical of Biblical works, Ecclesiastes, and in Cicero's *Academics*. He also knew the moderns – Pico della Mirandola, for example, and Cornelius Agrippa; he borrowed much from Agrippa's declamation *On the Vanity of all learning and on the Excellence of God's Word* when developing his 'Apologia for Raimond Sebond' – the chapter which gives full scope to his Catholic scepticism (II. 12).

Montaigne was a hard man to convince. He found no ultimate certainty in any branch of human inquiry. If scholars claimed to base their certainties on natural reason, Montaigne emphasised his mistrust of all human reason when working by itself, without the guidance of divine grace. Even Copernicus's theory did not impress him over much: somebody would eventually come along with another one. As, of course, they did: the stately circular motion of Copernicus's planets was soon to be superseded by Kepler's discoveries.

Claims to human knowledge based on *experience* – experience and experiment, that is – he found just as uncertain as those based on reason; if anywhere, experience should be on its own dunghill in medicine, and yet doctors disagreed about the simplest matters. Experience was evoked as 'the Certain Master in uncertain things'. Not, however, by Montaigne. Man is finite, truth is infinite; so our experience will always fall short. We can never know enough to talk of certainty, solidly based, about any subject whatever – unless, that is, we can enjoy revelation. In most matters Montaigne was sure that we cannot.

3.   The good life

In terms of Renaissance science he was of course right. Schoolchildren nowadays see the error of much of what was then taught as fact. But Montaigne had wider ambitions than simply to demolish the pretentions of the doctors and natural scientists of his day. His main concern was with ethics. He wanted to find out, by human inquiry, how he should live and how he should

die. The Church supplied the answers in her own terms.
Montaigne, especially after the Roman censors gave a friendly
jog to his arm, protested his complete acceptance of her
conclusions and then – in the *Essays* – set them firmly aside, to
be brought in when solutions were sought, not at the outset or
when he was enjoying the chase. He acknowledged his Church's
right to censor, but he also asserted that Theology (with a capital
T) best kept her dignity by remaining apart from the mere
humanities. As a humanist he enjoyed seeking after truth, even
though truth, by human means alone, can seldom if ever be
found within this life. Such an attitude strikes some as insincere,
as though Montaigne were writing tongue-in-cheek. But
Montaigne, in one respect, shared something with those
university Aristotelians who were called Nominalists. They, like
him, maintained that human inquiries and Theology were better
kept apart for their mutual good. Then Theology could display
her truths and have them accepted on the Church's impregnable
authority, while human inquiry proceeded to explore doubtless
lesser truths in humbler and more tentative ways. Of course,
such a claim opens the way to cynical lip-service to one sort of
truth and a real concern with the other. That is not, however, the
essence of this claim.

Aristotle lies behind some of Montaigne's most novel
conclusions, for Montaigne was original but not timeless. He
thought mainly with the tools of inquiry which Renaissance
philosophy gave him.

The scepticism is obvious enough to anyone who reads the
Essays. Following a long tradition, stemming from Plato,
Montaigne used the word 'opinion' mainly for convictions resting
on grounds insufficient to establish them with certainty. Opinion
(*doxa*) was typical of the limited wisdom and knowledge of
mankind lodged in a sublunary world of change, decay,
disintegration and coming-into-being. To find certainty – not
mere opinion – one needed to have access to permanent, stable
truths which are not subject to the flux of the world and of
humankind. Claims of mere men to have access to such
unchanging truths were more and more distrusted by
Montaigne. He contrasted particularly sharply human opinion
on matters of religion – the opinions, say, of even the wisest and
most pious pagans – with the shining certainties of divine
revelation vouched for by the Church. There is no room for

opinion within Christian truth; there is room for little else within all the human disciplines put together.

4.   The self

Of Montaigne's originalities none was greater than his decision to write about himself, to make himself the central subject of a constantly expanding book. The idea did not come to him all at once. Originally the *Essays* were conceived on a much more modest scale. At first he was content to write down his reactions to particular pieces of conventional wisdom or controverted assertions. Soon he was so disturbed by strange fancies that he decided to write them down too. Later, he thought he would leave behind a portrait of himself in words for his family to remember him by. (Self-portraiture was a feature of some Renaissance painters: Montaigne was probably influenced by their example.) His last step was to believe that by studying himself he could find out what the nature of mankind really was and so how he, or anyone else, should wisely live and wisely die, in accordance with Nature's leadership alone.[1]

Montaigne's decision to write about himself merits not only the approval implied by the word 'original' in English but the oddness implied by *'original'* in French. Nobody in Western culture had ever done what Montaigne set out to do. A thousand years earlier, it is true, Augustine had given a partial portrait of himself in his *Confessions*, but the Renaissance placed that work far below the *City of God*. Montaigne may not even have read it, though he certainly read the *City of God* and cites it. The *Confessions* lead from Manichaeism to Catholicism, and show the effects of original sin on fallen man. Montaigne was not exploring himself in that way. It was precisely natural man – fallen man no doubt – which interested him and which led him

---

[1] That the wise man follows the footsteps of Nature, the best of Guides, is a commonplace going back especially to Cicero but also to Seneca. There was no necessary opposition between the claims of Nature and those of God; for many Renaissance Christians, including Montaigne's beloved Etienne de la Boëtie, Nature was God's minister to whom were delegated general powers. Barthelemy Aneau includes an emblem to this effect in his *Picta Poësis* (Lyons, 1568, p. 59). The emblem asserts that 'Nature, the best of Guides, is to be followed' (*Natura optima dux sequenda*). Aneau explains that to struggle against Nature (*reluctari Naturae*) is to act like the foolish giants in the Greek fable and rashly to fight against God (*'et temerè pros Theon antimachein'*).

from a study of himself as man to a study of mankind as a whole.

Aesop had condemned self-love (*philautia*) as the prime source of human error. Self-love, so the Latins said, was blind. The authoritative commonplaces which conveyed these moral imperatives are given, with commentaries, in Erasmus's *Adagia* (1.6.85ff. – Rabelais drew upon many of them for the *Tiers Livre de Pantagruel*, making them even more widely known). Christians of all persuasions had made these ideas part of their own moral system, equating *philautia* with the Old Adam in man. To write about yourself without overwhelming cause was to stand condemned by towering and august authority, both ancient and modern. A few Renaissance authors were tentatively beginning to breach this interdict. Montaigne went far beyond them; yet there was nothing narcissistic about his study of himself. He came to believe that such a study provided him with the only effective way of assaying the worth of moral teachings or examples. The words or deeds of even Socrates, Plato, Aristotle, Alexander the Great, Epaminondas, Cato, Seneca or Cicero are weighed against Montaigne – and Montaigne is weighed against them. He was a judge who prided himself on schooling his power of judgment, and who strove to be fair and to compensate for the blindness which self-love entails. A prerequisite of his work was truth. If self-love led him to flatter himself or devalue others, his enterprise would collapse like a pack of cards.

Montaigne felt the full force of the oddness of his undertaking. So did many of his contemporaries, including those who read him with fascination. That he persisted, and brought his *Essays* to a conclusion in a work which has delighted and instructed readers ever since, is proof of his emotional balance and of his sanity. Yet he feared that there was an element of madness in what he had taken on. Other men turning in upon themselves have indeed produced monsters, not manifest wisdom. The Rousseau of the *Rêveries*, for one. Yet Montaigne's *Essays* arose from wild *rêveries* too. There is, of course, a paradox in claiming to study yourself, and a danger in trying to do so. What part of you can conceivably stand apart and weigh you up dispassionately and fairly? Montaigne reduced tensions and avoided unbalanced judgments partly by refusing the temptations of naked introspection. To study himself he ceaselessly studied others, past and present – what they did, what they said, what they wrote, what they were like in repose, in crisis,

in death, and how their comportment when dying corresponded to
their lives and doctrines. All this matter he 'brought home' to
himself. He peopled his solitude, in the end, with something other
than wild fantasies: with thoughts about himself in relation to all
sorts and conditions of men. Rousseau came to believe that he was
alone of his kind – overflowing with love, hated, yet impassable
like God himself. Montaigne took the opposite road, which, he
found, led him to think little of himself and to bring all men and
women together, in their confusing variety, within the wide span
of humankind and to laugh out of court anyone mad enough to
draw comparisons between himself, a creature, and his Creator.

The conclusions seem so wise – and the winding paths of the
Essays are so fascinating – that it is easy to forget that
Montaigne had moments of great misgiving about what he was
doing. His worries were not random or vague; they were quite
specific. Indeed it was because of an association of ideas in which
insanity played a part that Montaigne was led to write the
Essays, a book 'consubstantial with himself'. These associated
ideas derive from theories of melancholy and its effects.

CHAPTER TWO

Genius

1. The nature of genius

A Renaissance author setting out to question the received
wisdom of his day had far from finished his task when he had
demolished faith in reason and experience. What he had to
tackle were revelatory ecstasies. From the outset ecstasies play a
preponderant rôle in Christianity. Without ecstasy, Paul's
teachings as an apostle have no authoritative foundation.
Montaigne had to come to terms with religious ecstasy, and with
many other kinds as well. Huge claims to infallible knowledge
depended on their reality: no discipline taught in school or
university was without its authorities, who were often venerated
sages from remote antiquity. Many maintained that these
authorities were inspired geniuses, specially gifted men to whom
wisdom or knowledge had been unveiled during ecstasies.
Genius, since Plato and especially Aristotle, was believed to be a
privileged capacity for experiencing ecstasies and profiting by
them.

All Christians affirmed the reality of the revelatory ecstasies of
the Apostles – but, from the earliest times, disagreed about those
claimed for pagans. In the mediaeval universities, Abelard and
Roger Bacon taught that 'special illuminations' had been
vouchsafed to Pythagoras, Socrates, Plato and Aristotle, in order
to bestow divine sanction on to their doctrines. Others such as St
Bernard or Duns Scotus limited such claims or rejected them. The
quarrels continue through the Renaissance; for Erasmus the great
pagans are inspired forerunners of Christianity; for Rabelais, all
true learning in all disciplines is 'manna from heaven'. That was a
standard humanist doctrine.

This view of genius depends upon a theory of man's nature which was widely held, being accepted by doctors and lawyers with as much certainty as by philosophers and theologians. Man, it was thought, was composed of body and soul. The body tied man to the earth and made him akin to the beasts: the soul had affinities with the divine and linked him with the angels. Geniuses are the men or women whose souls at least partially detach themselves from the restraints and pollution of their bodies; while in this state they may be influenced by good spirits or glimpse divine Truth and Beauty. More sinister, such people can also be possessed by evil spirits. Or they may be mad.

Christianity came to limit spiritual possession to diabolical forces, though Platonic doctrines – which do not so limit them – proved very resilient; belief in good daemons was widespread during the Renaissance in the highest intellectual circles. More at home with traditional Christianity is the belief that the soul, once freed from the restraints of its body, catches glimpses of the divine; in specially privileged cases it may even become for a while 'one with God'. These ideas are Greek in origin. By New Testament times they had found their way into Latin and Jewish thought. With such modifications as orthodoxy required they became widely accepted by the Fathers of the Church. Christian mysticism depended upon these doctrines. By returning to the sources, Renaissance scholars gave them a new and vigorous life in almost every field of human activity.

Not all ecstasies were high, spiritual ones: the soul might strive to leave its body for many different reasons. Ecstasies of various sorts were a common experience. Drunkenness was a form of ecstasy; so was falling in love; so were sexual climaxes; so was bravery on the field of battle; so was scholarly devotion to selfless inquiries; so was poetic inspiration; so were the revelations which made Socrates, say, and Hippocrates the authorities they are; so too were several kinds of madness, which share some spiritual powers with genius itself. 'Ecstasy' covered them all.

2.   Genius and melancholy

Most studies of the *Essays* bring out the stages on Montaigne's journey towards wisdom and self-discovery: his critical interest in the Stoics, Sceptics and Epicureans; his wide reading of Latin literature – and of Greek in Latin or French translation; his passion for Latin poetry and for Plutarch's prose in Amyot's French; his unique friendship for Etienne de la Boëtie; his travels in Europe (especially Italy); the effect on his thought of the new horizons opened by the discovery of the East, the Antipodes and the Americas.

This book looks at the *Essays* from a different point of view. It goes back some thirty years to a day in the early 1950s when I was troubled by misrepresentations of the final pages of the *Essays*. These misrepresentations are still common. If they were minor it would not matter. As it is, they distort some of the most challenging pages of an attractive writer and thinker who delights undergraduates, in my experience, more than any other. As so often, the problem is one of context, and of the meanings of words and of the force of the allusions to authoritative commonplaces. Towards the end of the *Praise of Folly*, for example, Erasmus, enthusiastically championing a form of ecstasy all but indistinguishable from madness, alluded to I Corinthians 2:9: 'Eye hath not seen, nor ear heard, neither have entered into the heart of man, the things which God hath prepared for them that love him.' For a thousand years and more before Montaigne that verse of St Paul (partly because of its eventual source in Isaiah 64:4) was a standard commonplace to cite in ecstatic contexts. It remained so for centuries to come. Merely to allude to it was enough to evoke association with ecstasies, visions and revelations. Shakespeare could use it for complex jesting in *A Midsummer Night's Dream*, when Bottom the weaver awakes from his dream:

> ... a dream, past the wit of man to say what dream it was ... The eye of man hath not heard, the ear of man hath not seen, man's hand is not able to taste, his tongue to conceive, nor his heart to report, what my dream was (Act 4, Scene 1).

By mangling this commonplace, Shakespeare made Bottom give an appropriately low degree to his popular, comic vision and ecstatic transport. Erasmus and Shakespeare could count on their public's recognising the force of their allusion. So too could Montaigne, who evoked I Corinthians 2:9 to telling effect in his apology for Sebond (see below, Chapter 18, n.1.). There are several such authoritative 'ecstatic' commonplaces in the *Essays*. Once they have been noted it becomes possible to approach

Montaigne with less erroneous conceptions in mind. Some of these texts, such as St Paul's 'desire to be loosened asunder and to be with Christ', help to cut through obstacles to an understanding of the cultural world within which Montaigne explores and expounds wisdom as well as the limits which he sets to his inquiries.

It has long been possible to read the *Essays* without even recognising this cultural world. When that is so a convenient way to begin to recover the lost context would be to read in succession the last few pages of Erasmus's *Praise of Folly*, a few chapters of Rabelais (*Tiers Livre*, 37; 44-45: *Quart Livre*, 55-56), the first dozen sonnets of Du Bellay's *Regrets* and the closing pages of the *Essays* themselves. Erasmus and Rabelais exemplify attitudes which Montaigne came to distrust outside strictly limited Christian subjects; both associate authentic revelations and rapture with Socrates and mad-seeming Platonic 'enthusiasm'. In Montaigne the same associations lead to negative conclusions. Nevertheless all share in the common language of Renaissance ecstasy, with analogous, interrelated terms appearing widely in French, English and Latin. Time has emptied most of them of their force. Some pose little difficulty once this fact is recognised – they include such French words as *ardeur*, *frénésie*, *furieux*, *ravissement*, *transport* and, of course, *extase* itself. Some of the most important phrases are easier to overlook; they include terms which show a man to be 'above' himself (*au-dessus de luy*), 'beyond' or 'beside' himself (*au-delà* or *hors de luy*). Verbs such as *ravir* and *s'eslancer* often have the sense of the soul's being plucked from its body or leaping outside it; so, almost always, does the adjective *vehement*, taken to mean 'bearing the mind away' or 'depriving of mind'; so does any suggestion that the soul wishes to 'part company' with its body (*se dissocier du corps*), to rise upwards from it (*s'eslever*) or to escape from it (*s'eschapper*). Increasingly Montaigne saw this as a desire to escape not simply from 'the body' but from *l'homme*, from 'Man' as such. Any suggestion of spiritual possession – including *enthousiasme* and Montaigne's pejorative *daemoneries* – also entails a theory of ecstasy. When the soul is deeply disturbed (*agitée*, *distraicte*, *estonnée* or *transye*) the ecstasy concerned was classed as a form of *admiration* (amazement) – a common yet often vitally important variety of trance or ecstatic confusion. All of these states overlapped various forms of madness caused by the

maladjustment of soul and body: common terms for them are
folie, *resverie*, *fureur* and *manie*.

3.   Essays and assays

Montaigne did not write 'essays'. He wrote a volume called
Essais de Michel de Montaigne, and we call them his *Essays* for
convenience. *De l'experience* is not an essay which happens to
come at the ₊nd; it is the last chapter of the third and last book of
the *Essais*. Each chapter contains numerous *essais*. *Essais* are the
work of an apprentice: a craftsman has already produced his
masterpiece, Montaigne's title claims that he has not. His wisdom
is an 'apprenticed wisdom'. Not by accident, the last word in
Book I is *apprentissage*.

As well as being apprentice-pieces, *essais* are 'assays' of
Montaigne's character undertaken by himself. This gives a
special double sense to the title of his book. The *Essais de Michel
de Montaigne* are Michel de Montaigne's 'assays' of Michel de
Montaigne's form of mind. They are assays, too, of his ideas and
of those of the authors he read and of the people he met, judged
against his own. He is like the smith in the Assay Office, testing
the silver and gold, stamping a hallmark on the good and
rejecting the counterfeit. The last word of Book II is, again,
revealing: *diversité*.

Essays, in a modern sense, can be read in any order. They do
not necessarily lead back to earlier ones or forward to later ones.
Montaigne's chapters do. The last pages of the last chapter, *De
l'experience*, form the climax of all three books. They are the end
of a long quest.

The chapters of Montaigne's books are not assembled by date
of composition. The order corresponds to a higher preoccupation.
In none of the hundreds of modifications which Montaigne made
to his text is the order of a chapter changed. The final pages are
modified in the final version, but they remain the final pages. In
them, the three books of the *Essays* gather up like a huge wave
and break upon the reader in the last few paragraphs. To weaken
their force is to falsify the work as a whole. For Montaigne, at
the end of his quest, had come to terms with melancholy and
ecstasy – and so with religion, life and death, and with his being
as a man.

4. Ecstasy interiorised

Before Montaigne, generations had raged or laughed at the
universities for teaching how to argue *pro et contra* – for and
against any thesis imaginable – but not teaching wisdom. When
Montaigne cast his earliest writings for the *Essays* in the *pro et
contra* mould he was following suit, showing how easy it was to
be wise after any event. But he was soon led – by his natural
bent, it seems – to a much more personal mode of writing. The
temple at Delphi in Ancient Greece bore commandments which
had been divinely revealed, the most famous of which was *Know
Thyself*; Socrates strove to know himself. He was judged to be
the wisest of men by the Oracle because he knew one thing only:
that he knew nothing at all. Socrates is one of Montaigne's
principal models.

Today many of the great figures of the past have been belittled
and brought low. The tendency was not unknown in Montaigne's
time, but in those days it was still an awesome task to emulate
Socrates. Montaigne was confronted with a Socrates whom
many had made a companion of the saints and patriarchs. For
Erasmus Socrates was an inspired prefiguration of Christ; for
Rabelais he was a figure entrusted with divinely revealed
wisdom. Plato, the disciple of Socrates, was regularly called
divine, like his master. Aristotle might be either divine or
daemonic (a term which claimed spiritual enlightenment for
him, but not the very special revelation claimed for Plato and for
Socrates). These philosophers could be surpassed by the
Christian revelation (which in any case they had helped to form),
but by little else. As time went by, Montaigne rejected such
ideas: Plato was great – but with 'human greatness only'.
Socrates too came under criticism for just those aspects of his life
which some accounted superhuman or divine. Montaigne had no
time for the fashionable debunking of ancient heroes; he believed
the ancients to have been better than the degenerate men of his
own day in an ageing world. But the raising of Socrates or Plato
to divine or saintly heights ranged them above the bounds of
common humanity. Mankind had its limits. They, like all
pagans, were firmly within them. A few, very few, Christian
mystics might escape in their ecstasies to greater heights and
enjoy them constantly. Not so Socrates, Plato or any sage of the
ancient world, nor many in the Christian: ecstasies they might

have, but they were lesser ones, lay ones. And they exacted a price.

5.   **Montaigne's earlier writings**

Before Montaigne published a word of the *Essays*, readers could have formed a picture of him as a very special man. In 1569 he published his French translation of the *Theologia naturalis* of the theologian we all call Raimond Sebond. Sebond was a Catalan, professing in fifteenth-century Toulouse; his book claims to establish Christian truths by natural reason and the world of nature, without calling on Scripture or revelation. (Sebond was strongly influenced by Raymond Lull's theology, it seems). Montaigne translated the *Theologia naturalis* for his father, who had heard of it as an antidote to Lutheranism; the translation shows sophisticated theological awareness. Montaigne's preface as translator hints at some of his later themes, including his mistrust of 'words and language, a merchandise so vulgar and vile that the more a man has the less he is probably worth'.

Montaigne consistently contrasted words with actions (*effets*) and things. His main criticism of universities was that they were 'yap-shops' (*escoles de la parlerie*). His preference for action over words needs no comment, but his contrast between words and things may.

The Renaissance continued the old debate which went back to Plato: are words the mirror of things, or are they simply labels stuck on to objects and concepts by an act of arbitrary will? Extreme Platonists could hold that one of the ways of getting to know objects or concepts was to study words and their etymologies. There is little of that in Montaigne, though plenty in Rabelais. In the *Essays*, Plutarch, the fluent Greek, is cited as feeling the concrete reality behind Latin words, but not in a fully Platonic sense. For Montaigne, words are a *pis aller*. As for French, it changed rapidly all the time. How could stable truth be held in such leaky vessels? Right to the end Montaigne distrusted words. Yet they were all he had.

The year after the appearance of Montaigne's version of Sebond came his preface to an edition of La Boëtie's French version of Plutarch's *Consolation to his wife* – a tender piece of writing addressed by Montaigne to his own wife who had just lost a child. Such a production was rare in the French Renaissance, when wives were kept in the background. But Montaigne classed both La Boëtie and his own wife as *amis*. 'Friendship' will never do as a translation of Renaissance *amitié*: *amitié*, like the Greek *philia*, is a term embracing love of friends, parents, children, wives. Within *amitié*, the soul (the *âme*) was thought to dominate. Montaigne, a hater of novelty – 'which in truth has cost our wretched country so dear' – hankered after the good old days when man not only took a wife but married her. La Boëtie had asked Montaigne to share his work with those he loved – with his *amis*. 'I believe I have none', he wrote to his wife, 'more intimate than you.'

Metaphors based upon married love which only death can sever are vital to Montaigne's mature thoughts.

The dedication of his edition of La Boëtie's version of Plutarch's *Matrimonial precepts* is interesting too. It is addressed to Monsieur de Mesmes, to whom Henry Estienne had dedicated his Latin translation of the *Hypotyposes of Pyrrho* in 1562.

This book of Sextus Empiricus was unknown to the Latin middle ages. For the Renaissance it was the most influential work of scepticism inherited from ancient Greece. In writing to Monsieur de Mesmes it may seem tactless of Montaigne to have dismissed as 'follies' man's ingenuity in shaking received opinions which bring comfort. But Renaissance scepticism was an ally of tradition. It destroyed the validity of arguments for change, throwing man back on to traditional virtue and faith. To clever reason, used destructively, Montaigne preferred childish trust and the guidance of Truth personified:

> Not without good reason, childhood and simplicity have been highly commended by Truth himself.

La Verité mesmes is Christ. Of his triple claim to be the way, the truth and the life, Montaigne was most concerned with the second. Christ, not as man but as Truth, placed children in their simplicity above all the wisdom of the world. In the Renaissance this old doctrine took on a new urgency as it merged into the theme that Christianity is a certain kind of folly and Christians are a particular kind of holy fool. This folly of the Gospel is Erasmus' theme in the *Praise of Folly*. Montaigne read it also in

Cornelius Agrippa. Rabelais expounded a version of it in the *Tiers Livre de Pantagruel*. To some extent Montaigne made it his own in his apologia for Sebond.

Christian folly was always connected, from the New Testament onwards, with madness, real or apparent; with men wrongly accused of being insane, – 'beside themselves' or diabolically possessed – and, above all, with ecstasies. A major form of Christian folly is to live 'outside oneself' in this world. Christian folly and insane folly often look alike. There is a madness about them both.

No critique of Renaissance quests for truth would be anything like complete without reflexions on the nature of ecstasy and rapture and their place in lay knowledge and wisdom, let alone in the Christian experience.

6. The hunt for wisdom

Montaigne enjoyed hunting truth as noblemen liked hunting game, and he used the language of the chase to describe the search. But, in the last resort, truth is not to be found in men. In all Montaigne's writings only one body is allowed to resolve disputed points: the Church. And, to the end, only one person is called the Truth.

Montaigne affects a gentlemanly disdain for midnight oil and long periods of study, but study he did. His syllabus was wide enough to last a lifetime. Soon after he retired to his estates and his library tower, he set about 'assaying his natural faculties':

> What I look for in books is pleasure from an honourable entertainment; if I do study I only look for knowledge of myself, teaching me to die and to live well (II.10, p.103).

Quite a syllabus! As an exercise of natural faculties it covers most of what would, then as now, be classed as ethics, as well as some of what would then have been classed as physics and metaphysics. Montaigne's territory is that of Plato and, increasingly, of Aristotle, as well as Plutarch and Pyrrho, of Seneca and Cicero – of all the ancient Greek and Latin authors who were avidly studied in the Christian schools and universities of the Renaissance for guidance on ethics and philosophy.

Such authors, working by the fitful light of natural reason, could reach the conclusion that revelation was needed; they could even reach true conclusions about the essence of God. But they gave access to neither. Earlier generations were not so sure. Montaigne was adamant: to have access was a privilege, requiring God to intervene. Natural reason could get so far, but there was a threshold; from then on theology took over. And that was not Montaigne's domain. Ever since the conclusion of the Council of Trent (1564), Roman Catholics left theology to the professionals. It was no task for laymen. Montaigne was a moral philosopher who touched on the fringes of theology only when his subject required.

The Reformation had made the Bible dangerous reading for Roman Catholic laymen. Montaigne cites it rarely, mainly for purposes connected with natural reason, revelation and ecstasy. His biblical quotations are often loose, not rigidly textual. This was perhaps a deliberate affectation. Protestants argued about jots and tittles: Montaigne did not.

Similarly, his arguments for the truth of Roman Catholicism are those of natural reason: since truth should be the same everywhere, the variations of the Protestants must be wrong; the schismatic English must be wrong, too, since they change their church by act of Parliament; a strong human argument for the Christian religion is that Christ lived and was put to death under the rule of law. And so on. Christ is the Truth; he is also an example. When Montaigne argued from his example, it was from his humanity, not his divinity.

In the few cases where Christ is cited in the *Essays* as speaking directly he is treated as God incarnate: there is nothing to do but to hear and obey him – under the guidance of the Roman Catholic Church.

That applies to Montaigne's chapters on any religious theme such as repentance or the need to judge God's *ordonnances* with restrained sobriety. It was not Montaigne's right to speak as an Old Testament prophet or a professor of theology. It was even less his right to bandy arguments based on New Testament texts. That right was claimed by his armed Protestant opponents. For Montaigne Christ, *la Verité mesme*, entrusted such truths to nobody but his Church.

Montaigne's professions of submission to the Church carry conviction, but they do not prove anything. Nothing is easier to counterfeit than devotion – as Montaigne says himself. But these professions are reinforced in the final version; the *Essays* make good sense if they mean what they say. Some want Montaigne to convince them of his sincerity, but that can never be demanded of Montaigne or of anyone who ever lived.

Montaigne is prepared to doubt everything in his Roman Catholic layman's search for ethical truth and self-knowledge. He likens himself to the schoolmen who try out 'disputable opinions' in debate. He can be as bold as he likes: the resolution of such topics is reserved to his Church alone. But theologians can be wrong, especially about matters outside their field of revelation. Much that man seeks to know he will never know in this world.

Montaigne's *Essays* are the account of a hunt – a well-read layman's hunt for self-knowledge and for ethical guidance on how to live and how to bear that painful separation of body and soul which is death. *Quiconques meurt, meurt à douleur*, 'Whoever dies, dies in pain': Villon's line held a ghastly truth. Death in Montaigne means the act of dying. He treats it as a layman, not a priest. The after-life is not within his territory of how to live and die aright.

In the course of his happy hunting, Montaigne gaily shook many of the foundations of what had long passed for wisdom and certainty. Is that what makes him seem so modern? But the errors he had to meet head on were those of the Renaissance, and they were enough in all conscience. France was torn by religious wars; fallible men interpreted infallible books; fallible men squabbled within and without an infallible Church; new quarrels split the universities without driving out the old. Everywhere one was met by claims to infallibility or special status: by a divine Socrates, a divine Plato, an inspired Aristotle, an Hippocrates who could not err; by prognostications, portents, visions, revelations, ecstasies.

A man with melancholy in his complexion must have been tempted to join the band and stake a claim to be inspired. His humour was one which might tempt him to seek revelations and ecstasies rather than to look at them critically. Montaigne was brought to be critical by his very melancholy. How that happened is a constant thread which I have pursued throughout this book.

7. Wider doubt

Montaigne ousted ecstasy, rapture and revelation from the
privileged places they had occupied in philosophy, the natural
sciences and the humanities as ultimate guarantees of certainty.
That led to a vast widening of the sea of doubt. Not one single
ancient classical writer retained final authority in any matter
whatever. Men such as Montaigne's much admired Turnebus
were discovering the classics in context, as pagans not as
prophetic proto-Christians.

Rabelais had been unable to recognise the validity of criticism
of Hippocrates or Galen, even when based on recent anatomical
dissections. Now, as Montaigne delighted to show, the art of
medicine was in disarray as never before.

For Montaigne all the disciplines, however venerable, are
based on human reason, human judgment, human authority.
None have sure foundations; all are open to doubt and
questioning. They are matters of opinion, of possible facts to be
accepted tentatively. There are no criteria for judging some
things to be natural and others miraculous; mankind does not
know the limits set to nature.

Montaigne was born with a mind made for doubt. He throve
on doubt. The Greek Sceptics strengthened this cast of mind but
do not explain it away. It was their arguments and his native
temperament which, together, led to his stripping Plato,
Socrates and others of the divine sanction claimed for them
because of their ecstasies. Once that was done, Platonic teaching
could no longer vouch infallibly for the spiritual realities.

By humanising Socrates and Plato Montaigne did not bring
them into contempt. But he did bring them down to the same
level as other great men. If Socrates is preferred at times to
Aristotle it is not for what he said but for what he was. Students
of Aristotle were making similar points: a good example is the
Jesuit Pedro Fonseca in his *Commentaries on Aristotle's
Metaphysics* (1559, I, col. 10ff.).

Montaigne had no respect for the average product of the
philosophy schools in the universities. He oversimplified the
issues, mocking graduates who merely recite chunks of
undigested Aristotle. But he himself could not manage without
Aristotle – nor, to some extent at least, without the
commentators. Perhaps it was Aristotle who helped him to

distinguish uncertain opinion from certain knowledge (*epistēmē*; *scientia*), though the *locus classicus* for this is Plato in the *Timaeus*.

Montaigne came to wonder whether man ever acquired knowledge at all. He eventually placed most that passed for knowledge in the category of opinion. Much was simply wrong. Moreover 'almost all the opinions we do have are held on authority or on trust' (III. 12, p. 322, first sentence).

Montaigne was not prepared to be impressed by either. For example, his view of medicine was even lower than Molière's. Pedro Fonseca considered that Hippocrates, 'the founder of medicine', was 'a great philosopher', with 'philosophical truths hidden in nearly every word'; his doctrines are so unshakeable and definitive that 'for nearly two thousand years he has never been proved wrong in any but trivial matters, and cannot be accused of error'.

Such authority Montaigne simply overturned. Even the Socrates of Plato's dialogues was esteemed by most people, he thought, for the wrong reasons. Such a man would have few admirers if he lived and taught today.

From Montaigne's pen that was a challenge and a claim.

CHAPTER THREE

Montaigne's Melancholy

1. The earliest hints of melancholy

Aristotle and Cicero among the ancients, philosophers and authors of *chansons de geste* among the medievals, theologians, poets and moralists during the Renaissance, all saw friendship as something special. It was a virtue, potentially the highest form of the kind of love called *philia* by the Greeks or *amicitia* by the Romans. It bound men together at the highest level of their humanity. Centuries might go by without a single example of such friendship coming to light. Or so Montaigne thought.

The friendship of La Boëtie and Montaigne was one of those rarest kinds. Then, within six years, La Boëtie died (in August 1563). The effect on Montaigne was profound and lasting.

The death – from an illness which was 'somewhat contagious' – was ugly and distressing. La Boëtie, who was concerned for Montaigne's 'natural disposition', since the disease was 'unpleasant and melancholic', begged his friend not to stay at his bedside for more than short periods at a time.

Montaigne did as he was asked. That is the first hint that melancholy played a part in his character, or *naturel*. All versions of the *Essays* confirm it. Chapter Two of Book I is devoted to sadness (*tristesse*). Chapter Three explores the fact that our emotions may carry us *au-delà de nous*, 'beyond ourselves'. Both have links with melancholy as the Renaissance understood it.

In late medieval and Renaissance France *tristesse* was an aristocratic emotion, a sign of sensitivity and depth. Such delightful delicate sadness gradually merged into the more ambitious state of melancholy affected by many noble figures of fact and fiction. Dürer captured the mood in his portrayal of Melancholia, as did Milton in *Il Penseroso*. Melancholy also shared much with *acedia*, the pensive sloth that afflicted contemplatives in monasteries.

Burton catches the feeling of this pensive melancholy. Melancholy is as 'Albertus Durer' paints her: 'like a sad woman leaning on her arm with fixed looks, neglected habits.' Some think her proud; others, half mad:

> ... and yet of a deep reach, excellent apprehension, judicious, wise, witty: for I am of that nobleman's mind: 'melancholy advanceth men's conceits more than any humour whatsoever' (*Anatomy of Melancholy* I. 3; 1,2; p. 392).

A man who imitated Melancholia's pose could hope to be admired for his intelligence (wit) and for the profundity of his mental concepts.

2. Fashionable melancholy and sanguine melancholy

Tristesse suggested noble sensitiveness; melancholy suggested genius – no wonder so many thought they were marked by it. No affectation was so widely cherished. Empty-headed men pretended to be stricken with it; at the other extreme characters as diverse as Hamlet and Alceste (Molière's *Misanthrope*) were cast in the mould of high melancholy.

Montaigne took care to distance himself from the affectation. In 1580 he used amusingly belittling terms for his melancholic humour; he was, he said, not so much a melancholic as an empty dreamer (*non melancholique, mais songecreux*). There is an edge to the word *songecreux*, the stage-name of the best comic actor of his youth, Jean du Pont-allais.

Montaigne also displays more than a hint of the same playful mock-modesty as led Cicero to affect to believe that his melancholy meant backwardness: 'Aristotle says that all geniuses are melancholic. That makes me less worried at being slow-witted' (*Tusculans* 1.33.80). Cicero is juggling with the fact that in Greek and Latin *melancholia* covered many states, ranging from genius to stupidity and madness. The Renaissance inherited all these senses, with a millennium and a half of thought and comment attached to them. When Montaigne (as he often does) refers to himself as sluggish, heavy and slow, he is probably making the same sort of statement as Cicero – and emphasising his melancholy. As he wrote of his disposition in childhood: '(A) Beneath this (C) heavy (A) complexion I nourished bold imaginings and opinions above my age' (I. 26, p. 227).

When Montaigne eventually decided to make the *Essays* a book about himself, he was defying one of the basic taboos of all civilised society and one of the great interdicts of European culture. Lovers of self, blind to their own faults, were thought to be lynx-eyed for those of their neighbours. Montaigne took pains to show that he was not like that.

Quite the contrary. The first chapter in which he wrote about himself is devoted significantly to presumptuous vainglory. By dwelling on his shortcomings he quietly showed that he was not blinded by self-love. This lends an unbiassed air to much of what he has to say, including his account of his complexion (his physiological and psychological disposition). 'My face', he says, 'is not fat but full; my complexion is between the jovial and the melancholic, moderately sanguine and hot' (II. 17, p. 421). If Montaigne's complexion was *entre le jovial et le melancholique* he had reason to be pleased – all the more because it was *moiennement sanguine et chaude*.

A complexion such as Montaigne's was the sign of genius. His melancholy was not to be confounded with *tristesse* – that refined sadness paraded by men of fashion; at the very beginning of *De la tristesse* (II. 2) Montaigne asserted that he was 'among the most exempt from that passion'. In the margin of the edition he was preparing when he died, he explained himself more clearly: he neither liked *tristesse* nor esteemed it, though the fashionable world had decided 'to honour it with particular favour'. Men dress Wisdom, Virtue and Conscience in her garments. Such tawdry ornaments are silly and monstrous. The Italians are much wiser; they use *tristezza* to mean 'malignity', for it is a quality which is always harmful, always mad (*folle*). Since it is always cowardly and low, the Stoics forbid it to their Wise Men (I. 2, p. 9).

Montaigne realised that melancholy *tristesse* could be cultivated for the pleasure it gave. He touches on this in the chapter which asserts that none of our tastes are pure and unalloyed (II. 20). In ancient times Metrodorus said that there is always a trace of pleasure in sadness; Montaigne was not sure that he understood what Metrodorus meant, but was convinced that in his own times people did indeed complacently cultivate melancholy, quite 'apart from ambition, which can also be mixed up with it'. For them it was like a dainty thing to eat. Some 'fed on melancholy'; in melancholy there is a 'shadow of *friandise*' (as though we were dealing with sweetmeats). 'Some complexions make it their only food.'

Montaigne wrote as though he knew the taste of such *friandises*. But his account of his complexion as one balanced between the jovial and the melancholic, moderately sanguine and moderately hot, is quite another matter. It takes us out of the world of fashionable affectation into the world of humanist erudition.

3.   True melancholia

In medieval French *merencolie* was used for both fashionable *tristesse* and for serious mental illness. By the early sixteenth century these twin meanings were strongly reinforced. Throughout the century many theologians, philosophers, moralists, lawyers, doctors, poets and writers of all sorts were agreed on one essential, however much they might differ over details or implications: melancholy might lead to genius; it could also lead to many forms of madness.

Renaissance theories of melancholy reinforced the astrological aspect of traditional medicine. Terms such as saturnine, jovial, lunatic, solar or mercurial were given a new lease of life. Some played down or excluded the planetary influences, but even those who did so often used the same terminology.

Montaigne was inclined to question everything except the Church in her inspired counsels. Lay authority, however venerable, did not blunt the edge of his criticism; medical authority he laughed at; yet he never questioned the dominant theory of humours and complexions nor the place of melancholy within them. On the contrary, he explains his own personality in just such terms.

'Melancholy' was used in two distinct ways by Renaissance writers, as the name of an illness and of a temperament. As an illness it was, as in mediaeval times, used for particular kinds of madness. As a temperament it was the subject of more comment than all the other temperaments put together.

Body and soul were believed to be affected, for better or worse, by the balance – or temperament – of the four primary humours found in the bloodstream. These primary humours were liquids: blood itself, phlegm, bile (or choler) and black-bile – *melancholia* in Greek, *atrabilia* in Latin. The ideal temperament would hold these four humours in exactly equal proportions. That never happens, in fact. When one humour predominates, a person is sanguine, phlegmatic, bilious (choleric) or melancholic. Two can dominate jointly, producing, for example, a temperament which is a sanguine modification of the melancholic.

The man of melancholy humour did not have to worry too much about melancholy madness, provided he remained within reasonable limits. There was little reason in theory why a melancholy temperament should lead to insane melancholy, but since the same adjective 'melancholy' was used for both, they seem always to have been associated in people's minds. In his authoritative discussion of the subject, the French royal physician André du Laurent dwelt at length on the dreadful manias, catalepsies and epilepsies classified as melancholic, but then reassured his patients and his readers: 'not all those whom we call melancholics' are troubled by 'pitiful afflictions'. Many remain within the 'bounds of health which, if we trust the ancients, embrace a not exiguous latitude' (*Opera therapeutica*, 1627, I. 3).

Trouble started when a complexion became dominated not by the melancholy humour as such but by 'burnt' melancholy. It is this burnt melancholy (called 'melancholy adust' – the adjective coming after the noun) which so troubled Burton that he leisurely explored the topic in the *Anatomy of Melancholy*. Burton's book remains the most fascinating account of melancholy adust in any language. He believed in it and was sure that he suffered from it.

Melancholy adust, despite its name, could be produced in the body by the burning of any of the four primary humours. While Greek medicine probably restricted it to the corruption of yellow bile, from Avicenna onwards any form of the four humours was held to produce it. Burnt melancholy itself produced melancholy adust, but so did burnt bile (choler), burnt phlegm or burnt blood. No matter what a man's natural temperament might be, melancholy madness was always a possibility once the balance was upset, especially by the burning of his dominant humour. Many assumed that the melancholy humour was more likely to become adust than the other three; this made melancholics particularly inclined to be anxious about madness.

The old categories still linger on in English. We know more or less what to expect if someone is described as phlegmatic, bilious, choleric, sanguine or melancholic. The characteristics we associate with these terms derive from the old beliefs but are not identical with them. Du Laurent is a clear guide, so I follow him here, but he is one among many. Happily, to understand Montaigne's melancholy it is not necessary to go into great historical detail.

Phlegmatic people were thought to be lacking in feelings (*stupidi*), hesitant, backward, with the higher qualities of their souls sunk in torpor. They are useless for any task requiring judgment and nobility of mind. Such people ought to be 'banished to dining-rooms and kitchens'. Montaigne agreed. In the chapter devoted to education he wryly suggested that tutors should quietly strangle children who were incapable of higher interests. Even sons of dukes may best be made pastry-cooks (I. 26, p. 211). No one held out any real hope of changing humours for the better, but they could be modified.

Bilious or choleric people are subtle and quick but not profound. They are unfit for tasks requiring application.

Sanguine people delight in good companionship and friendship, in laughter and joking. They are ill-suited to graver matters and are easily distracted by their senses.

This leaves the melancholics, a category which embraces the best and the worst.

4. Melancholy: genius or madness?

Today the *Problems* are not the most widely read of Aristotle's works. Yet two or three pages of them have influenced the interpretation of human genius as much as anything ever written. Few doubted the book's authenticity: it was cited as genuine by Plutarch and Cicero, as Ludovicus Septalius points out in his commentary (Lyons, 1622, p. 348).

The *Problems* are divided into 38 short books, dealing with a number of related questions. Book 30 treats matters concerned with thought, intelligence and wisdom. Aristotle was often tentative in his answers but not in the opening question: 'Why is it that all men who have become outstanding in philosophy, politics, poetry or the arts are melancholic?' The implications of his answer remained disturbing across the centuries; the certainty of his assumptions proved irresistible. Seneca alluded to it in the closing sentences of one of his most influential treatises devoted to praising peace of mind (*De tranquillitate animi* 17.10-12). Montaigne cites it.

Among the great melancholics Aristotle ranged 'Empedocles, Plato, Socrates and many other well-known men.' If you were a Renaissance melancholic you might hope to be classed with them. On the other hand, you might be a candidate for chains in Bedlam, since Aristotle took the vital step of explaining the genius of melancholics in terms of that Platonic madness (*mania*) which the Latins called *furor*. Such people were 'furious'.

5.   The ecstasy and madness of melancholics

Montaigne drew on Aristotle's interpretation of genius and madness. He knew how Ficino had made this interpretation conform closely to what is conveniently called Renaissance Platonism. He examined such theories in several parts of the *Essays*. These doctrines are important for the understanding of Montaigne, partly because the *Essays* assume that the reader knows them; they are also important in that Montaigne's melancholy made him subject to the hopes and fears which Aristotle and Ficino raised.

Expressions such as 'to keep body and soul together' go back to a time when the reality of the soul and body as the two major divisions of man dominated thinking, in medicine as in law, in philosophy as in theology. The body and soul can be badly joined or loosely joined. The joints can be strained or come apart. Their final dissolution is death; their temporary severance or loosening can be madness (when due to illness), or ecstatic inspiration (when due to higher causes).

The philosopher who gave the highest place of all to the soul was Plato. For him it was immortal. Man dies: his soul does not.

The real man is his soul. In essentials a human being is a soul using a body destined to be discarded. The true philosopher partly discards it already in this life.

Christianity eventually rejected that doctrine; it teaches instead that the soul of man, immortal as created by God, will be reunited with its body at the general resurrection. Nevertheless the influence of Platonic asceticism on Christianity was immense, leading at times to a Platonising suspicion of the body which came close to supplanting orthodoxy. That is true of some of the fathers of the Church. It is truer still of many Renaissance humanists, who often write as if Christianity were primarily concerned with a Greek belief in the soul's immortality rather than with that resurrection of the dead which dominates the New Testament.

Plato taught that the soul is not at home in the body. It belongs to heaven. It is in the body as a punishment. It yearns to return to heaven and, in the case of lovers of wisdom, strives to do so. These teachings, especially as expounded in two dialogues, the *Phaedo* and the *Phaedrus*, underlie much classical and post-classical mysticism. Suitably adapted, they entered into the heart of Christian mysticism. During the Renaissance some, such as Ficino, can seem more Platonist than Christian. Others, like Erasmus, were Platonising Christians, probably without ceasing to be orthodox.

Plato asserted that the soul existed before it was born into this world. Belief in the pre-existence of the soul became incompatible with Christian orthodoxy about the time of Augustine and was largely dropped, at least in theory. As battles against heretics such as the ecstatic Montanists were waged by the Catholics in the second century, Plato's belief that the souls of the prophets were driven from their bodies by *daemons* – angelic spirits who possessed them – was also modified, but not abandoned. There is hardly a hint of the immortality of the soul in most books of the New Testament. The gap was filled with later works, sometimes innocently antedated. But already in New Testament times a Jewish philosopher like Philo of Alexandria was Platonising Judaism. Platonic influences can be found in St Paul; more can be read into him.

Platonic beliefs remain closely interwoven into the Christian theology of the Renaissance. One such belief is that Christian philosophers, no less than ancient Platonists, practise dying.

The chapter entitled *Que philosopher, c'est apprendre à mourir* (I.20) starts off with a reference to this philosophical 'dying', taken from Plato through Cicero. Death is the separation of body and soul. Philosophers train their souls to die – to leave, that is, their bodies, so far as they are able – in order to contemplate divine truth and beauty. This detachment from the body is made possible by the soul's kinship with the changeless world of heaven (*Phaedo* 80A-81A). The Greek fathers of the Church used such terms; the Latin fathers did too, following Jerome (PL XXII, 598). Christian mystics followed suit; such ideas were championed by some of the most influential thinkers of the Renaissance. When the soul leaves the body – or strives to do so – there is ecstasy or rapture. Rapture, strictly speaking, is an ecstasy in which the soul is caught away to God, but Montaigne and others use *ravissement* for any ecstasy, even for one brought on by natural causes.

Plato's teaching in the *Phaedo* about soul-departing philosophy became closely linked with similar doctrines in the *Phaedrus* about good and bad madness. Since wisdom is a good, men might conclude that insanity (*mania*) is bad, but Socrates denied that this was so. Plain insanity attributable to illness is, of course, bad. But lovers are insane too, so are philosophers, prophets, poets. They are insane in that their souls are all striving to leave their bodies. In the case of lovers their souls yearn to merge with the beloved; in the case of philosophers their souls yearn to soar aloft towards divine Truth and Beauty; in the case of prophets and seers their souls are taken over or driven out by spirits. These notions are not simply metaphorical.

Platonic ideas of inspiration found room for spiritual possession, posing problems for Christians who wished to follow the example of Plato or Socrates. Sibyls were possessed; so were poets and seers; so was Plato, so was Socrates. Spirits (daemons) took over a person so that he might not even know what he said or did. Christians rejected this in the case of good daemons, who do not obliterate anyone's responsibility for what he says or does. Evil daemons (devils) do.

When, for whatever reason, the soul was leaving the body or striving to do so, the person concerned was said to be 'beside himself', 'furious' or 'outside himself'. One reason why Renaissance Christianity found it easy to accept the Platonic linking of melancholy with ecstatic madness was that Aristotle (or Pseudo-Aristotle) had done so. For centuries before Montaigne philosophy was in a sense a commentary on Aristotle. In some matters of great importance, Aristotle rejected the teachings of Plato, but not where melancholy madness was concerned.

Aristotle adopted the Platonic doctrine of ecstatic possession to explain the genius he attributed to melancholics. A genius may be mad in a good sense, in that his soul is striving to leave his body in order to rise to a higher order of things. In addition he may be mad because of inspiration or enthusiasm – caused by the prompting of the good daemon who strives to possess him. Melancholy made a man or woman especially open to both.

The fusion of Platonic and Aristotelian doctrines with Renaissance Platonism was made by Ficino in his interpretation of *Problems* 30. 1: a philosopher is a man who seeks truth and beauty where they exist in stable permanence. Nothing in this sublunary world is stable or permanent; such beauty as there is is a reflection of beauty as it exists in the mind of God. So too for truth. These doctrines encourage philosophers and artists to seek ideal truth and beauty in ecstatic revelations or from spiritual inspiration. A philosopher, artist or prophet will detach his 'soul', 'spirit' or 'mind' from his body and send it winging its way aloft to the realm of permanence in the mind of God. When he cannot actually do so, he will strive to do so. Great lovers, as a step on the way to this, will have souls which leap ecstatically toward union with the beloved so as to 'live in him'.

For those who accepted their authority, the sources of these ideas made it impossible to separate melancholy genius from madness. In the *Problems*, the first example that Aristotle gave of an outstanding melancholic was Hercules (Heracles) and his 'sacred disease' (epilepsy, considered to be a case of spiritual possession). Aristotle mentioned Hercules' 'insane frenzy towards his children'; linked this frenzy with Ajax 'who went completely mad' and then recalled the case of Bellerophon who craved for solitude in places where no men were. Without a break he went on to 'Empedocles, Plato, Socrates and others', as examples of geniuses associated with melancholy frenzies.

Aristotle explained these frenzies and inspired madnesses by analogy with men drunk with wine. This was a classical commonplace; it became a Stoic one, then a Christian one. Plato, Aristotle, Seneca, Gregory of Nyssa, Erasmus or

Montaigne pass just as easily as Rabelais does from questions of drink to questions of ecstasy and melancholy madness.

Melancholics, like men inflamed with wine, may become variously 'maniacs, clever, amorous or talkative'. The melancholy humour may become heated. When this heating occurs near the seat of the mind, men become 'madmen or enthusiasts'; when their condition is not caused by illness or disease, they are the seers, prophets and *entheoi* – men like Socrates, inspired by a 'god within' (Aristotle, 954a).

These Greek ideas were transmitted to the Renaissance partly in the original but mainly through Latin translations. Montaigne used the Latin rather than the Greek. Both languages employ words which carry their own associations. In Aristotle, Heracles betrayed his melancholy 'by his *ekstasis* (frenzy) towards his children'; such melancholics are *manikoi* (madmen) or *enthousiastikoi* (men possessed and inspired). These terms require the reader to associate melancholy with madness, manias, inspirational revelations and ecstasies (Aristotle, 953a-954a).

The keyword is the *ekstasis* of the original, as that enabled Aristotle's view of melancholy genius to be associated with the Latin terms used to translate it, especially with *furor*, a word which had many meanings, including most of the forms of Platonic mania and embracing the fury of the man who is mad with anger, the frantic bravery of the warrior and the distracted inspiration of seer or poet. Latin versions of the *Problems* do not underplay the madness. For the *ekstasis* of Heracles, Theodore Gaza used 'mental disturbance' (*motio mentis*) and Ludovicus Septalius a stronger variant, *commotio mentis*. Where Aristotle wrote of *entheoi* (persons with a 'god within'), Gaza wrote of 'people who are believed to be goaded on by a divine in-breathing' (*divino spiraculo*), and Septalius, more classically, wrote of *numine afflati*, people 'breathed on by the godhead'.[1]

---

[1] The relevant section of *Problems* 30.1 (in Latin forms in which it was widely known) is given in Appendix B. For the extent to which Plato and Aristotle were taken as being in agreement over the necessary association of genius with melancholy 'madness', see for example, the authorities gathered together by Valleriola in his *Enarrationes medicinales*, Lyons, 1554, Book 6. *Enarratio* 10 is largely devoted to discussing Aristotle's assertion in *Problems* 30-1, and the nature of both melancholy and genius. On p. 428 the 'divine Plato in the *Theaetetus*' is given priority over Aristotle for having recognised that 'most geniuses are violently stimulated and mad' ('*ingeniosos concitatos, furiososque*

These ecstasies may arrive unbidden. Philosophers may encourage them by practising dying; yet even great melancholics may topple over from good ecstasies into genuine insanity – not merely into the high madness of poetic *furor* affected by the poets of the Pléiade, although Ronsard linked his own poetic *furor* to his melancholy. The madness feared by melancholics led to chains and padded cells.

But fear of madness went hand in hand with hopes of genius – a form of genius which gave special access to revealed truth. Not only were Socrates or Plato *divini* – mad ecstatics enjoying the privilege of special revelations – but so was St Paul, whose rapture to the third heaven became the greatest ecstasy of them all.

Astonishment, too, was associated with melancholy. Since *estonnement* is an ecstasy, it is not explained simply in terms of the soul's being stunned within the body but as the soul's striving to leave its body behind. Such men and women ecstatics are 'beside themselves' or 'outside themselves' for joy or fear or wonder. When they recover they are said to be 'given back to themselves' or to 'come back to themselves'. Many experience ecstasy in the sudden presence of goodness, beauty, truth, bravery or any great-souled action, especially when unexpected.

6. Montaigne's sanguine melancholy

As a man subject to melancholy, Montaigne could hope for genius and fear lunacy. In his case, genius was more likely than madness, since his complexion was, as we saw, 'between the jovial and the melancholic, moderately sanguine and hot'. But this balance could be upset. In Montaigne's case it was.

To say that you are jovial is another way of saying that you are

---

esse solere'). Democritus reached the same conclusion, asserting that 'there are no great men apart from those who have been excited by a form of madness (*furor*)'. This is linked to Socrates' teaching about inspired madness in the *Phaedrus* and discussed in relationship to Galen's largely incompatible opinions. Valleriola knew Ficino's writings and admired them but, like Montaigne, was not prepared to accept that most geniuses were inspired by divine or angelic spirits who drove them to fits of good, creative melancholy madness, raising them above the level of ordinary humanity. Where melancholy is concerned Valleriola is only one author among many, but he is a good one to read for background to Montaigne's attitudes towards the subjects under discussion in this book.

sanguine. Each humour was associated with a planetary influence; Jupiter (Jove) influenced sanguine people; Saturn influenced melancholics. Montaigne was saturnine with jovial influences. Such a complexion brought hope and assurance. It put you firmly on the right side of those thin partitions which divide great brains from madness. Du Laurent describes in some detail a complexion like Montaigne's:

> Melancholics are considered particularly capable of great responsibilities and high undertakings. Aristotle in his *Problems* wrote that melancholics are the most ingenious. But this passage must be understood aright, for there are several sorts of melancholy. One kind is entirely gross and earthy, cold and dry. Another is hot and adust – we call it *atrabilis*. There is another which is mixed with a little blood, but with more dryness than humidity. (*Des maladies mélancholiques*, 1598, p. 244, or *Opera therapeutica*, 1627, I. 3.)

Many agreed with Du Laurent that it was this third kind of melancholy alone which marked out men of genius. Indeed, cold and earthy melancholy is 'asinine'; it makes men gross and slow in mind and body. Hot and adust melancholy makes men mad, unfit for any office or responsibility. 'Only that kind of melancholy which is mixed with a little blood makes men ingenious, excelling all others.'

But probably few melancholics were ever totally at ease with their complexion. Montaigne was not. Scholars agreed on many things to do with melancholy, but disagreements there were. When pundits disagree, laymen doubt. Burton is worth reading on this point too:

> Why melancholy men are witty, which Aristotle hath long since maintained in his *Problems* – and that all learned men, famous philosophers and lawyers *ad unum fere omnes melancholici*, have still been melancholy – is a problem much controverted. Jason Pratensis will have it understood of natural melancholy, which opinion Melanchthon inclines to, in his book *de anima*, and Marsilius Ficinus, *de sanitate tuenda lib. 4 cap. 5*, but not simple [melancholy] for that makes men stupid, heavy, dull, being cold and dry, fearful, fools and solitary.

Some say that melancholy must be mixed with other humours, 'phlegm only excepted, and they not adust, but so mixed with blood as to he half, with little or no adustion.' For Du Laurent, as Burton reports him, melancholy humour

> must be mixed with blood, and somewhat adust, and so that old aphorism of Aristotle may be verified, *Nullum magnum ingenium sine mixtura dementia*, no excellent wit without a mixture of madness.
>
> Fracastorius shall decide the controversy: 'Phlegmatic are dull; sanguine are lively, pleasant, acceptable and merry, but not witty; choleric are too swift in motion, and furious, impatient of contemplation, deceitful wits.

And then we come to melancholy:

> Melancholy men have the most excellent wits but not all; this humour may be hot or cold, thick or thin; if too hot they are furious and mad; if too cold, dull, stupid, timorous and sad; if temperate, excellent, rather inclining to that extreme of heat than cold. (*Anatomy of Melancholy* I.3: 3, p. 422).

The genius which Aristotle attributed to melancholics – sanguine melancholics according to Du Laurent and others – makes men 'outstanding in intellect and exceeding others in sharpness of judgment' because it clears the mind of waste matter, makes the imagination more subtle and profound and 'when the melancholy humour is heated by sanguine vapours it excites a kind of holy *furor* called enthusiasm, bringing out unusual effects in philosophy, poetry and prophecy, so that something divine seems to come forth' (*Opera* I. 3).

It is precisely because genius consists in a drive on the part of the soul to leap 'outside itself' and leave the body behind that madness is a constant risk. Anyone whose *complexion* was sanguine-melancholic would have had cause for worry if he fell victim to an access of melancholy *humour*. Montaigne complacently noted that his own complexion normally tended the other way, towards a more 'stupid' form of melancholy which gave him some modest experience of 'vehement' disturbances but not enough to thwart his Socratic desire for self-knowledge:

> (A) Being of a soft and heavy complexion, I certainly do not have a great experience of those *agitations vehementes*, most of which

suddenly take our soul by surprise, without giving it time to know itself (II. 12, p.320).

But things were not always like that ... Nevertheless Montaigne's 'heavy' melancholy became his strongest ally against the flightier, vehement, disturbing kind. And he prided himself on his judgment.[2]

---

[2] A man's natural complexion did not exclude changes of mood – as when he was 'out of temper' or affected by an access of a particular 'humour'. Montaigne distinguishes at times between a temporary melancholy 'humour' and the 'complexion' (melancholy modified by blood) which gave him his basic character; cf. II. 12, p. 316 (V/S. p. 566; Platt. p. 346, Pl. p. 549):

(A) Il se faict mille agitations (C) *indiscretes & casuelles* (A) chez moy. Ou l'humour melancholique me tient, ou la cholerique, à cet'heure le chagrin predomine en moy, à cet'heure l'alegresse.

Elsewhere Montaigne follows the confusing Renaissance practice of also using *complexions* to mean passing humoral states; cf. III. 11, p. 313; (V/S. p. 1033. Platt. p. 134, Pl. p. 1011) – the context is usually enough to make the distinctions needed to avoid confusion:

(B) Certes, j'ay non seulement des complexions en grand nombre, mais aussi des opinions assez, desquelles je desgouterois volontiers mon filz, si j'en avois.

Passing 'complexions' or 'humours' do not supersede the basic complexion which forms a man's temperament, but they can fundamentally modify it or even pervert it.

CHAPTER FOUR

From Genius to Madness:
Torquato Tasso

1.   Poetic madness, or a lunatic's chains?

Genius may plunge down into a bestial form of madness. Such a conviction is fundamental to Montaigne and deserves a short chapter to itself.

The traditional explanation of this linking of madness and genius derives from the ancient belief that both madmen and geniuses have souls and bodies more loosely knit together than other men do.

In a short final addition to the chapter on drunkenness Montaigne resumed Platonic doctrine with a direct borrowing from the *Timaeus*:

(C) Plato contends that the faculty of prophesying is 'above ourselves'; that we must be 'outside ourselves' when we treat it; our prudence must be darkened by sleep or illness or else snatched out of its place by a heavenly rapture (II. 2; end).

Here we find the commonplaces of ecstasy, including *audessus de nous* (above ourselves), *hors de nous* (outside ourselves); they lead easily on to prudence which is *enlevée de sa place par un ravissement celeste* (snatched out of its place by a heavenly rapture).

All acknowledged that such rapture was akin to madness. Montaigne did, in the earliest version of his apologia for Sebond: from the actions of madmen we can properly see how close folly comes to the most vigorous operations of our soul:

(A) Who does not know how imperceptible is the neighbourhood

dividing folly from those lively elevations of a free spirit, and from
the effects of the highest extraordinary virtue? Plato says that
melancholics are the most able to learn and the most outstanding;
but there are also none who have a greater propensity towards
folly. An infinite number of spirits are ruined by their own force
and suppleness (II. 12; p. 212).

Genius may become sheer madness; the example which
Montaigne gives concerns one of his most famous
contemporaries, Torquato Tasso, the Italian Renaissance poet
(1554-1595). He describes him as a man 'judicious, ingenious'
and formed in the classical school of poetry, whose last years
were marked by squalid lunacy. Montaigne believed him to have
been 'blinded by the light'; the force of his reason had brought
him to unreason.

Was it Tasso's careful and toilsome quest for learning,
Montaigne asked, which brought so great a poet to such *bestise*,
to such animal-like madness? *Bestise* – a favourite word of
Montaigne's – is impossible to translate. It means silliness of
course, but also stupidity and animality. In the *Essays* a man
may be a beast in a great many ways. Montaigne included in
Tasso's *bestise* the squalor of his madness, its subhumanity.
Tasso had raised his soul to the heights only to fall below
humanity, down to the state of a beast. Madness, madness
alone, is recognised by Montaigne as the means by which a man
may cease to be fully human and so slip down the scale to bestial
status.

When he was in Ferrara Montaigne – typically – went to see
Tasso for himself. He felt less compassion than anger. He
wondered whether it was Tasso's 'rare aptitude for the exercises
of the soul' which had deprived him not only of exercise but of
the soul itself. The soul's *exercises* (in ecstatic terminology) are
the same as its 'practisings' when it practises dying. Tasso had
practised dying in order to write inspired poetry: he ended up as
a madman in chains. Goethe and the Romantics honoured Tasso
even in his madness as a higher, Platonic maniac, a genius still.
Montaigne emphatically did not. He did not even feel pity for
him. He was more inclined to feel irritation:

I had more irritation than compassion at seeing him at Ferrara in
so pitiful a state, surviving himself, not recognising himself or his
works ... (II. 12, p. 212).

Given his own complexion, Montaigne's interest in Tasso as a melancholic genius turned bestial madman is to be expected. It was a natural association for a well-read man to make. Ludovicus Septalius did the same in his commentary on Aristotle's *Problems* (p. 350). He pointed out that Aristotle was writing about those who had been 'endued with melancholy by nature', and added: 'As we know, in our own day Torquato Tasso, easily the prince of Italian heroic poets, was at times in the toils of insanity.'

2. Drunkenness and Platonic mania

Melancholy madness fascinated Montaigne; so, too, did melancholy genius. But he did not always like what he found. His interest became increasingly marked by suspicion, distrust and rejection. At first he was positive: men of genius rise above humanity by the elevation of their free spirit. Yet he did not look for wisdom there. And he did not see this as one of the ways God ordinarily speaks to man.

Roman Stoics, hard on emotion, were strangely indulgent to occasional drunkenness. In his own chapter on drunkenness ancient associations led Montaigne from a concern with tipsy excesses to great-souled ecstasies: Platonic ecstasy is a sort of spiritual drunkenness; a man's soul cannot reach the heights if it remains in its normal seat:

> [The soul] must leave it and rise upwards, taking the bit between its teeth; it must bear its man off, enrapture him away so far that he astonishes himself by what he has done; just as, in the exploits of war, the heat of the combat often makes the valiant cross such hazardous steps that they are the first to be struck with astonishment, once they have come back to themselves (II. 2, p. 20).

Soul-departing ecstasy is explained by classical analogies which noblemen could understand – in terms of drunkenness but also of bravery in battle. It was not only an analogy. 'Furious' bravery is a form of ecstasy.

In peace as in war, ecstatic souls practise leaving their bodies, enjoy their liberty and then 'come home'. When that happens men may be said to have 'come back to themselves' – the term

Montaigne employs. The immediate source is Seneca, *De tranquillitate animi* 17.11. As a Stoic, Seneca is associated less with ecstasies than with constancy and tranquillity, with mastery over the body and the emotions by use of right reason. But like other Roman Stoics he made a distinction between some senses of the Greek word *mania* and the word *furor*, which often stands for it in Latin: one sense of *mania* is madness or foolishness; the Stoic Wise Man cannot be mad or foolish, so he cannot experience that form of *mania*; but *furor* in the sense of frenzied rapture he can experience. Cicero made the same point in the *Tusculans* (3. 5).

Montaigne was long attracted by many aspects of Stoicism. Even when that attraction was at its height he had no cause to question on stoical grounds the reality or the desirability of those frenzied ecstatic raptures to which the melancholy complexion made men of genius subject. For the mass of mankind – even for philosophers – the great ideal was, indeed, *tranquillitas animi*, peace of mind. Yet Stoics admitted that there was an even higher form of wisdom, namely that good *furor* of which the *furor* of occasional drunkenness could act as a reminder. It was called (not least by Christian theologians) *nēphalios methē*, *sobria ebrietas*, sober drunkenness. But Montaigne detested drink taken to excess, and it may have been this antipathy that led him to question the desirability of even those ecstasies of genius which were akin to drunkenness. He did not intend to get drunk; he eventually made it plain that he had no desire to be philosophically or theologically drunk either. For his taste, such *fureurs* came too close to *folie*.

And indeed the distinction between *fureur* (as frenzied madness) and *folie* is not always maintained in French, or, *mutatis mutandis*, in Latin. Montaigne pointed out that poets, like soldiers, are often 'seized by astonishment' when they realise what they have done. They cannot explain how they did it. 'It is what we call, in their case, *ardeur* and *manie*':

> And just as Plato says that a sedate man knocks in vain at poetry's door, so too Aristotle says that no outstanding soul is free from a mixture of folly. He is right to call *folly* any leap upward – however praiseworthy it might be – which goes beyond our own judgment and discourse. All the more so in that wisdom is a controlled handling of our soul, carried out with measure and proportion (II. 2, p. 21).

The linking of the ecstasy of admiration with astonishment in the face of both bravery in arms and great literary creation was an important theme in Renaissance writers. One French poet, Barthelemy Aneau, invented an emblem to signify this. He called it *'stupor admirationis* from the presence of arms and literature'. *Stupor* is a regular word for ecstasy when caused by wonder (*admiratio*). It suggests a dazed amazement caused by the soul's distraction. The emblematic picture shows Pallas, the goddess of Wisdom, clad in the full panoply of a knight. The poem which accompanies it explains that great praise is due to arms and letters. In the emblematic picture, petrified men stare at Wisdom; 'so great an astonishment had enraptured' them, that you could 'take them for stones'. The association of bravery and similar great-souled actions with the soul-departing ecstasy of philosophers and mystics goes back to Plato and Aristotle – in Aristotle's case yet again to *Problems* 30, 1.

Given the way in which his classical sources had linked drinking with rapture a less independent man than Montaigne might well have done the same. Rabelais did so, holding that wine quickened the spirit. For Montaigne there was nothing spiritual about it; drunkenness is 'gross and brutal', *corporel et terrestre*, an affair of the body and earth, not of the soul and heaven. The only *stupor* it produces is a bodily one: *il estonne le corps* (II.2, p. 11). It is an ecstasy, no doubt, but a gross and bodily one – not a case of the soul rising above its normal links with the body but of the body cutting itself off from its normal links with the soul.

The reality of ecstasies of all sorts is never in question (their causes are). As type after type of ecstasy is examined in the *Essays* the frontiers of wisdom are strengthened against them. In the end most ecstasies are firmly excluded from the wisdom which the *Essays* gradually uncover.

CHAPTER FIVE

Privilege and Grace

1. Privileged ecstasy

The apostles derive much of their authority from particular ecstasies or raptures. Apart from Paul's rapture there is the ecstasy of amazement of Peter at the Transfiguration and the ecstatic vision by which he learned that no food was unclean.

The Renaissance Church rated religious ecstasy very highly. Theologically speaking, all such ecstasies are privileges. No human being can ever merit them. This applies to all grace (*gratia*) which, in the last analysis, is *gratis*; but saintly ecstasies are very special privileges, special miracles wrought by grace quite outside the whole order of Nature. Ancient philosophers were allowed to glimpse the need for them: they were wrong (Montaigne thought) in believing they had ever experienced them.

Ecstasies such as those which Peter and Paul were granted, appearing as they do in the basic texts of Christendom, were commented upon by scholars, preachers and mystics, becoming embedded in the Christian teaching and conscience. When Montaigne alludes to them he is treating matters of importance. The example of Paul's ecstasy is Montaigne's answer to an anti-religious contention of Lucretius; it was also a challenge to the lukewarm religion of ordinary Frenchmen, including, in a sense, himself.

In the first version of his apologia for Sebond, Montaigne called upon Paul's ecstasy in a very effective manner. Paul wrote (Philippians 1:23) that he 'wanted to be loosened asunder and to be with Christ'. Montaigne exploited that with great sophistication and to considerable effect, in a way which shows that he knew what his contemporary theologians made of it:

> (A) Those great promises of everlasting blessedness – if we were to receive them as having authority like that of a philosophical discourse, we would not hold death in such horror as we do. 'I wish to be loosened asunder,' we would say, 'and to be with Jesus Christ.' The force of the discourse of Plato on the immortality of the soul led some of his disciples to death, so as to enjoy more promptly the hopes which he gave them (II.12, p. 149).

To deal first with the appeal to Paul: this text was taken to mean that, although he would go on living for the sake of his flock, he really wished to die, so as to enjoy more fully the blessedness he had known in his rapture. Paul wrote of 'having the desire to be loosened asunder' – in the Latin Vulgate, (*desiderium habens dissolvi*. The force is in the verb, *dissolvi*, What is being 'loosened asunder' is the soul from the body. The Vulgate text lies behind this passage of Montaigne, but a little indirectly, since the expression long used in Latin to refer to Paul's yearning for the ecstasy of death was regularly simplified to *cupio dissolvi*. That is the source of Montaigne's version, *je vueil estre dissout*: 'I want to be loosened asunder.'.

Montaigne appealed to this same text of Paul in the chapter devoted to 'a custom of the island of Cea', in which there is much discussion of suicide. Montaigne makes, more fully, the same association of ideas as in the apologia for Sebond:

> (A) But one may sometimes desire death out of hope for a greater good. 'I want', said St Paul, 'to be loosened asunder so as to be with Jesus Christ', and 'Who shall deliver me out of these bonds?' Cleombrotus Ambraciota, having read the *Phaedo* of Plato, entered into so great a yearning for the life to come that, without further cause, he cast himself into the sea (II.3, p. 37).

This was an important point for Montaigne: such a 'voluntary sundering' of body and soul gives the lie to those who say that the desire to die means sinful despair. There can be not despair but solid judgment based on burning hope. A warrior bishop who threw himself into the heat of battle under St Louis exemplified this.

What, then, about the Christian interdict on suicide, which Montaigne is often said to have tossed aside in favour of a stoical admiration for suicide in its proper place? Was that old bishop a

Platonist or a Stoic, not a Christian? That question cannot be answered without looking at what Renaissance teaching on the subject of suicide really was; Montaigne, far from being bold or whimsical, is simply following – in detail – Renaissance theologians. Others beside Montaigne linked Paul's *cupiò dissolvi* with Cleombrotus, the impetuous young Platonist who leapt to his death and the world of the spirit. The reformed theologian Simon Goulart does so in a work translated in English in 1621 as *The Wise Vieillard* (p. 170f.); he insists, however, that Plato would never have approved of Cleombrotus and that true consolation is to be found in Paul: 'It is to be unshackled and delivered out of a galley or prison, to be with Christ (Philippians 1:23).' The Franciscan court preacher Boucher made somewhat similar points in 1628 in his *Triomphes de la Religion Chrestienne* (p. 794). But Montaigne's linking of Paul and the example of Cleombrotus may be found, used exactly as he does, in theologians nearer to his own heart than Goulart or Boucher. Indeed the association of Cleombrotus with the two verses of Paul alluded to in the *Essays* shows that Montaigne was writing within an established tradition. Montaigne's reproach to Christians for not even receiving the promises of the true religion with the zeal shown by others for mere philosophical promises can be thrown into relief by excellent theologians. For example, the *Exposition* of Thomas Aquinas by Bartholomew of Medina of the order of preachers explains that we abhor death through our 'sensitive appetite', since that appetite knows nothing of the world to come. 'But it is right that we should seek death through our rational appetite', out of desire for that 'perfect blessedness' which cannot be had in this mortal life. 'That is why many philosophers promptly killed themselves in order to acquire this happiness, even though they only had a very tenuous knowledge of it.' Cicero's *Tusculans* are cited to show this, because of his mention of the 'man named Ambrosiastes ... who cast himself into the sea after reading Plato's book on the immortality of the soul.'

> But to pass over these, which are uncertain, St Paul, most truly, in I Philippians, says *cupio dissolvi*, 'I wish to be loosened asunder and to be with Christ'; and in Romans 7: 'wretched man, who will free me from this body of death?'

Ambrosiastes and Cleombrotus Ambraciota are the same man. Montaigne also alludes to Romans 7:24, though more loosely. 'This body of death' is cited as 'these bonds' (*ces liens*). This is a conflation of Paul with standard Platonic-Christian vocabulary, found also in Bartholomew of Medina (*Expositio in IIam IIae*, 1588, p. 302).

It is not impossible that Montaigne took his material from this commentary on Aquinas, who was in his mind in the apologia for Sebond, since 'Adrien Tournebus, who knew everything', assured him that Sebond's book was the 'quintessence of Aquinas' (II. 12, p. 143). At all events there is no difficulty about reconciling the protestations of Roman Catholic orthodoxy in the *Essays* with the attitudes of Montaigne towards suicide. On the contrary, his attitudes are exactly what one would expect them to be at the time that he wrote.

But man is 'loosened asunder' in death as in ecstasy. This enabled Montaigne to use the exclamation of St Paul also against classical pessimism. It gave force to his interpolation of a quotation from Lucretius in the 1588 edition of the apologia for Sebond, immediately before alluding to *cupio dissolvi. Dissolvi* is classical as well as Christian in the sense of the loosening asunder of soul and body; so Montaigne wryly associated a sceptical verse of Lucretius with the joyful confidence of Paul. The juxtaposition of classical irreligion and Paul's ecstatic yearnings is a fruitful one: The passage, as expanded, now reads:

(A) Those great promises of everlasting blessedness – if we were to receive them as having authority like that of a philosophical discourse, we would not hold death in such horror as we do.

(B) *Non jam se moriens dissolvi conquereretur*
Sed magis ire foras, vestémque relinquere ut angis
Gauderet, praelonga senex aut cornua cervus.

[The dying man would not then complain that he is being loosened asunder, but would rather rejoice to be 'going outside', like a snake casting off its skin, or an old stag casting off his overlong antlers.]

(A) '*Je vueil estre dissout*', we would say, 'and to be with Jesus Christ' ...

Lucretius, scoring points off believers who are afraid of dying, asserted what would happen if men really believed in eternal bliss: when dying, no one would complain of being loosened asunder. Montaigne assumed that his readers knew a Biblical tag as current as *cupio dissolvi* and so jumped a step in his argument. Instead of citing *cupio dissolvi* in Latin, translating it and attributing it to St Paul, he simply assumes that we know it; without explanation he alludes to the traditional French version, *je vueil estre dissout*, which, indeed, all but the illiterate must have known. But it is the unstated Latin verb *dissolvi* which links St Paul's *estre dissout* to Lucretius, so making the dutiful Paul – who felt poignantly the desire to die, but who went on living for his flock – into a powerful reply to Lucretius and his sarcastic pessimism.

Paul's privileged rapture also shows how far ordinary Christians fall below the saints. As Montaigne put it, 'We are Christians by the same title that we are Perigordins or Germans.' The point is a sharp one: Germans suggest Lutherans; Perigordins suggest Roman Catholics. For many this is all that religious differences mean; yet zealous Christians should be yearning, like St Paul, to die, even though they go on living because it is their duty to do so.

Before the end of the *Essays* Montaigne became less demanding of others – and of himself. In fact he turned all this upside down. His praise of suicide is nevertheless quite orthodox. Theologians such as Bartholomew of Medina show that any good man – Montaigne as much as Seneca – may yearn for death with his rational appetite; indeed that his rational appetite should urgently wish for death, even though his earth-bound sensitive appetite never can. Heresy only arises if the rational appetite is allowed to have the very last word. For Christians the Church's revealed teaching overrides natural reason just as it overrides the example of Cleombrotus. As a pagan Cleombrotus lacked grace; he had no way of knowing infallibly that 'the Almighty had fixed his canon 'gainst self-slaughter'. Without that canon, Hamlet would have been right to put an end to his own life.

2.   Grace

Montaigne's religious world is a world of grace – though reason has to manage without it in the *Essays*. Montaigne stresses that anything to do with true ecstasy is *un estude privilegé* (III. 13, end). No human creature can ever, of himself, see God as he is. Standard works such as the late mediaeval *Pantheologia* of

Raynerius of Pisa show this as clearly as did Montaigne: the essence of God is, by nature, inaccessible to man; but God is not bound by nature; he may grant men privileges:

> It was conceded to Moses and to Paul, *ex singulari privilegio*, that they should see the essence of God in rapture (*Pantheologia*, 1585, p. 806).

Plato wrote of a kind of religious conviction based on fear, which makes believers out of atheists. That meant nothing good to Montaigne. It might just do for 'mortal and human religions'; but it 'does not touch a true Christian'. All Christians know they need grace. Montaigne defended Sebond and his 'natural theology' as a useful book for Christians, but he never saw natural theology as having any effective power apart from grace.

Two verses of the New Testament are conflated in the *Essays* to modify and justify Sebond's claim to prove the Christian verities from nature and by natural means. Montaigne, who always treats the Bible as verbally inspired, cites them as 'God's own word speaking to mankind':

> (A) It is not believable that in all this fabric of the world there should not be some mark printed by the hand of this great Architect; that there should be no image in the things of the world referring somehow to the Workman who built them and formed them. He left within these great works the imprint of his divinity; it is only because of our weakness that we cannot discover it.
>
> It is what he tells us himself: that he makes manifest his invisible actions by the visible ones (II. 12; p. 151).

There is no scriptural text which corresponds word for word to Montaigne's account of what 'God tells us himself'. He was, I think, idiosyncratically alluding to the Vulgate text of Hebrews 2:3, which Aquinas took to have a sense in conformity with Plato's teachings. If so, he linked it with another text, central to Sebond's argument in the *Theologia naturalis*: Romans 1:20:

> 'The invisible things of God,' says Saint Paul, 'are seen by the creation of the world, perceiving his everlasting wisdom and divinity through his works.'

Sebond had used this text, but Montaigne applied it in a more orthodox way.[1]

In the *Theologia naturalis* Sebond believed that he had proved from nature that Christian doctrines are true and necessary: Montaigne more prudently, and more traditionally, asserted that this can only be done for men already touched by grace. He used an analogy from Aristotelian physics, in which every object consists of form and matter: 'Human reasons and arguments are like heavy sterile matter; God's grace is the form.' That is why Socrates or Cato, for all their virtue, were, in the end, 'vain and useless'. They never knew the love and obedience due to the 'true Creator of all things'.

> (A) It is the same with what we imagine and with our arguments; they have some 'body', but it is a formless mass, without shape, without light, if faith and the grace of God are not joined on to it. When faith comes to give colour and light to Sebond's arguments it makes them firm and solid. They are capable of serving as travelling directions and a beginner's guide for an apprentice to put him on the road to this knowledge. They give him a certain fashioning and make him 'capable' of the grace of God ... (II. 12, p. 152).

That is what makes man, 'according to our belief', perfectible.

---

[1] (a) God himself, according to Montaigne, said, 'que ses operations invisibles, il nous les manifeste par les visibles'. That may be an echo of Hebrews 11:3, Vulgate: *ut ex invisibilis visibilia fierent* ('that from invisible things visible things might be made'). Platonic interpretations were given to this text, which was taken to mean that God had created the world after the pattern of the divine Forms (or Ideas). See, for a dense discussion of this verse, Cornelius à Lapide's commentary on the Epistles (Lyons, 1660, p. 865).

(b) Romans 1:19-20 was regularly interpreted as Montaigne did. In the Vulgate it reads, 'Deus enim illis manifestavit invisibilia enim ipsius a creatura mundi, per ea quae facta sunt intellecta conspiciuntur sempiterna quoque eius virtus et divinitas' ('For God has manifested it unto them. For the invisible things of him, from the creation of the world, are clearly seen, being understood by the things which are made; his eternal power also, and divinity'). With this text Cornelius à Lapide (p. 36) justifies the theological insight of Gentiles such as Hermes Trismegistus, Socrates, Plato and Aristotle, let alone saints such as Athanasius or Bernard. Montaigne's argument may derive from Duns Scotus, who associated Hebrews 11:3 and Romans 1:19-20 in much the same way. Cf. *Scriptum Oxoniense*, on Sentences I, dis. 3, qu. 1, art. 10, §4, *Sed econtra* (Venice, 1612, p. 145).

(c) Raymond Sebond exploits Romans 1:19-20 in the *Theologia Naturalis* (Book 2, chapter 16).

A fundamental Christian doctrine is underlined here by repetition: Sebond's arguments are said to be made effective (*capables*) by prevenient faith and grace. They in turn make an apprentice-Christian *capable* of further grace. These are technical theological terms. Montaigne is asserting that Sebond's book may help a Christian beginner who reads it with the eyes of faith to move on to higher things, indeed, to become *capax Dei*: able to receive the grace of God in all its plenitude.

Montaigne never wavers: natural reason can stumble on to Christian verities and hold ideas or imagery identical with Christian ones. Yet without grace man would have no reason to put all his trust in Christianity. And he would certainly be no closer to God.[2]

Grace is outside Nature. For Montaigne any advance in a man's religion always depends on it. In the final version of the *Essays* frequent interpolations of words and phrases emphasise this. One word frequently so interpolated is *extraordinaire*: divine intervention does not follow the *ordo rerum*, the natural order of the world; it is always *extra*, always outside, that order.

God, for Montaigne, is transcendent Being: man is contingent and so has nothing to do with absolute Being (*Essence*). If Man and God are to meet, the initiative must ever and always come from God. In the chapter on repentance Montaigne wrote that he 'rarely repents'. No wonder! He was writing not of acts of penance but of that repentance by which a man sees his whole life and his whole person as through the eyes of God. To do that he needs grace (III. 2, pp. 32-5).

The apologia for Sebond ends by quietly stressing the need for grace. Plutarch knew that God is absolute Being. But Plutarch affords no means of access to that divine Essence. Seneca condemns men who fail to rise above their mere humanity. That is quite 'absurd'. You cannot, unaided, make the pace greater than the stride. Man cannot, of himself, 'climb above himself or above humanity':

---

[2] What Gentiles could and should learn from natural reason is that God is one and eternal, the prince and judge of the world. For a brief discussion of the issues involved, see Cornelius à Lapide, pp. 35-6 and, on the essentialness of grace for effective Christian belief, p. 30. Raymond Sebond believed that essential and specifically Christian truths can be obtained by man's *enlightened* natural reason rightly reading God's 'book' of Nature.

(A) He will rise if God lends him his hand; he will rise by giving up and renouncing his own means, letting himself be raised and supported by *divine grace, not otherwise.*

At this point Montaigne made several changes for the edition he was preparing when he died. He interpolated, for example, the adverb *extraordinairement* to emphasise that a miracle is required: 'he will rise if God lends him, extraordinarily, his hand.' And the last words of this extract, shown here in italics, are replaced by the following:

... (C) purely heavenly means. It is up to our Christian faith, not to his Stoic virtue, to claim this divine and miraculous transfiguration (II. 12, end).

With such uncompromising certainty his long doubting chapter ends.

The verb to rise (*s'elever*) alludes to that *elevatio* by which the mind of man is raised by grace up towards God, in contemplation or selfless charity. Similar assertions are made in the chapter on repentance. Christians may repent in a manner worthy of God, the searcher out of men's hearts, but only through divine intervention: *Il faut que Dieu nous touche le courage'*, 'God must touch our hearts' (III.2, p. 37).

This is an echo of I Kings 10:26: 'hearts God had touched'. The source may seem a bit out of the way, but in fact it was not; a contemporary of Montaigne, Georgette de Montenay, has a picture and poem on this theme in her *Emblemes ou devises chrestiennes*, designed to represent *Frustra* (In vain): all man does is 'in vain, if God does not touch his heart'.

By the time Montaigne reached the end of his apologia for Sebond he had discredited reason when deprived of grace. With Christian scepticism he defends Roman Catholicism at the expense of reason itself. In this he was following tradition. A generation earlier Rabelais's wise old evangelical king, Gargantua, had been pleased to note that all the best thinkers were pyrrhonist sceptics now (*Le Tiers Livre*, 1546, TLF, 36, 130).

Sceptical orthodoxy was certainly in the air. Quite independently of Montaigne, in nearby Toulouse, François Sanchez wrote an exciting little book in the 1560s or 1570s, which he then kept in a drawer for years. He entitled it, 'That Nothing is known', *Quod nihil scitur* (Lyons, 1581). Montaigne was more hesitant; he struck a medal and stamped on it, '*Que sçay-je?*' (What *do* I know?).

CHAPTER SIX

Everyman's Ecstasies

1. Sexual ecstasy

Montaigne championed the classical ideals of the golden mean, temperance, peace of mind and, up to a point, controlled emotions. To modern ears ecstasy sounds incompatible with these ideals. But classical moralists found no difficulty in reconciling ecstatic mania or inspired *furor* with the staider virtues. Socrates reconciled them by teaching and example.

In the *Phaedrus* Plato asserted that the mutual love of true lovers is the happiest form of mania. Lovers exchange souls. Each lover dies, his departing soul living in the other; true lovers live therefore in permanent ecstasy, their souls sojourning outside their own bodies. For Renaissance Platonists, 'to die with love' was not a jaded metaphor. It expressed a vital truth.

High Platonic love is largely an affair of the soul; bodies play only a minor rôle in it. It is, nevertheless, considered to be a form of *eros*, not of *philia*. When these ideas became more widely spread in Latin, the distinction became blurred. This was even more the case in French, where *amitié* might be used for many kinds of love and several kinds of friendship which were represented in Greek by different words, sometimes sharply distinguished. Montaigne did not express his friendship for La Boëtie in terms of *eros* or of ecstasy; there was no claim to be 'living in' his beloved nor of 'dying to him'. On the other hand, Platonic love is exclusive: you can only exchange souls with one person. Exclusiveness is also central to Montaigne's highest *philia*. No third person could, at this highest level, share in it. It was of course quite compatible with other forms of affection, including that intimate form of *philia* which binds husband and wife together in mutual tenderness.

In Plato, the ideal love is male-homosexual. Many admirers of Plato in the Renaissance did not see this, partly because Ficino obscured it in his Latin translation and commentary. Montaigne did see it: he dismissed Greek homosexuality as incompatible with 'our manners' and as a mere parody of heterosexual love. With that, he let the subject go. It did not worry him. But in his own way he played it down; when Socrates was older than Montaigne his soul was still susceptible to passion; in Xenophon Socrates described how his heart went a-flutter as he shared a book with a handsome pupil; Montaigne calls the pupil *un objet amoureux*, thus effectively obscuring his sex.

By reflecting on this incident, Montaigne humanised Socrates. Even at the height of his career as a moral philosopher, Socrates had weaknesses. He remained a great man but human, not more than human. Montaigne at first marvelled: 'A mere touch, by chance, on the shoulder, was enough to warm and disturb a soul chilled and enervated by age! And that soul, the first of all human souls in reforming itself!' But he finally wrote in the margin: 'And why not? Socrates was a man: he never wanted to be, or to seem to be, anything else' (III. 5, p. 137).

Montaigne's love for La Boëtie was in no way physical. It concerned the soul and was therefore solid and stable, in life as in death. It burnt with a 'general, universal, temperate and equal heat', being 'spiritual, with the soul refining itself by usage'. The souls of women may not be firm enough to experience so great a friendship, but the question is left open.

It is here that Socrates and his homosexual affections come to the fore in order to be criticised. Such love is a parody of the love Montaigne feels for 'fair and honest women'. His ideal would be an application of this Socratic parody to his own circumstances: if only a man could feel the *philia* of friendship and the *eros* of sexual love for one and the same woman ... If it were possible, then such a love as that would surpass even the highest form of friendship he had experienced with La Boëtie: 'Not only would their souls have this total enjoyment, but their bodies would have their share in this engagement too.' But there has been 'no example so far' of women ever reaching these heights. The final version adds that the ancients rejected such a possibility. Yet a love which could bind a man and woman, by soul and body, would be one where *l'homme fust engagé tout entier* – where man and woman were engaged with all their being (I. 28, p. 243).

Such love was indeed unknown to Plato, though not to Renaissance theorists, poets and novelists who accommodated Plato's doctrines to Christian manners. Most of them continued to make love into an ecstasy, with the man and woman 'dying' to themselves and reliving in each other. Montaigne did not. But he did, in the one case of his rare loving friendship for La Boëtie, isolate the soul from the body. There is not the slightest hint that the body played any part at all in the genesis or course of their love. But it is not presented as an ecstasy.

2.　Sexual climaxes

It was reflexion on sexual love which, more perhaps than anything else, led Montaigne to conclude that all but a few should strive to keep body and soul closely bound together, avoiding ecstasy constantly and effectively.

In theory Christianity accepts the body. To reject it is heresy. Yet many traditional moralists and philosophers – especially those influenced by Platonism – remained suspicious of the body, which they treated as not only lower than the soul but as a clog, a prison, a set of fetters for the soul. Moralists dwelt on the grossness of the body and the animality of the sexual embrace. Philosophically sexual climaxes were regularly seen as affairs of the body alone and therefore bestial in the full sense of that word: an activity shared with lower creation and so somehow unworthy of man's higher nature. In philosophical, moral and ethical writings the sexual embrace was only grudgingly admitted as a second-best for those who could not aspire to worthier ends. It was hedged about with provisos and limitations. All the books ever written on the subject had been written by men – most of them unmarried; women often appeared in books as dangerous creatures, naturally inclined to unlimited lust. It was man's duty to try to hold them in check. It was his duty to control his own sexual urges too. Philosophy saw sexual intercourse as one of the bodies 'necessary' functions, like eating and drinking, but not one to be allowed free play. Montaigne rejected the teaching that would make sex into a purely bodily ecstasy and concluded that 'male and female are cast in the same mould; education apart, there is not much difference between them' (III. 5, end).

Those who did engage the soul as well as the body in sexual intercourse could be worrying. Hippocrates believed that sexual climaxes were a form of *petit mal*, a 'small epilepsy'. Moralists dwelt on that theory for nigh on two thousand years.

Tiraqueau, the jurisconsult and friend of Rabelais, wrote an authoritative treatise on the *Laws of Marriage* which grew into a compendium of almost everything ever said on sex and marriage. It makes sombre reading. The fifteenth law expounds a long litany of illnesses caused by sexual intercourse. No part of the body was exempt. On sex as epilepsy, it is uncompromisingly certain:

> Hippocrates the greatest of doctors whose property it is never to deceive nor to be deceived (as Macrobius attests in Book One of the *Dream of Scipio*), considered that sexual coîtus is part of that terrifying illness which the Greeks call *epilepsia* and the Latins *morbus comitialis* (*De legibus connubialibus*, 1586, p. 289).

Aulus Gellius (19.2), citing Hippocrates, talks of 'a small, or if you prefer, a brief epilepsy'.

If sexual climaxes are a form of epilepsy, then they are a form of insanity or sick ecstasy – and one to which melancholics are peculiarly prone. Aristotle is definite about that (*Problems* 30.1).

Montaigne examined sexuality above all in *Sur des vers de Virgile* (III. 5), a chapter which takes its title from passionate verses in the *Aeneid* (8. 387f., 404f.), which Montaigne considered to be a delightful evocation of love enriched by poetry, though rather too passionate for sex within marriage. Aulus Gellius had already been struck by them (9.10); it was quite usual to express some surprise at their intensity.

In most of the treatises on morals one can look in vain for any advice on marital relations, other than to cut sex down to the minimum; François de Sales cannot bring himself even to mention the subject: he likens the need for sex to 'the need for food' and lets you draw your own conclusions. Not untypically, in his treatise on divine love, he jumped straight from the holy mystical ecstasy, which he venerated, to coîtus, treated as an ecstasy both brutal and 'epileptic'. In Montaigne, on the contrary, there is room for love and tenderness, which for him are what marriage mainly concerns – together with children.[1]

---

[1] François de Sales stresses, of course, the honourable nature of the nuptial

Several times Montaigne contrasted, to its disadvantage, the burning fire of sexual passion with the solid constancy of marriage. Finally he went back to what he wrote to his wife in his preface to Plutarch's consolatory letter: 'To wed without marrying is treachery.' He found, to his surprise, that he had kept his marriage vows better than he had ever expected (III. 5, p. 85).

Sexual passion he assumed to be extramarital, in the tradition of mediaeval mistresses and servitors. But he never called it an epilepsy. Unlike most, he never suggested that it leads, by its nature, to illness of any sort. Quite the contrary. In one of his few criticisms of university theologians (*Nos Maistres*, as they were called) he stakes the claim of sheer good health in provoking ecstasies of many, less 'distracted' kinds:

> (C) *Nos Maistres* are wrong when they seek the causes of our spirits' extraordinary transports. Leaving aside the attribution of some of them to divine rapture, to love, to the harshness of war, to poetry, to wine, they do not give its due part in them to good health (III. 5, p. 73).

The *Essays* amply show that Montaigne is not just rejecting the Platonic theory underlying the teaching of *Nos Maistres* nor all later developments of it. But his own life had taught him that youthful good health has a part to play in whàt was classed as enthusiasm, passion or ecstasy. When he was young, in 'boiling health' and with time on his hands, he found this to be true:

> This joyful fire gives rise to flashes in our spirit; they are lively, bright, beyond our natural reach; they are some of our most

---

couch. But his suspicion of the sexual embrace transpires even in the chapter in which he asserts its purity (*Introduction à la vie dévote*, Part 3, chapter 39). In this chapter he is, however, less morose about sex than a married layman like Tiraqueau. Nevertheless on sexual intercourse as a brutal ecstasy he is quite uncompromising in *De l'amour de Dieu* (Book 7, chapter 4: *Du ravissement*): Man is certainly in a true, though brutal, ecstasy when enraptured by carnal pleasures; he is, in fact, cast 'outside himself'. The soul is said to be 'ravished and caught away outside itself, because these bestial pleasures put it beyond the use of reason and intelligence with such a mad violence that, as one of the greatest Philosophers said, man, being in this state, seems to have fallen into an epilepsy'. In François de Sales the love and tenderness of married couples is seen as something distinct from sexual intercourse, not as something expressed through it.

spritely enthusiasms even though they are not the most distracted.

Old age, of course, does the contrary. Montaigne does not think that old men should ape youth, but he does think that commerce with women may have good effects on a man's declining years. Some old men are spurred on by avarice or ambition: he could more easily be spurred on by love, which would make him take more trouble over his appearance and help to lighten the burdens which old age brings in its train:

> (B) it could divert me away from a thousand painful thoughts, (C) from a thousand melancholy sorrows (B) which idleness burdens us with in that age (C) and from the bad state of our health (III. 5, p. 139).

It was a standard belief that melancholics were prone to the power of love, but that is not Montaigne's point. He saw commerce with women as a palliative for senile melancholy. It is striking, however, that the verbs he uses to say this are all in conditional tenses. It is how things might be, not how they are. As he wryly commented, with a laugh at blue-stockings who made sex a matter of the mind, no beautiful woman was ever ready to trade her young thighs against the decrepit wisdom of Socrates – nor, by implication, of himself (III. 5, p. 143).

In the *Timaeus* (91Aff.), Plato made both the male and the female organs of generation into wilful parasitic creatures, working havoc on their hosts when thwarted. Montaigne increased the element of frenzy beyond what he found in Plato or his translator Ficino. For the male he uses *furieux*; for the female *forcené*, 'raging mad' (III. 5, p. 94). Yet this aspect of the sexual embrace did not please him. Montaigne coarsens his language. However indulgent he was to Socrates when his soul was disturbed by a chance touch, philosophers like Zeno and Cratippus are roundly condemned for the frenzy of their sexual passion. He uses the language of ecstasy, but these ecstasies are bad ones. He disliked the 'rage' that finds its place in sexual intercourse; he dislikes 'the face inflamed with *fureur* and cruelty' at the very 'sweetest point of love' as well as 'that grave, severe and ecstatic face in so mad an activity'. Sexual intercourse should not be like

that; for the wise it is a happy, foolish, madcap activity, more akin
to Cupid than to Venus.

At this point, as a stage in his argument, he dwells upon the
animality of it all – as so many moralists did. Sexual intercourse
makes fools and wise men alike; it makes men like beasts; eating
and drinking are shared with other animals without our losing
our advantage over them, not so sexual intercourse; it 'drives out
all the theology and philosophy' of Plato; it is a mark of 'original
sin, or human vanity' (III. 5, p. 118).

This is then answered in terms which lead eventually to the
ringing convictions at the end of the *Essays*. Philosophy teaches
moderation, not rejection. But can she be right to assert that
'bodily appetites must not be increased by the spirit'; that we
should not find ways of sharpening our appetites:

> ... just as, in the service of love, Philosophy orders us to take an
> object which simply satisfies the needs of the body and which does
> not disturb the soul; the soul must not make it its concern, but
> follow nakedly along, accompanying the body – *suyvre nuement
> et assister le corps*? (III. 5, p. 137-8).

These last words are worth noting. Montaigne returns to these
terms a few lines later to make a telling point.

Philosophy certainly took a low view of sexual intercourse.
Rabelais can quote ancient sayings interpreted by Erasmus as
meaning that a philosopher should lie with a woman with
complete indifference, as far as his soul is concerned, so that he
can be said to have had the woman, but not she him (*Tiers Livre
de Pantagruel*, TLF, 35, p. 50ff.). Montaigne felt the weight of
such assertions, but refused to be overawed. He was feeling his
way, so the reply is a tentative one:

> But am I not right to think that these precepts – which are by my
> standards rather rigorous – concern a body which is doing its
> duty?

In the case of a sickly or ageing body, may not art and fantasy
play a part in bringing back lost appetites and joy? He then
ventures to compare ordinary human beings in their sexuality
and saints in their penances. His point is all the more forceful,
since he uses the language of Platonic asceticism – the body
being thought of as the 'prison' of the soul:

May we not say that there is nothing in us, during this earthly prison, either purely corporeal or purely spiritual and that it is injurious to tear a living man apart?

Can we not do for pleasure what saints do for pain? 'Pain, for example, is vehement to the point of perfection in the souls of the saints doing penance.' Medicine established a natural link, a *colligantia*, between body and soul: 'By right of this *colligance*' the body plays a part in penance even though it could have had 'but a little part in the cause' – the sins of saints being spiritual ones.

Montaigne then takes up the terms just applied by philosophy to the soul, inverts the situation and applies them challengingly to the attitudes of holy penitents towards their bodies:

The saints were not content that the body should follow nakedly along, accompanying the afflicted soul – *qu'il suyvît nuement et assistât l'ame affligée* (III. 5, p. 138).

Saints, that is, chastise their bodies, which in this way share in the penance of their souls.

A man who holds those convictions is well on the way to rejecting ecstasy as an ideal for most people. Far from freeing the soul from the body, he gives each the rôle of sharing in the pains and joys of the other. If it is right for saints to inflict pain on their bodies, it must, at the other extreme, be right for ordinary mortals to encourage their souls to join in the sexual joys of their bodies.

3.   Poetic ecstasy

On Platonic authority true poets were believed to enjoy revelations of truth through inspiration. Many believed that these revealed truths were then 'veiled' by the poets in fable. By veiling truths the poets clad them in beauty and disguised them. In this way they saved them from profanation: anyone could enjoy their poems for their beauty, but only a privileged few could lift the veil and uncover the divine yet hidden truth. When they did so, they were astonished and enraptured.

Theories such as these were all the more easily acceptable in that similar ones justified both the allegories which Christians found in the Old Testament and the use of psalms in Christian worship. David, it was said – like all the Old Testament writers – had been vouchsafed knowledge of Christian truths, which he had hidden beneath a Jewish veil. To some extent poets other than David could be treated as inspired, including pagan ones such as Homer, Hesiod, Virgil and others – which is why they were called 'divine'.

Montaigne accepted poetic rapture and used its language very freely but, so far as he himself was concerned, with nothing like the full Platonic sense. The Bible he treated as the word of God, which no pagan writings ever were. Montaigne probably read his Plato in Ficino's edition, with Ficino's notes and Latin translation; but that seems to have been for convenience. He rejected Ficino's Christianising of *Plato noster*. Plato's teachings, like those of any other man not enlightened by revelation and vouched for by the Church, were open to discussion.

Ficino was a prime authority for the reality of poetic ecstasy. Montaigne went back beyond him to the two original sources of his theories in Plato: the *Phaedrus* and the *Io*. These dialogues were widely read. Ronsard exploited them in a famous poem to a famous man: his *Ode à Michel de l'Hospital*. Ronsard, in other words, made the theories his own. Montaigne did not.

According to Plato, poets compose in trance or rapture; they are seized by a divine spirit which inspires them to rise above human limitations. Their driving force is a yearning to glimpse divine truth and beauty. The insights vouchsafed them in their inspiration are then passed on through their poetry. Inspiration works like a magnet.

This poetic rapture is also a case of mania, of *furor*, of ecstatic madness. The normal expression for it in Renaissance French was *fureur poëtique*. (Doctrines such as Plato's have to be adapted if they are to be seriously accepted as true in the light of developed Christian doctrine. As myth the Renaissance found them quite acceptable.)

Montaigne made a major addition to his final version of the chapter on the Younger Cato in order to expound briefly the doctrines of Plato: poets are at their best when they sing the virtues of great men, composing not plodding verse (an 'art' which follows rules) but the poetry of inspiration. Great poetry cannot be coldly judged: it ravishes the judgment. As in Plato's *Io* (533D) this is explained in terms of magnetism, with inspired 'poetry' contrasted with mere 'art' (I. 37, end).

Plato's terms are there in the *Essays*: ecstasy, *furor*, enrapturing beauty. What is missing is an influence literally divine. Who – or what – inspires the poets, we are not told. Do poets actually glimpse the beauty of the living God? Nothing suggests that this is so. For Plato, as for Ficino, the goad which prods the poet on to painful creativity is a truly divine one. Divine too is the inspiration. For them poetic *furor* is genuine. It was specifically classed by Ficino with St Paul's privileged rapture.

In Montaigne poetic ecstasy is not even remotely in the same category as the rapture of Paul or of Christian contemplatives. If ever a man talked of being enraptured by the beauty of poetry, that man was Montaigne. But he does not suggest that the great classical poets were truly inspired, nor that they were God's mouthpieces for revealed truths, nor that they were privileged interpreters of God. Nor does he make the ecstasies induced by reading poetry into anything like a Platonic trance. For such attitudes we can turn to Rabelais, but not to Montaigne.

As a frenzy – an inspired mania – poetic *furor* was too close to madness for Montaigne's taste. Ficino acknowledged the closeness of the two sorts of *furor* or mania in the opening words of the dedication of his Latin translation of the *Phaedrus* to Lorenzo de' Medici:

> Our Plato, most excellent Lorenzo, defined *furor* in the *Phaedrus* as an alienation of the mind. He taught that there were two kinds of alienation. One comes from human illness: the other from God.

The first is plain *insania*; the second divine *furor*: Ficino taught that madness – insane *furor* – makes man subhuman, 'in some ways changing him from man to beast', while poets enjoy a divine *furor*, 'which raises man above nature so that he crosses over to God' (Plato, trans. Ficino, 1539, p. 167).

Montaigne found bestial madness real enough – witness Torquato Tasso. But there he stopped. Geniuses may be 'ravished' only by their own heady thoughts; poets may enrapture others with the beauty they create, but of rapture in the strict sense, Montaigne is suspicious; he would not allow that

mere man can ever 'cross over to the divine'. A gulf unbridgeable
to unaided man separates creature from Creator. It can be
crossed only by a privileged few. Any author who obscures that
fact is eventually smashed to the ground – Cicero for one. He was
only a poor creature subject to calamities, yet when he talked of
man and of the human condition you would think he was talking
of an 'all-living, all-powerful God'. Even the greatest of the
pagans fell into that stupid error; Aristotle, Democritus,
Chrysippus, Seneca ... (II. 12, p. 208).

As a reader of poetry Montaigne experienced rapture of a sort –
but not such as to bring him face to face with the divine. He saw
poetry as being like fair and honourable women: beautiful, the
beauty enhanced by art and all on display. Poetry contains no
revelations of theological truths and no wisdom other than the
exquisitely human – and philosophy is a better vehicle for
human wisdom. When Montaigne talked of poetry in his own
name, not Plato's, he called it an 'art'. That is why women can
read poetry, if read they must:

> ... it is an art, playful, subtle, feigning, wordy – all pleasure and
> all display, like they are.

Women are welcome to read and enjoy it. But if they want to
learn how to limit their desires, prolong the pleasures of life and
put up with harsh, unfaithful husbands and ugly old age, they
must turn to moral philosophy (III. 3, p. 46).

By calling poetry an art, Montaigne rejected what Socrates
says of art and inspiration in the *Io*. Indeed, without spiritual
possession or divine inspiration, Plato's teachings have no literal
force. If his terms continue to be used by those who do not
believe in them, it is to serve for conventional poetic decoration –
or else they are applied hyperbolically to purely natural
ecstasies, which are real but not divine.

Montaigne's raptures on reading great poetry were like his
copious quotations: glimpses of poetic beauty in a sea of prose.
Poetic rapture was for him a thing apart, even though it did
take him out of himself. In other matters he intended to regulate
his life by the natural order: 'all actions which go beyond the
bounds of the ordinary' are open to sinister interpretations; 'you
risk not rising above the *ordo rerum*; you may fall below it.'
There is a lesson to be drawn from those philosophical martyrs of

classical times who jested under torture. They are impressive, yet not to be followed:

> You must confess that there is some change for the worse in those souls, some frenzy (*fureur*) however holy (II. 2, p. 20).

With the one exception of the vehement, joyful but natural rapture derived from reading poetry, such frenzies are best avoided or played down.

It is the same with Stoic bravado. Antisthenes exclaimed that he would rather be mad (*furieux*) than a voluptuary. Such bravado, it was said, comes from a heart soaring above its natural range. It recommended itself less and less to Montaigne as he went more deeply into himself.

CHAPTER SEVEN

Privacy

1. Melancholy retreat

Melancholy tends to be imagined as the gloom of an older man
such as Molière's Alceste, sulking 'alone with his black sorrow in
his dark little corner.' Traditionally, however, it covered both
public and private states and could be found even in children.
Aristotle asserted in the *Eudemian Ethics* (229a) that 'passion
makes a man ecstatic'; the frenzied bravery of soldiers who are
beside themselves in the heat of battle was certainly often to be
attributed to ecstatic melancholy. (Montaigne notes the bravery
but does not advise emulation.) Renaissance ways of thinking
linked these madly brave soldiers with vehemently devoted
scholars in their bookrooms, with gloomy, irascible dominies in
school and with suspiciously studious pupils poring over their
books.

Schools should not be gaols. Montaigne distrusted melancholy
in the schoolroom; as a complexion and as an illness it should be
closely watched.

> (A) I do not want a pupil to be left to the melancholy humour of a
> furious schoolmaster ... (C) When you see a boy over-devoted to
> studying his books because of a solitary or melancholy
> complexion, it is not good, I think, to encourage him in it (I. 26,
> p. 212).

Yet, at least when Montaigne took up his position in the country
on the death of his father, he had much in common with that
bookish boy. Schoolboy melancholics creep culpably off to their
books. So did Montaigne. Reading 'honest' books in some

compensation to an older man for losing the company of 'honest' friends and fair 'honest' women. Books afford a slackish pleasure, but you can shut them up at will. And you can have conversations of a sort with them.

Montaigne was no hermit; his withdrawal to his estates was marked by pomp and paint. Two inscriptions on his walls recorded his action for posterity. One lamented the death of La Boëtie; the other, dated from Montaigne's thirty-eighth birthday (28 February 1571), dedicated the ancestral home to *libertati suae, tranquillitatique et otio*. These are philosophical ideals, not mere peace and quiet.

Libertas is power over your own life; Cicero called it the power to live as you wish. *Tranquillitas* is serenity of mind – a stable, lasting state. Cicero called it *placida quietaque constantia*. As for *otium*, it is studious leisure, made possible by disengagement.

Such was Montaigne's ideal: peaceful study at his own pace, in his own place. It all went wrong. He was plagued by melancholy humour. By way of escape he started to write. He gave an account of all this to explain how he came to begin what he calls 'this daft undertaking'. *'Cette sotte entreprise'* is a strong expression; it stuck. Pascal echoed it, referring to the 'daft project' which Montaigne had of painting his own portrait (*Pensées* II. 62).

At this stage Montaigne wondered what could save him from damning criticism – perhaps only the strangeness and novelty of it all. How odd his book must seem! Perhaps its 'phantastical' nature would see it through:

> It was a melancholy humour – and therefore a humour very inimical to my natural complexion, produced by the moroseness of the solitude I cast myself into a few years ago – which first put into my head this *resverie* of meddling with writing (II. 8, p. 69).

Resverie is one of those misleading words: here it means not vague dreaming but mad frenzy. (François de Sales uses it the same way in his *Traité de l'amour de Dieu* VII. 9: 'in *resverie* and frenzy, beyond use of reason.') Under the influence of melancholy adust, peculiarly dangerous to a man newly plunged into a life of retirement, Montaigne conceived the idea of portraying himself, of assaying himself. It was the kind of notion that might have occured to a lunatic.

Any author may play down his work: Montaigne went well beyond convention. His terms mean that people might judge his undertaking to be insane. His self-imposed task was *farouche et extravagant*, 'wild and abnormal'.

It is understandable that he felt that way. He was breaking absolutely new ground. We do find self-awareness in' the Renaissance – in the exiled poet Clément Marot, in the melancholy Du Bellay of the *Regrets*, in an erratic scholar like Cardano of Ferrara. But Montaigne outstripped them all. He looked into himself and found things strange and monstrous. According to Burton (I. 3, 1, 3) sufferers from an access of melancholy do just that: 'there is nothing so vain, absurd, ridiculous, extravagant, impossible, incredible, so monstrous a chimera', that they will not imagine.

Montaigne found that out for himself. He had hoped that his soul would 'entertain itself'. Nothing of the sort happened; on the contrary, his soul bolted off like a runaway horse, giving birth 'to so many chimeras, so many fantastical monsters, one after the other, without order, without sense, that, so as to contemplate their ineptitude and strangeness', he started to write them down (I. 8; end; cf. II. 8 beginning).

In the chapter in which he admits the role of an access of melancholy humour in the genesis of his work, he was led to reflect on one melancholic he knew who was brought to such a sorry state by his melancholy that, when Montaigne visited him, he had already spent twenty-two years in his room, without once going outside (II.8, p. 79f.). Even less extreme cases could be troublesome to a man withdrawing to his country fastness. Montaigne learned that a soul left to its own devices was like a fallow field: the 'agitations' which shook it might well bring forth a crop of madness: 'There is no *folie* or *rêverie* which it will not bring forth in that agitation' (I. 8, beginning). Strong words indeed.

The melancholy humour which beset Montaigne, high up and isolated in his bookish retreat, was indeed, as he states, hostile to his natural complexion: it upset the balance of his native temperament (melancholy tempered by the sanguine), tilting it toward melancholy adust. Montaigne risked becoming 'unbalanced', with the distinct possibility of mental disturbances.

In *Il Penseroso* Milton wrote of 'the Melancholic in his lonely tower'. Such, quite literally, was Montaigne.

2. Bravery and pedantry

Montaigne conquered this melancholy adust with its drive towards mad extremes by the strength of his recovered balanced temperament. Meanwhile he meditated on the curious links which brought frenzied scholars and soldiers close together.

The most interesting example of this comes in the chapter on solitude:

> That man you can see over there, furiously beside himself, scrambling high up the ruins of that battlement, the target of so many volleys from harquebuses; and that other man, all covered with scars, wan, pale with hunger, determined to burst rather than to open the gate to him! Do you think they are in it for themselves? It could well be for somebody they have never seen, someone plunged, meanwhile, in idleness and delights, who takes no interest in what they are doing.
>
> And this man over here, rheumy, filthy, blear-eyed, whom you can see coming out of his workroom after midnight! Do you think he is looking in his books for ways to be better, happier, wiser? Not a bit. He will teach posterity how to scan the verse of Plautus and spell a Latin word, or else die in the attempt (I. 39, p. 314).

Both soldier and scholar are furiously 'beside themselves'; prepared to die for things that do not really matter.

3. A place of one's own

The remedy for such frenzies is one which a balanced melancholy complexion provides for the man who knows how to cultivate it – especially when he is older. When he is young a good man must espouse his wife, not simply take her. But now, with old age, the time approaches when every knot must be untied save one. The exception is that last knot of all, the knot by which the soul is espoused to the body till death it do part; that must be strengthened. Now even the claims of a beloved wife and the sexual embrace must be relaxed:

> (A) God gives us time to make things ready for our departure. Let us prepare for it. Let us pack our bags and take our leave of the company in good time; let us untangle ourselves from those violent holds which engage us elsewhere and take us away from ourselves. We must unknot those strong binding obligations and,

from this day forward, love this and that but marry nothing but
ourselves (I. 39, p. 315).

Montaigne is writing about solitude – about being alone in lonely
places. He insists – from experience – that a wise man does not
wildly retreat to a wilderness. Solitude must be prepared for. In
any case real solitude is within us. We must learn how to be
alone, how to lose those we love. In death we shall lose the lot.

We must not allow the soul to roam wildly about on fantastical
flights of fancy, as unbalanced melancholics do. It is at home in
the body. Bring it home and keep it there. That is the way to find
real solitude. It is not enough to 'get away from the crowd out
there: we must get away from the crowd inside ourselves'. We
suffer from an illness of the soul: the soul needs the whole of man
to help it; by itself it cannot escape outside obligations:

> (A) So we must bring it back, pull it back to us. That is what true
> solitude is. You can enjoy it in the midst of towns and in the
> courts of kings, but more conveniently apart (I. 39, p. 312).

The wise man, unlike the man of furious enterprise, binds his
soul to his body; that is the antithesis of ecstasy. It enables wise
people to carry their own solitude about with them. It is not a
question of rejecting those whom we love but of slackening the
ties which bind us to them; in one way or another all will be
broken, if only by death: 'We should have wives, children, goods
and, especially, health – if we can. But we must not so bind
ourselves to them that our happiness depends on them':

> (A) We should set aside an *arriereboutique*, a room, just for
> ourselves, at the back of the shop, keeping it entirely free and
> founding there our true liberty and our principal place of retreat
> and solitude (I. 39, p. 313).

Montaigne delighted in expressing his wisdom in everyday
words. *Arriereboutique* is one of them: everybody can be a
philosopher, if all you need is a private room at the back of the
shop where no public business is allowed to enter and take over.[1]

---

[1] Huguet (*Dictionnaire de la langue française du XVIes*) lists many examples
of *arriere boutique* in the sense of *arrière pensée* or dissimulation and once only in
the sense of 'ultimate resource'. Randle Cotgrave's *Dictionairie of the french and
English Tongues*, 1632, after the literal definition ('a back-shop; or back roome,

This famous passage comes in the first version of the *Essays* (1580). It expresses a conviction which Montaigne never departed from. Man's soul is peculiarly fitted for this kind of solitude:

> (A) We have a soul capable of turning in on itself; it can keep itself company; it has means of attacking, defending, receiving, giving. Let us not fear that, in a solitude like this, we shall be crouching in boring idleness.

The *Essays* are largely an account of what went on inside Montaigne's 'private room'. But Montaigne could do what he did because he had a temperament fitted to it: 'There are some complexions', as he admitted, 'more suited to these precepts than others are' (I. 39, p. 316).

This calm withdrawal into self was the mark of the equable, sanguine melancholic. Its greatest contrast is with the solitary wildness of the man suffering from melancholy adust, as Montaigne had been when he first came home to live in studious idleness.

It may help us to get closer to Montaigne if we read what others wrote about the same subject. Such matters are attractively expounded, for example, by Jacques de Bosc in a treatise of general interest to male and female psychology, confusingly entitled *L'Honneste femme* (best known from its enlarged edition of 1635). As *The Compleat Woman* it had a considerable influence in England too. Du Bosc insists on the constancy of people blessed with a balanced melancholy complexion. 'They always reserve for themselves a privat roome, where the tempests of Fortune cannot reach. There it is that the soule retires, to maintain her self in an eternall serenity.'

This 'privat roome' (*place secrette*) is the only place where we can 'consider with an attention less distracted, what we are, when our imagination represents us to ourselves.' Du Bosc

---

used for privat wares, or working in') gives the same two figurative senses: *sans arriere boutique* he renders by 'plainly, openly, wholly' etc., whilst *Il a une arriere boutique* or *il se reserve une arriere boutique* he translates as 'He dissembles, or suppresses as yet his courage or cunning; he reserves, or spares them for his last cast, or for his last effort'. Montaigne uses the term in neither of the figurative senses listed by Cotgrave or Huguet. I know no author before him who did so in his sense.

contrasts this with 'the ecstasies which the poets feign.' The image for these is Narcissus gazing in his pond, dangerously seeking himself 'out of himself' (*L'Honneste femme*, 1635, p. 122f.; *The Compleat Woman*, 1639, p. 40f.).

The best complexion of all, according to Du Bosc in his concluding words on melancholy, is one which adds a little sanguine gaiety to the melancholy temperament.

Montaigne did just that.

CHAPTER EIGHT

Love and War

1. Amorous zeal

The Wars of Religion were civil wars, fought to an end or to a standstill. They were marked by the great cruelties of the rival armies. Religious zeal merged into anger (*cholère*), finding satisfaction in exceptional cruelty. Montaigne often described such fighting as *furieux*. He cited the Byzantine theologian Nicetas who condemned the factions of Christian princes in his own day, 'armed not with zeal but with anger' (I. 56, p. 414).

In battle (as in other activities traditionally marked by frenzy, fury, inspired madness or ecstasies of soul or body) Montaigne counselled the control of the various manias connected with them or else their outright rejection. Sometimes, as was the case with sexual intercourse, he sought to replace them by more humane qualities which acknowledge the fact that men and women are souls united with their bodies.

It is, tellingly, in the chapter on cruelty that Montaigne rejects, from his own experience, the kind of sexual embrace that 'transports us outside ourselves' and 'enraptures us in voluptuousness'. In amorous affairs he prefers the image of the chase to the image of the kill (II. 11, p. 131).

2. Religious zeal

Christian culture is badly placed to condemn cruelty. Cruelty is not one of the seven deadly sins. Traditional works of piety or ethics did not usually treat it as a sin at all. Montaigne considered the ferocity of his countrymen pitched against each other and of the Conquistadores with their base mechanical triumphs over simple people close to nature; he loathed it. The desire for vengeance is a *furieux appetit*, an appetite with a streak of madness in it. He was shielded from it by his natural complexion, which was opposed to all vehemence. If he had been born with 'a more unruly complexion' things would have gone 'pitifully' with him. He had assayed himself and found 'no firmness' in his soul capable of 'maintaining passions' which were even slightly 'mind-departing' (*vehementes*). As for justice, if it goes beyond straight-forward executions of the guilty, then it becomes cruelty too (II. 11, pp. 120, 127, 130, 133).

This absence of passion was cultivated by Montaigne to an extent which can mislead. He refused to use the distorting language of hate even about religious opponents, past or present. The Calvinist leader Beza is condemned for his wrong theology but admitted to be a good erotic poet. Praising Beza's love poetry is partly a way of embarrasing a man later known for his austerity, but it is more than that. The Roman censors objected to his ranging Beza, a heretic, among great contemporary poets. Montaigne believed he was right and stood his ground; he held that 'the magistrate' had exceeded his charge. He never blackened a man he did not agree with.

This would lead one to expect Montaigne to have been in favour of religious tolerance. No doubt he was, but mainly from necessity. 'Freedom of conscience' – religious toleration – was forced on to exhausted warring enemies. Montaigne doubted the wisdom of the policy and accepted it only reluctantly. He believed – out of respect for 'the honour' of the 'religious devotion' of French kings – that 'not being able to do what they wanted, they pretended to want what they were able to do' (II. 19, p. 463).

This policy gave rise to a chain of thoughts within him which afforded him the opportunity of being publicly fair to one of the almost legendary enemies of Christianity.

Freedom of conscience had been the policy of the fourth-century Roman Emperor Julian who compelled rival Christians to tolerate each other in the hope that this *licence* – abusive freedom – would weaken all forms of so quarrelsome and so despicable a religion. Christians in power traditionally did not allow freedom of conscience to rival Christians. Julian did.

Julian had become, like Ganelon or Judas Iscariot, one of the figures from the past whom it was good to hate. It is intriguing to see how Montaigne treats him. His chapter on freedom of conscience follows hard upon his condemnation of lying and his reminder that, in earlier times, merely verbal attacks of enemies were overlooked by potentates (II. 18, end).

The legends which had been foisted upon Julian by pious hatred are stripped away. Christians had called him the Apostate; his life and morals were decried. As Swinburne recalled, it is alleged that at the end of his life he conceded victory to the pale Galilean. Montaigne examined this legend critically and cast it aside. Julian is presented as an emperor who avoided cruelty and even let his Christian enemies rail against him to his face in public. He was a philosopher who despised the things of this world and who believed in the immortality of the soul. His death was 'somewhat like that of Epaminondas' – high praise: Epaminondas was a very special hero for Montaigne.

Julian was a ruler who was good for the Empire, bad for the Church. It is only after having listed his many good qualities that Montaigne abruptly asserted that 'in matters of religion he was totally vicious' (*vicieux partout*). Montaigne is sometimes said to have tried to 'rehabilitate' Julian the Apostate. He was doing something more unusual: giving a lesson to his warring countrymen. Religious hatred and anger were splashed over books as over battlefields. Montaigne was not worried by the verbal attacks and, by implication, could tolerate any amount of railing or blaspheming. He himself drew strength from a surer Christian age – that of Prudentius, the Catholic poet who lived as a child under the very emperor whom Christians had been encouraged to regard with detestation.

Prudentius is best known to English readers for the Christmas hymn, *Of the Father's heart begotten*. His praise of Julian comes in another poem on the divinity of Christ:

> I remember that in my boyhood there was the most valiant leader in war of all the emperors, a founder of laws, famed for his skill with tongue and hand. He was devoted to our country but not to the maintenance of true religion – loving as he did three thousand gods. He was faithless to God, not faithless to the world he governed:
> *Perfidus ille deo: quamvis non perfidus orbi (Apotheosis, 450-5).*

This serene judgment, which upset Gibbon (*Decline and Fall of the Roman Empire* XXII, end), since he wanted Christians to appear as intolerant bigots, is the one adopted by Montaigne. He certainly adopted the same tone. No one is gratuitously attacked in the *Essays*. The good qualities of enemies are noted and praised. Nowhere does Montaigne's zeal become vehement anger. This does not mean that he thought it wise to follow the policies of Julian, though one might be forced to. He would tolerate Reformed worship reluctantly if he had to. He would loyally have served a legitimate Protestant king. When he fought for the Roman Catholic faith he fought with no needless cruelty. Against influential opinion in his Church, he was convinced that torture or quartering were wanton cruelty. And, in real life, he supported the legitimate claims of Henry of Navarre even when a protestant.

One of the fruits of his meditation is a calm refusal to advocate ecstasy in battle or in quarrels about the true religion. What he came to appreciate was moderation in all things. 'Even when it does not offend me', he wrote, 'the lack of moderation astonishes me – even towards that which is good' (I. 30, p. 258).

CHAPTER NINE

Person to Person

1. Change and decay

In certainty and uncertainty Montaigne was no hater of those
who disagreed with him. He found very little to be certain about,
in any case.

Where do we find such truths as may be accessible to the
natural reason of natural, philosophical man? As far as morals
are concerned, sceptics of Montaigne's bent normally took refuge
in conservatism, accepting traditional moral and social
imperatives as practical guides to conduct. But, conservative
though he was, this was not in itself enough for Montaigne. He
needed some certainty somewhere, as a base from which to enjoy
doubting everything else. Could such a base be found? The
Renaissance had its answers. There was little new about many of
them, but wider horizons opened even venerable solutions to new
criticisms.

Those who knew no Latin were not debarred from an
awareness of such questions and solutions, as they spilled over
into French, partly in works of vulgarisation but also in great
literature. The works of Rabelais alone would suffice to show a
Renaissance reader how much could be doubted and where
wisdom was said to be available to man. (The only French
author picked out for high praise in Montaigne's chapter on
books is Rabelais.)

The major division in philosophy was between Platonists and
Aristotelians, though in practice many found it possible to
harmonise them. Those who followed Plato sooner or later turned
for help to the supernatural world. Those who followed Aristotle
– especially if they were 'Moderns' or 'Nominalists' – did not

seek any philosophical truths in revelation, which they restricted to the higher discipline of theology. It was possible to be a Platonist in theology and an Aristotelian in philosophy. Montaigne took his matter where he found it. His respect for Socrates did not turn him into a genuine Platonist; he certainly made recognisably important use of the writings of Aristotle, that 'monarch of the Moderns', as he called him, but he read him without 'biting his nails over him' (I. 26, p. 187).[1]

The Renaissance seeker for truth – especially for such truths as can be expressed in language – might turn to Plato's *Cratylus* and *Theaetetus*, or to works deriving from them. In the first of these dialogues, Cratylus, like Homer and Heracleitus before him, is portrayed as believing that everything is in a state of flux. Such a notion disturbed Socrates – or Plato, who tells us so – though it was characteristic of Montaigne (III. 2, beginning).

If everything is in a state of flux, so too is language; in which case nothing is knowable in the sense that nothing can be expressed immutably and clearly in language, unless we can discover something unchanging which communicates its stability to both thing and word.

Platonists did not seek this 'something' in the material world. If it was to be found anywhere, it would be in the world of the spirit. This spiritual element may, however, lend some of its stability to things and words as known to man.

Aristotelians, unless influenced by Plato, did not agree. For them there was stability in the world (which is itself eternal). Language, on the other hand, was an arbitrary construct. You would not expect to find truth in words as such – words as such have no link with the superhuman.

These are the kind of problems that form the backcloth to the

[1] It was once normal to dismiss out of hand Aristotle's influence on the *Essais*, to ignore Aristotelianism in general and to pass over scholastic influences completely. Even Villey does so (*Sources et évolution des Essais*, 2nd edition, 1933, pp. 69-72). As for Hugo Friedrich, he is wildly misleading (cf. *Montaigne*, Berne, 1949, p. 74); so are many others. But there is now a considerable interest in these questions, some of which were brought up in Dr Sharratt's Edinburgh colloquy, and in Dr Bolgar's Cambridge one, in 1974. Useful is Edilio Traverso's *Montaigne e Aristotele*, Florence, 1974. The only work I know which overlaps some of the preoccupations of this present book is an original study by A. Compagnon, which repays struggling with: *Nous, Michel de Montaigne*, Paris, 1980. His conclusions are different from mine but very challenging. Among other scholars interested in similar problems is Dr Ian Maclean of Queen's College, Oxford.

Essays when they treat matters related to Renaissance scepticism or Renaissance dogmatism.

2. Platonic forms

A stable language could convey truths about stable things. But language is not stable. How can we overcome this?

One of the ways suggested in the *Cratylus* is to uncover the etymologies of words, so giving access to their *etymon*, the 'truth' which the word allegedly conveys. This theory depends on notions which later views of the world have rendered strange and improbable. It assumes that at the beginning of language there were inspired lexical creators who made words as mirrors of the things they stood for.

This theory presupposes Plato's doctrine of forms (or ideas). The effects of his teachings are still with us, though even in Plato's time the unphilosophical laughed at them.

Since all is in flux in the world of matter, Plato concluded that there must exist, in pure reality, in the higher world of souls, 'forms', which are the ideal patterns of all things which do come into being. Once those forms are even partially known, discourse is possible. Everything there is in the material world of change corresponds to a stable form, which, for Christian Platonists, is an unchanging pattern in the mind of God. Behind the mere fleeting appearances of the material world, there lies the spiritual world of stable, immutable Being (*ousia*). Montaigne believed that Man, on his own, had absolutely no contact with Being:

(A) Finally there is no constant existence, either in our being or in that of objects. We and our judgment and all mortal things are ceaselessly flowing and rolling. And so nothing certain can ever be established from one to another: both what we judge and what we judge with are in continual change and movement. We have no communication with Being (II. 12, p. 366).

3. How to know individuals

What, then, is to be done? Are Plato's ideal forms the answer? Certainly his doctrine of forms was used to account for what philosophers term universals and individuation – a problem central to Montaigne. If you call one particular man 'Socrates' – and if he alone bears that name – you know where you are; but how is it that we can use a single universal term, Man, for countless individual human beings? What is the meaning of any such universal term? Is there such a thing as Man apart from countless individual people? How can you know what Man or, indeed, what any universal term means? This matters to Montaigne, whose main concern in the *Essays* is how to live and die as Man.

Revelation apart, the Platonic answer relies on the pre-existence of souls. We are born trailing clouds of memory; our souls dimly recall the forms which are the patterns on which individuals are made. We recognise individuals because we remember forms.

There is a form, Man. It really exists in the spiritual world. Philosophers can get to know that form. They may glimpse it as mirrored in the etymologies of words used for it; they may recall it to mind by the memory within their souls; they may practise dying and so glimpse the spiritual reality of form. Anyone who recalls or glimpses the forms – or is taught by one who has done so – knows what constitutes the humanity, the 'Man-ness', of each individual human being.

This applies to every kind of individuation. For Platonists, certainty begins and ends with the forms. No certainty is to be found anywhere else. If this is true, Montaigne's hunt seems hopeless:

> (A) It is impossible for the pieces to be arranged by anyone who does not have in his head a form of the whole (II.1, p.8).

4.   The forms of Aristotle

Aristotle rejected these doctrines of Plato. He did not believe that forms, as Plato described them, existed at all; nor did he have constant recourse to divine promptings when human reason proved inadequate. He did not believe that words have ingeniously or divinely placed etymologies which reveal stable truth about forms – or about anything else. Indeed, apart from onomatopoeias and the like, Aristotle taught that words result from the 'arbitrary imposition' of sound on meaning and so cannot have any genuine links whatever with the things they signify. Words do not picture things nor do they mirror them.

There is no real connexion between word and thing: you cannot get at the truth about a thing from the word used for it in any language; nor is there any need to. Forms for Aristotle are not ideal patterns in the divine mind, but moulds which give common characteristics to all the individual members of a genus and, more particularly, of a species. (Those who did not reach such things in their philosophy schoolbooks could have read them in their Cicero: *Topica* 7.31.)

In Aristotelian physics everything is composed of form and matter; an individual human being is composed of the form Man (which is in some way common to all individuals of the human species) and of matter (which is unique to him as an individual person). The matter makes him a separate individual; the form makes him human.

There are forms so demanding that they use up all the available matter, such as the form of the sun. But as far as mankind is concerned the matter is, for practical purposes, limitless. The form of Man is capable of limitless individuation.

Followers of Aristotle believed in strict definitions. All individuals belong to a genus and a species: an individual human being belongs to the genus Animal and the species Man. We should be able to grasp the essentials of a particular individual from the full definition of its general and specific qualities. In the case of an individual man – Socrates, say, or Montaigne – we should be able to approach him from the 'general' characteristics of the 'genus' Animal and from the 'specific' characteristics of the 'species' Man.

5.   Real or nominal?

These Platonic and Aristotelian theories lie behind the claims of the Realists and Nominalists of philosophy before, during and after the Renaissance. Realists claim that universals have a real existence, and thus that the form Man is a reality; Nominalists say that it is only a name.[2]

[2] For an excellent study of the ways in which Realist and Nominalist affected early Renaissance and Reformation thought, see H.A. Oberman, *Masters of the Reformation*, Cambridge, 1981. Sixteenth- and seventeenth-century glossed editions of Aristotle are also very helpful. I have used particularly (but by no means exclusively) the edition of Pedro Fonseca, that of the Jesuits of Coîmbra and that of Antonio Scaynus.

Montaigne addressed himself to these matters. He had to, if his work was to have validity. Rational theism is impossible if there are no universals. Christian Nominalists do make Christian doctrines irrational, since they insist that such doctrines exist independently of reason. They are matters for faith alone. On the other hand, Christian Realists tend to devalue the material world, preferring spiritual reality to unstable material things. They place souls not only above bodies – everyone did that – but immeasurably far above.

From the earliest times attempts had been made to reconcile Plato and Aristotle. Divisions between Platonist and Aristotelian, Realist and Nominalist, are not always stark and sharply defined, but Montaigne could not avoid taking up positions. He wanted to know an individual person: himself. He also wanted to know what natural philosophy had to tell Man about wise living and wise dying.

He 'assayed' himself in order to find out.

CHAPTER TEN

Assays and Resolutions

1. The footloose soul

Montaigne contrasts assays with solutions: 'If my soul could only find a footing, I would not be assaying myself but resolving myself' – *je ne m'essaierois pas, je me resoudrois* (III. 2, p. 21).

No final resolution of the problem of identity is, in human terms, possible: the world is compounded of constant and age-long change (*une branloire perenne*). Even great natural features such as the Caucasus and huge man-made buildings like the Pyramids are not exempt. Man, more volatile, changes from moment to moment. What one calls constancy is merely a slower rate of change – a body blow aimed at Stoics for whom constancy is the principal virtue.

Montaigne cannot portray absolute being, only his becoming-and-passing-away – *Je ne peins pas l'estre, je peins le passage.*

These themes, developed at the beginning of his chapter on repentance (III. 2), take up what was said even more powerfully at the conclusion of the apologia for Sebond:

> 'the whole of human nature is always in between birth and dying, so that it gives only a dark appearance and shadow of itself, an uncertain, weakly opinion.' (II. 12, pp. 366-7; quoting from Plutarch).

Since the gulf separating man from the Being of God is absolute, to cross it man needs a miracle; God must go beyond the order of things and lend him a hand. Plato's ideal forms are not part of the natural order of things. Even if they do exist, the mass of mankind has no contact with them.[1]

In matters of truth and human psychology Montaigne was no
Platonist. His *Essays* had to do without his soul's reminiscences
of spiritual forms, without Platonic glimpses of them in ecstatic
revelation, without hints from spirits or from daemons. Even
poetic ecstasy gave pleasure, not privileged truth.

2. No help from words

None of Plato's approaches to knowledge afforded any certainty
to Montaigne. His own emphasis on flux and change put him on
the side of Heracleitus and Cratylus. The French language was
prone to change, but so were all languages, to a greater or lesser
extent. He conceived of language in an Aristotelian way: as a

[1] Heracleitus' teaching that all is in a state of flux was best known from Plato's
complex dialogue the *Cratylus*, in which the rival theories of flux and
permanence are discussed, sometimes whimsically. Renaissance interpreters
variously believed that Socrates held one or the other of the opposing views or
even both of them at once. Ficino in his commentary on the *Cratylus* explains
that Socrates applied the doctrine of permanence to the supercelestial world of
Forms (or Ideas) and the doctrine of perpetual flux to everything in this
sublunary world. Montaigne firmly limits his natural philosophy to sublunary matters, restricting them therefore to the world of constant flux. The
Heracleitean doctrine of flux is faced by commentators on Aristotle, who accept
that, if literally everything is in a state of flux, then knowledge is impossible. Montaigne, by using the adjective *perenne* to explain the totter-
ing 'Perennial' seesaw movements of all worldly things, attaches his reflexions to this train of thought. Fonesca, for example, (on *Metaphysics* III,
cap. 5, cols. 895-6) considers that the *perennis fluxus rerum omnium* applies to
quantitas (material properties) but not to *qualitas* (whatever pertains to form). If
that is so, form is stable, and so potentially knowable, whilst matter is
unknowable, since it endlessly flows from change to change. Antonio Scaynus
treats the subject in his *Paraphrases de Prima Philosophia Aristotelis* (Rome,
1587, p. 56f.). He asserts that Plato misunderstood his master, misapplying to
the moral sphere of Socratic definitions the flux which Socrates had restricted to
material objects. At all events, certain knowledge concerns permanent form not
flowing matter. Montaigne accepts that he can only portray *le passage* (Man in
his changing state) not what was traditionally called the 'quiddities' of Man. If
he could discover the nature of the Being of Man (his *essence*) he could describe
what it was like (its 'quiddity'). At this stage at least he had no such pretensions.
Montaigne's inclusion of the Pyramids as examples of change is not original to
him. Erasmus, in his commentary on the 38th Psalm, *Dixi custodiam*, makes the
same point, incidentally showing how consonant with Christian doctrine
Montaigne's concern with perennial flux can be. (Cf. Erasmus, *Opera Omnia*,
1703-06, vol. 5. coll. 448F-450F and col. 461E: 'Where now are the pyramids of
Memphis? ... Nothing is stable, except that which the spirit of Christ builds up
within us.')

matter of convention, not as a divinely vouchsafed means of conveying truths. There is no place whatever in the *Essays* for truth-revealing etymologies. Proper names as a possible source of revealed truth are important to Platonists, but not to Montaigne. It is precisely in the chapter on names that Plato gets short shrift; some alleged derivations of French names are condemned as being 'as bad and as crude' as Plato's!

Names are simply 'pen-strokes common to a thousand men'. How many people are there 'in all races, who have the same name and surname?' Montaigne reinforced this in his last version:

> (C) And in different races, centuries and countries, how many? History has known three Socrates, five Platos, eight Aristotles, seven Xenophons, twenty Demetriuses, twenty Theodores – and guess how many history has overlooked! (A) What is there to stop my ostler from calling himself Pompey the Great? (I. 46, p.359).

Wherever Platonism and Neoplatonism flourished there were those who looked for divinely placed truth veiled in proper names. This was at least as true in Montaigne's time as in any other. He did not seek truth about himself in his own name; nor did he seek truth about others in theirs. He was just not interested in names. He did not admit them as possible sources of divinely certain knowledge. We know his father was called Pierre – but not from the *Essays*, where the fact is not even worth mentioning.[2]

The revolution worked by Montaigne can be seen by comparing him with Pantagruel. No Socratic daemon came to

[2] On what they took to be the authority of Socrates in the *Cratylus*, most Renaissance Platonists attached importance to etymologies as a way of getting at the true nature (the *etymon*) of the object named. Some however interpreted the *Cratylus* differently. Petrus Calanna, for example, may be cited to represent this view. In his *Philosophia Seniorum Sacerdotia, & Platonica* (Palermo, 1599, p. 72), he asserts that, in the *Cratylus*, 'Plato said that knowledge is not to be looked for from names or from their properties, since they are in a state of flux ... knowledge is to be studied from Ideas and sought from them. The Peripatetics [the Aristotelians] neglect our philosophy and laugh at these necessities, confuting them as useless and superfluous since, they say, things ... can be known from their quiddities and definitions.' As a sceptic Montaigne is neither a Platonist nor a thorough-going Aristotelian: he does not believe that he can find knowledge from Platonic forms nor from Aristotelian or scholastic definitions and quiddities.

prompt him as it did Pantagruel; no 'divine' Socrates ever gave
him 'superhuman' knowledge; no words bear for him the stamp
of veiled divinity and convey religious truth to those privileged to
know their true origins; no proper names are God-given
prophecies or divinely ordained labels, providentially attached
to people who truly correspond to what they mean; no serried
ranks of authors vouch for arts or sciences revealed to man
through their inspired genius; no enraptured judge is defended
by the celestial Intelligences; no judge receives the gift of
prophecy, making him 'beside himself'; no hero receives from
God the special 'gift of wisdom' ... Almost all that made the
Pantagruel of Rabelais's maturity heroically wise in his genial
splendour is dropped by Montaigne into the bin of error.

Rabelais and Montaigne present us with worlds belonging to
different orders of reality. To pass from the *Tiers* and *Quart
Livres* of *Pantagruel* to the *Tiers Livre* of the *Essays* is to relive
an intellectual revolution.

CHAPTER ELEVEN

Metaphysics

1. Experience

Montaigne chose to end the *Essays* with a deep bow towards Aristotle, the 'monarch' of the New Way, as well as with many a laugh at those who claimed to follow him. The chapter on experience, which brings the long inquiry of the *Essays* to a close, starts with a resounding echo of one of the most famous of all Aristotle's authoritative statements:

> There is no desire more natural than the desire for knowledge (*Il n'est desir plus naturel que le desir de connoissance*) (III. 13).

That is a vital commonplace of scholastic and humanist philosophy. What Aristotle wrote (in Cardinal Bessarion's Latin version) was *omnis homo natura scire desiderat* – 'every man naturally desires to know'. That contention and its close association with all empirical knowledge mean that even mere beginners could have placed the concerns of *De l'experience* in their philosophical context. A schoolboy knowledge might have sufficed. Montaigne is evoking the opening words and immediate preoccupations of Aristotle in the first chapter of the first book of the *Metaphysics*.

Montaigne, like Aristotle, plunged directly from this to reflexions on empirical knowledge. Men seek knowledge:

> We assay all the means which can lead us there. When reason fails, we try experience (III. 13, p. 360).

In Bessarion's version as, indeed, in philosophical usage

generally, the word used is *experientia*: both experience and experiment.

Aristotle and Plato held that 'experience produces art; inexperience, fortune'. That puts inexperience in the same category as human reasoning in its ineffectual chanciness; Montaigne had ended an earlier discussion of the uncertainty of human judgment by suggesting that human deliberations actually depend not on logic but on fortune. The final version went farther, finishing up with the challenging assertion that Plato was right: both men and their discourse are largely matters of *hazard* – of mere chance (I. 47, p. 368).

As far as natural inquiries are concerned, if human reason joins inexperience, then empirical knowledge is left holding the field. But Montaigne now proceeds to reduce experience to inexperience too. In this way virtually the whole of what passed for rational thinking or empirical enquiry becomes haphazard chance.

Aristotle asserted that a man who is able to extract a single universal judgment from a series of 'experiences' has produced an art (*techne*; *ars*). Through an association of ideas almost inevitable then, Montaigne first refers this *ars* to the art of medicine, the usual name for which was simply 'the Art' (*Ars* or, by a corruption of the Greek, *Tegne*). Throughout the *Essays* medical men are mocked and their mystery termed *leur art*. Law is associated with medicine, since common law and case law are based upon inductions made from numerous *experiences*.

The ancients placed empirical knowledge below reason, but valued it when reason ran out. Montaigne agreed that it was 'more feeble and less worthy'. In the end he allowed it perhaps just a little more validity than hazardous reason. Yet one of the many delights of the *Essays* is their concern to show the infinite variety of human beings and human situations. Montaigne dwelt on the limitless variety of it all. But where there is literally infinite variety there can be no certainty: no two patients are ill in exactly the same way; no one legal case corresponds to another in every respect. Some praised the ancient jurisconsult Tribonian for breaking up Roman law into gobbets in order to restrict the discretion of judges. (The expression for this was *tailler leur morceaux*, 'to cut their slices'.) Montaigne condemned him: his gobbets are useless. We are dealing not with what is numerous but what is infinite. No example overlaps any other sufficiently for definite conclusions to be made. No art can be drawn from infinite variety.

Some try to still philosophical disagreement by glossing the ancients, but experience shows that glosses and interpretations only increase the doubt: 'All I can say is that you can feel from experience that so many interpretations dissipate the truth and break it up. Aristotle wrote in order to be understood.' If he did not succeed, lesser men will not manage it for him.

Infinite doubts result from infinite cases. Infallible books are no answer: 'there is no book in the world, human or divine' where the glosses eliminate the difficulty. There are more books about books than anything else (III. 13, pp. 363-5).

One fruit which Montaigne did draw out of his experience is the wisdom of scepticism:

> (B) It is from my own experience that I acknowledge human ignorance which is, in my judgment, the most certain faction in the school of the world.

Those who will not accept this conclusion on his authority may do so on that of Socrates, '(C) The Master of masters' (III. 13, p. 375).

At no point did Montaigne ever allow finality to arts or sciences based on experience: 'Relationships drawn from experience are always weak and imperfect.' In other words, experience may lead a man of sound judgment to probable opinions: it will not lead him to certainty.

2. Words

Ancient philosophy consists in words. Macaulay summed it up in his essay *On Lord Bacon*: 'Words, and more words, and nothing but words, had been the fruit of all the toil of all the most reknowned sages of sixty generations ... The philosophy of Plato began with words and ended with words' (*Critical and Historical Essays* III, 1844, pp. 383, 386).

Montaigne anticipated this verdict: 'Our disputations are verbal ones' – a judgment which must be interpreted in the light of his contempt for such trivial merchandise. He made the point by reminding his readers of elementary steps in grammar and philosophy. Philosophy thrust you back to definitions –

definitions were needed to describe Platonic forms or to
characterise the species and genera of Aristotle. One of the best-
known definitions was that of Man. Plutarch cited it in his
treatise *On many friends*: 'it is all the same if you say Man, or
mortal and reasonable animal' – in Amyot's French: '*c'est tout
un que homme, mortel et animal raisonnable*' (*Oeuvres* I. 31).
Montaigne put it to good use in a passage calling upon schoolboy
memories of Priscian the ancient grammarian:

> Our disputations are verbal ones. I ask what is nature, pleasure,
> circle or substitution. The question is about words; it is paid in
> the same coin. – 'A stone is a body.' – But if you argue more
> closely, 'And what is a body?' – 'Substance' – 'And what is
> substance?' and so on; you will finally drive the answerer back to
> the end of his vocabulary-book. We change one word for another
> word – often for one less known. I know what a man is better than
> I know what is meant by animal, mortal or reasonable (III. 13,
> p. 366).

Priscian had said it all before, with the bland seriousness of
the grammarian explaining a platitude. To define anything that
can be defined we put forward a plain substantive and supply
adjectives:

> For example: 'What is an animal?' – 'An animated substance'. Or
> vice-versa: 'What is an animated substance?' – 'An animal' –
> 'What is a man?' – 'A rational and mortal animal'. And vice-
> versa: 'What is a rational and mortal animal?' – 'A man'.

Priscian added that you may do the same for all definitions,
including those describing the properties of genus and species
with regard to those 'general and specific forms which exist
intelligibly in the divine mind' before they go forth into bodies
(*Opera*, 1527, XVII, ii, p. 1180). The entire passage of Priscian
is cited in some source-books. (In the *Lexicon philologicum* of
Matthias Martinus it stands alone under the heading *Forma in
Deo Ideae*). For Priscian, definitions are ways of determining
the nature of those ideal forms in the divine mind which, he
held, give rise to genus and species.

So definitions ought to help us to understand what the species
Man is. For Montaigne, however, they do not. The nouns and
adjectives which may be used to define man do not help us to
know ourselves or others better.

Quite independently of Montaigne, Sanchez used the same argument to devastating effect in that sceptical little book, *Quod nihil scitur*. Either it was an argument that was going the rounds, or else two very original Christian sceptics hit on it at about the same time.[1]

Words were at best a secondary matter for Montaigne. For him, a good education formed not a grammarian or a logician but a gentleman. Teach a child 'things'; words will follow only too easily. 'Following' is what words are made for. Some people – like Quintilian – sought after fine words. We should do the contrary. Montaigne sought – and found – no help from words as such (I. 26, pp. 221-5).

Of course he venerated words when used in speech as trustworthy tokens for the honest exchange of ideas and opinions; of course he savoured them as an artist and as a lover of poetry. But he was impatient with the kind of reader who lingered over his style at the expense of what he had to say:

> (C) I am well aware that, when I hear anyone confine himself to the language of the *Essays*, I would prefer him to hold his peace. That is not so much a matter of raising up words as of thrusting down sense ... (I.40, p. 325).

3. The end of Man

Renaissance authors associated ideas in ways which now seem strange. We have to rediscover links and associations which were once evident enough to those within Renaissance culture.

For example: Montaigne's chapter on lying is largely taken up with a study of memory and forgetfulness. This seems whimsical, even perverse. But Quintilian put memory and lying together: 'Every liar had better have a good memory.' This was so well

---

[1] Sanchez's position in the dedication 'To the Reader' of *Quod nihil scitur*, (Lyons, 1581, p. 3) is close to Montaigne's: 'It is inborn to man to know how to wish; it is granted to few to wish to know, and to even fewer to know.' Sanchez exploits the *Animal rationale mortale* definition of Man on two occasions: (a) 'You say that you are defining a thing, not a word, with that definition *Animal rationale mortale*. I deny it. For I doubt again over the word *Animal*, about *rationale* etc.' (p. 2); (b) 'And that is not enough. Not being content with simple words, in order to make the matter more difficult' they 'use for *Man* the term *Animal rationale mortale*, which is more difficult than what we started with' (p. 5).

known that Rabelais used it in a minor work; Montaigne uses it in the same way.

We must consider Montaigne's echo of the opening words of Aristotle's *Metaphysics* in the same light. The phrase has a history of its own as a vital step in a well-known argument from natural reason proving the reality – indeed, the necessity – of an after-life. 'All men naturally desire knowledge' was used to prove that the 'end' of Man is not to be found in this world but in the next. Major versions go back to Socrates, Cicero and Scotus, but the argument was in wide currency and can conveniently be followed in Pedro Fonseca's *Commentary on Aristotle's Metaphysics* (1599, I. 73): Nature does nothing in vain. That is not in doubt; nevertheless 'all men naturally desire knowledge', yet 'experience shows that man's appetite cannot be satisfied by any one of this world's goods, nor by any combination of them'. Therefore only the world-to-come can offer hope of satisfying the thirst for knowledge with which Nature has endowed all individual human beings. In that way it can be seen that the desire for knowledge was not given by Nature in vain.

Such chains of argument were available to those who had no Latin. They could read it in Rabelais, who expounded the argument succinctly, though with his tongue in his cheek since he was no Scotist but an evangelical who intended his faith in the after-life to be based on a surer foundation than scholastic theology. Such arguments fall appositely here, nevertheless. Rabelais jumped with agility from the opening phrase of *Metaphysics* to the Biblical proof that the end of Man is life in the world-to-come, where, at last, he will be 'satisfied'. This notion of 'satisfaction' is found in all the authors treating this problem, including Montaigne. It is of the essence of the argument. Rabelais wrote:

The ancient philosophers who concluded that our souls are immortal did not have any argument to prove it or persuade of it other than the indication of an emotion within us, which Aristotle described (Lib. I *Metaphysicorum*), saying that all humans naturally desire to know – *tous humains naturellement desirent sçavoir* – ; that is to say that Nature has produced in Man a yearning, appetite and desire to know and to learn ... But, as men cannot come to perfect knowledge in this transitory life – for 'the eye is never satisfied with seeing nor the ear satisfied with hearing' (Ecclesiastes 1) – and as Nature has done nothing without a cause nor given an appetite or desire for anything which cannot be obtained (otherwise that appetite would be either frustratory or depraved): it follows that there is another life after this one, in which that desire will be satisfied (*Almanach pour 1535*).

In which case, adds Rabelais, you ought to echo St Paul's *cupio dissolvi* so that 'your souls may be taken from this dark prison and joined to Jesus the Christ'. It is as 'King David said (Psalm 16): I shall be satisfied, when I awake in thy glory' (Text in *Pantagrueline Prognostication*, Droz, pp. 45-6).

Montaigne makes the same points as cogently but more discursively. He likens the pursuit of knowledge to the sport of kings:

(B) It is only individual weakness which makes us satisfied with what others or we ourselves have already discovered in this hunt for knowledge. A cleverer man would not be satisfied. There is always room for someone to follow on afterwards (C) – indeed, for ourselves too – (B) always another way to follow.

The next sentence hammers the point home with the force of tradition. No hope is held out for a final understanding of anything in this life:

There is no end in our inquiries. Our end is in the other world (III. 13, p. 364).[2]

---

[2] Arguments such as these were also used to explain Cicero's statement in *De officiis* – itself linked to *Metaphysics* 1. 1, i – 'We are all attracted and drawn to a zeal for learning and knowing' (I. 6. 18). Cf. Xystus Betuleius in *De officiis*, with commentaries by Erasmus, Xytus Betuleius, Amerbach, Franciscus Maturantius, Calcagnini etc. (Paris, 1562), p. 23r: 'Socrates in the *Phaedo* seized upon this argument in favour of immortality, that the desire for knowledge and wisdom is natural to men, but, since this is achieved in this life by very few, or rather, by none, there is, without doubt, a future state so that this desire may be fulfilled elsewhere.' Amerbach (p. 23v) points out that 'Aristotle taught the same thing' as Cicero 'when he said: All men naturally desire knowledge'.

CHAPTER TWELVE

Contemplation

1. Satisfaction for the soul

The argument that Man's end lies in the next world did not exclude another arising from similar preoccupations. Many Scotists and others taught that Man was endowed with a natural and innate appetite for the 'enjoyment' of God. The numerous opponents of these teachings did not believe that such an innate appetite (if it did exist) could belong to the world of fallen nature; they emphasised the inordinate lack of proportion between such an appetite and the only means of satisfying it: God. Gulfs such as that cannot be crossed by natural means: they call for special grace. Ecstasy can be a means of giving man a foretaste of the joy he may experience from God's presence in the world to come; but such ecstasies will be rare and always provoked by supernatural means.

Questions such as these hung on interpretations of the opening sentence of Aristotle's *Metaphysics* with which Montaigne begins *De l'experience*. He might therefore be expected to touch on such questions too. He does, beginning like Aristotle, reaching the conclusion that there is no end to our inquiries (since Man's end is in the next world) and then closing the *Essays* as a whole with reflexions linked to privileged ways of enjoying a foretaste of heavenly bliss. He avoids being partisan, but his conclusions are far more Thomist than Scotist. A theologian of a Thomist bent would conclude that the natural desire to contemplate God is totally ineffectual and can only be satisfied through privileged grace. That is precisely the conclusion which Montaigne is to lead us to.

Montaigne wrote glowingly about contemplative rapture,

especially in the final version of the *Essays*. There he became
loud in praise of contemplation – for a handful of chosen mystics.
An important addition on this theme was written in the margin
of the chapter 'On Solitude' (I. 39, p. 318).

Montaigne contrasted two sorts of men: those who physically
withdraw from the world (like Cicero) but who fail to turn their
gaze 'outside the world', still clinging to its values and
judgments; and those who seek true religious solitude, 'filling
their hearts with the certainty of divine promises.' The latter
look out of this world to the world-to-come, contemplating God,
'an object infinite in goodness and in might':

> The soul finds matter there to satisfy (*ressasier*) its desires in
> perfect freedom.

The verb *ressasier* links this assertion with the train of thought
set off by the original echo of Aristotle, since (as many insisted)
man is 'not satisfied (*non satiari*) by this world's goods'; he will
be satisfied only by the glory of God.[1]

2. Asceticism

The saintly few can have a foretaste of this 'satisfaction' in their
ecstatic contemplations. Contemplation of this sort is marked, in
the *Essays*, by constancy and fierce asceticism: 'affliction and
pain are profitable' to such contemplatives; they use them to
acquire 'eternal health and joy'. For them death becomes
desirable, 'a passing over to so perfect a state'. Constant ascetics
can live with their bodies tamed by discipline; long custom
softens the harshness of their discipline; carnality is held in

---

[1] In his long discussion on *Metaphysics* 1.1, Fonseca raises the question, 'Does
man naturally have an appetite for an intuitive knowledge of the divine nature'.
In Question 2 (col. 72E. f.) he expounds the ideas of those who answer, Yes. The
fourth of those reasons is that 'we know from experience that man's appetite is
not satisfied (*non satiari*) by any one of the world's goods nor by any combination
of them'. He can only be satisfied by the Supreme Good, a clear, intimate and
familiar knowledge of God. Fonseca's own reply is given in Section 2 ('The true
explanation of the question', (col. 74B.f.) and in Section 3 ('The Removal of the
arguments of the adverse party'). Just like Montaigne, Fonseca insists that this
desire to be satisfied can only be slaked by means outside of Man's power (col.
74). There is no proportion between Man and his 'End' in the next world and
therefore no natural means of Man's achieving that End; the strength to do so
comes 'from the grace of God alone' (col. 145).

check by not being exercised. Only contemplation such as this is worth taming the body for. This alone, of all ecstasies, is held up for admiration:

> (C) Only this end, of another life blessedly immortal, loyally deserves our renunciation of the comforts and sweetnesses of this life of ours. Whoever can set his soul ablaze with the fire of this living faith and hope, really and constantly, builds in his solitude a voluptuous, delicate life beyond any other form of life (I. 39, p. 319).

This ascetic contemplation combines several key ideas: 'living faith and hope' echo the Gospels; constancy echoes the Stoics; pleasure and delight provocatively attributed to such a life – *une vie voluptueuse et delicate* – proclaim their source in Epicureanism.

In his colloquy *Epicurus*, Erasmus, partly following Lorenzo Valla, had confronted his readers with a similar paradox; the real Epicureans are rare Christian ascetics. They alone know solid joys and lasting pleasure.

CHAPTER THIRTEEN

The Church

1. Authority

The mass of ordinary Christians cannot and should not aspire to such heights. They should lead an ordinary life in this world, obeying the Church in every detail. Montaigne professed his complete submission to the Church of Rome. These professions increase in number and intensity in the final version. The chapter on prayer shows what an abyss there was between him and the *Eglise réformée*, which took the Bible not the Roman Catholic Church as the basis of religious certainty.

It is in this chapter that Montaigne most specifically claims that the *Essays* are 'unresolved fantasies', seeking truth not laying it down. The church authorities alone have the right.

> (A) to regulate not only my actions and my writings but even my thoughts. Their condemnation will be as acceptable as their approbation; (C) myself finding it execrable if anything has been said by me, ignorantly or inadvertently, against the ordinance of the Catholic, Apostolic and Roman Church, wherein I die and wherein I was born (I. 56, pp. 408-9).

The *Roman* attached to *Catholic* avoids ambiguity. All churches claim to be Catholic. That is why slick lawyers told you, if you were subjected to questioning about your faith by hostile authorities, to say that you were a Catholic. By insisting on his *Roman* Catholicism, Montaigne left the reader in no doubt about the identity of the Church to which he gave unqualified allegiance.

Montaigne took care to submit himself in public to the authority of his Church even before approaching what he called

'(C) the only prayer which I make use of everywhere' – the Lord's Prayer, the 'prayer prescribed and dictated to us, word by word, by the mouth of God', thanks to 'a special favour from the divine Goodness'.

It may be the Lord's Prayer, but its use and interpretation are subject to the Church. Hence the hesitation: 'I am not sure whether I am mistaken, but … ' (I. 56, pp. 408-9). The words of Christ-as-God need interpretation. The increased protestations of orthodoxy derive in part from criticisms made of aspects of this chapter when Montaigne submitted the *Essays* for comment to the *Maestro del Palazzo* in the Vatican. He withdrew little, but strengthened and clarified much. The Church authorities were apparently quite happy about it all.

For some readers, this makes Montaigne suspect. Yet from the outset he condemned those who presumed to judge the Church and her teaching by their own standards or by natural reason. To judge God and his ways by human standards is stupid. Take the case of miracles. To know what is or is not a miracle by human reason you would have to know 'the bounds of the will of God and of the power of our mother Nature'. But the 'power of Nature' is 'infinite'. So to judge miracles by the standards of mankind is madness (*folie*), as the title of Chapter 27 of Book I states. Montaigne had come to believe that no point of doctrine should be conceded to schismatics or protestants. Apparently minor concessions, which he had once thought not to matter, turned out to be vital: 'We must either submit ourselves totally to the authority of our ecclesiastical polity or have nothing at all to do with it.' Christians have no right to decide on their own 'how much obedience they owe the Church' (I. 38). But without her catholicity, her universality, the Church is nothing. The true Church is not local or national and does not vary from place to place or from time to time. Only protestants or schismatics chop and change. Truth is one and the same everywhere and for ever.

As he wrote in another context: 'the ultimate perfection is to add constancy' (II. 2, p. 18).

Montaigne is the authentic voice of post-Tridentine rigour. There is no room for compromise of any kind over religious truth.

2.   The body and the Church

The Roman Catholic Church found a place for joyful contemplation; it was as a privileged ecstasy for privileged souls. The mass of Christians must come to terms with their bodies. Montaigne had no patience with those who would try to make all Catholic Christians into saintly contemplatives.

> Those who, in recent years, have wished to build up for us so contemplative and non-material a religious exercise should not be astonished if there are those who think that it would have slipped and melted through their fingers if it did not keep a hold among us as a mark, sign and means of division, of faction, rather than for itself (III. 8, p. 186).

That can hardly be a condemnation, as some editions say, of 'leaders of the Reformation'. Montaigne would not have classed them as 'factions among us' nor dubbed them 'contemplatives'. He is condemning a party within his own Church, associated with an *exercice de religion* which did not give the body its due. These exercises did not work; but they did mark their devotees out as partisan. A faction was trying to foist on to the Church an excessively spiritualised soul-centred worship. (The context does not seem to fit the Jesuits and Loyola's spiritual exercises.)

It was not only ordinary sensual men who found such immaterial extremes excessive: so did celibate Sorbonne theologians. Rabelais and others had turned the wine drunk at high table and gaudy into a proverbial saying: *vin théologal*. Montaigne defended the *Magistri Nostri*: having spent their mornings working seriously and conscientiously, they deserved to dine well. In that way first soul and then body have their due. A good conscience makes a good sauce (III. 13, p. 420). Where most Christians are concerned, the right thing to do is to avoid giving comfort and satisfaction to only one of our two constituent parts.

3. Sebond's ecstasy: the risk of heresy

This conclusion is in keeping with Montaigne's growing distrust of ecstasy and spiritual rapture. Ecstasies are at the root of the Church's experience, but they are subjects of concern and scrutiny, since important heresies derive from claims to ecstatic revelation and from claims of enthusiasts to have found union with God. In the early Church there had been Montanism; in the mediaeval and Renaissance Church, Beghardism. These heresies were still felt to be very much a danger – enemies accused Erasmus of both of them. Particularly to be watched was any claim that the soul was made 'one' with God. A privileged soul may seek a kind of union with God, but not assimilation – union, not an absorption which would make it 'one' with a God who absorbs its identity.

Montaigne knew this; without warning he recast an interesting passage in his version of Sebond's *Theologia Naturalis*. By doing so he avoided praising even true ecstasy in terms which time had made open to suspicion. Sebond wrote:

> Oh! How close man comes to God! What assimilation, what unity, what goodness of God!

God's word goes straight from his heart to the heart of Man:

> And since there is nothing nearer to God than his Word, he completely draws the heart and soul of man to God whence he came, and makes the heart of man one with the heart of God.

In Montaigne's version all talk of assimilation, unity and oneness goes; this censoring of possibly heretical excesses took place well before the *Essays* were begun, and serves to remind us that Montaigne had a sophisticated theological awareness of the dangers involved when ecstasy got out of hand.[1]

---

[1] *Theologia naturalis*, chapter 216: *Ecce quanta propinquitas hominis ad Deum, quanta assimilatio, quanta unitas, quanta Dei bonitas, quia verbum quod exit, immediatemente de corde Dei, intrat cor hominis. Et nihil propinquius Deo quam verbum eius, ideo totaliter trahit cor hominis et animam ad Deum, unde exit, et facit cor hominis unum cum corde Dei.*

With that compare Montaigne's rendering (*La Theologie naturelle*, Paris, 1569, p. 251v): 'Voyez la bonté de nostre createur, & l'estroicte societé qu'il daigne dresser avec l'homme. La parole qui part de son coeur et de sa bouche entre en nostre coeur & en nostre ame: d'autant qu'à mesme qu'elle part de luy, elle emporte avec soy son coeur, son intention, & sa volonté, & vient loger en nous, ainsi honorablement accompagnée, il advient qu'elle moyenne un tres-heureux & tres-salutaire meslange & conjonction du coeur de nostre createur avec le nostre, et de nostre volonté avec la sienne. Et attendu qu'il n'y a rien de si près à Dieu que sa parole, il s'ensuit encore, qu'eschauffant & embrazant nostre coeur & nostre ame d'une saincte amour, elle les esleve & pousse contremont jusques à Dieu, duquel elle est partie, & les attache & coust à sa saincte divinité d'un noeud inviolable.'

A rendering as cautiously free as that betrays a keen awareness of the possibly heretical implications of Sebond's doctrine at this point.

Montaigne was not the kind of philosopher who 'practised dying' in ecstasy; nor was he the kind of Christian who sought religious strength, comfort or knowledge from enthusiastic ecstasies outside the direction of the Church. For him, the Church reigned supreme. Natural reason was fallible; experience was too; revelation needed the Church to interpret both meaning and application.

What Montaigne wanted to know was what Man is – and he wanted to know it from human sources and natural reason; the Church could not help him. He found his answer in his own highly original, indeed revolutionary, use of form and matter as conceived by Aristotle. He was helped to his conclusions by his deep distrust of ecstasy. If man is body and soul – i.e. matter and form – should we not keep them both together if we want to know what Man is? If Man is form and matter, firmly wedded one to the other, psychological knowledge alone is just as inadequate as purely physiological knowledge.

CHAPTER FOURTEEN

The Whole Form of Man

1. Physics or metaphysics?

The Church resolved problems about God and man raised by natural reason – in the *Essays* or anywhere else. Its power to resolve was not limitless. The Church established universities and afforded a large place within them to human inquiry. The moral system by which men lived was not an ecclesiastical monopoly. The four cardinal virtues are Justice, Prudence, Fortitude and Temperance; they do not derive from the Bible, from the Fathers or from Councils of the Church, but from Aristotle. They were taken to be 'natural' – ultimate moral platitudes, not open to doubt. The Church recognised them and added three theological virtues (Faith, Hope and Charity).

The Church had no power to decide whether or not there were inhabitants in the New World; that had to be decided empirically. But the Church did decide whether or not the inhabitants, once discovered, were fully human.

Montaigne conceived of philosophy, much as the Romans did, with a bias towards practical ethics. He wanted to get on with the job of living – and learning how to die (II. 10, p. 102). To do that he had to find out more about Man.

Aristotle's *Metaphysics* made it plain that the mere accumulation of experiences does not amount to knowledge and so cannot, of itself, lead to wisdom. Montaigne did not expect to find conclusions anywhere in Aristotle's writings, but he made good use of his philosophy; not only does *De l'experience* start off with its echo of *Metaphysics* I. 1 but arguments known from Books I, III and VII of *Metaphysics* form the background of his own argument. Yet Aristotle was, after all, only a learned author. 'Authors' are indeed held up in honour, in contrast to the glossators and commentators who seemed to have the contemporary stage to themselves (III. 13, p. 365); but no man has final authority. Men are *autheurs vains et irresolus* – empty authorities who resolve nothing.

The trouble is that even good authors can only tell you about their own experience – and such experience is outside ourselves. Something may be learned from outside experience, but it will not take you far. To be useful, experience must be our own inside experience:

> Whatever fruit we may glean from experience, that which we draw from outside examples will hardly contribute much even to our elementary education, unless we profit from the experience we can have of ourselves; that is more familiar to us and certainly enough to teach us what we need (III. 13, p. 371).

Then, with what amounts to a punch-line in a chapter written with a sustained concern for Aristotle's writings, Montaigne brings the section to a close:

> I study myself more than any other subject. That is my metaphysics; that is my physics (*C'est ma metaphysique, c'est ma physique*) (III. 13, p. 371).

Every man is his own Aristotle.

2. Forma mentis

Montaigne did not say that he never studied Aristotle but that his study of even the *Physics* and *Metaphysics* took second place to his study of himself. To study yourself need not be limiting: quite the reverse. For Montaigne it leads firmly back to the forms of Aristotle and scholastic theology and then on to Man himself.

Montaigne deepened his wisdom by a study of his character. In Greek, the word *character* meant the die-stamp on coins; it was also used to describe groups of different people having, as it were, the same stamp. In Latin *character* was rendered by *forma* which had a wider sense, being used both for a group and for individual people with the characteristics of that group. This sense of *forma* merges into the *forms* of Aristotle, into form as distinct from matter and into soul as the form of Man. All these senses are found in *forme* as Montaigne uses it.

The form which is 'character' is not the same as complexion or humour. It is more fundamental than that, and closer to *forma* in the expression *forma mentis* – the cast of a man's mind. It is the nearest thing to permanence in man.

Montaigne studied himself, observed himself and brought his reading and experience to bear upon himself. As a result he began to understand better his own form – the character of his own soul – but not until he came to terms with the fact that it was conjoined with his own body, in a union which alone made him a particular man.

The form which he discovered in himself and which gave him some characteristics which, in this world of change, are virtually permanent, he called his master mould, his *forme maistresse*. He discovered that, in his case, it gave him an inclination to doubt and to acknowledge his ignorance. He wrote of surrendering himself 'to doubt and uncertainty and to his *maistresse forme*, which is ignorance' (I. 50, p. 387).

The exact relation of this *forme maistresse* to *forme* as soul is not spelled out, but each man has a form peculiar to himself. No one can change it completely; everyone, if he tries, can examine his own: 'Nobody who listens to himself can fail to uncover a *forme* of his own, a *forme maistresse* which resists education and the storm of passions which oppose it' (III. 2, p. 29).

When Montaigne began his chapter on repentance with two allusions to the notion of form he was preparing his readers for what was to come:

(B) Others form Man; I give an account of Man and sketch a picture of a particular one of them who is very badly formed ... (III. 2).

But Montaigne came to realise that, badly formed as he was, his was the only form of Man he could ever know at first hand. He was the *only* example of individuation within the human species that he could study. If he could not get to know himself, he would never get to know Man.[1]

---

[1] Sanchez is more sceptical than Montaigne here: 'I know, you say, that while the same form remains the individual is always the same'. He counters this argument by stressing that the same form does not 'inform' a body in the same way, precisely because of the *perpetua mutatio* of the body (*Quod nihil scitur*, p. 45).

3. Honesty

To get to know the form of himself as a particular man he must
first listen to himself. He must then give an account of himself –
not a partial one but one which shows him roundly as Man:

> (C) Authors communicate themselves to the public by some
> peculiar mark foreign to themselves; I – the first ever to do so – by
> my universal being as Michel de Montaigne, not as grammarian,
> poet or jurisconsult (III. 2, p. 21).

Montaigne realised that there was far more to knowing a man
than simply knowing his profession. He intended to explore, and
then convey to the world, his 'universal being'. By his *estre
universel* Montaigne means the whole of his being, body and
soul. No part of his life can be left out of account if the picture he
is sketching is to be a true one. Hence the importance of his
protestations of truth. It is puzzling that even some of those who
like Montaigne believe that he was a liar.

Montaigne saw how vital truth was for him. Lying is an
ungentlemanly vice, but his hatred for it goes beyond that:
'Truly, lying is an accursed vice. We are men, and hold one to
another, by speech (*parolle*).' If we knew the 'horror and weight'
of lying we would burn people for that rather than for other
crimes. Montaigne, of all people, talks of burning in an age when
stakes and pyres had seldom been more frequent – a measure of
his detestation of the one vice that could sap the very
foundations of wisdom (I. 9, p. 40).

> (A) Lying is a villein's vice, a vice which an Ancient paints
> shamefully when he says that it gives testimony to contempt for
> God together with fear of men. It is not possible to show more
> richly the horror of it, its vileness and its disorderliness ... Our
> understanding is conducted by speech alone; anyone who falsifies
> it, betrays public society. It is the only tool by means of which we
> communicate our wishes and our thoughts; it is our soul's
> interpreter (II. 18, p. 456).

Montaigne's aversion to lying does not mean that everything
he wrote may be taken straight. There is his humour for one
thing; in that vein he has to be taken with a grain of salt. He
suffered from the anguished, suicidal pain of stones in the

kidney; he found arguments, both playful and serious, to help him bear that pain. Some of his arguments here and throughout the *Essays* are akin to rhetorical declamations – a *genre* which leaves an author free to exaggerate and sport with ideas. He frequently argues on both sides of a question or else marshals strong arguments for a case he is later to undermine. He can also be ironical and paradoxical:

> (B) Feeling you to be tense and prepared on one side, I make the case for the other with all the care I can – not in order to bind your judgment but so as to enlighten it.

Readers of Renaissance paradoxes know the importance of context (cf. III. 11, p. 318).

But Montaigne knew that lying or prudent ambiguity were not for him. If he consciously lied we might as well not bother to read him: saying one thing and doing another was no good; 'it cannot apply to those who relate themselves as I do' (III. 9, p. 265).

4.   The whole form of mankind

Montaigne has his master form. Others have theirs. What are the links between these particular forms and the form of the species Man? What constitutes common humanity? Is there any way of getting from Man to men, from species to a solid, certain knowledge of 'particulars'? Montaigne suggests that there is not. Indeed his quiet revolution lay in his interpretating the *Metaphysics* in such a way as to turn long-established notions on their heads. He took an Aristotelian commonplace, widely accepted in Latin scholastic philosophy, and eventually started from the other end – the end philosophers wanted to reach. This commonplace concerns individuation within species.

A good way to get at Montaigne's assumptions is through the Latin Aristotle of Renaissance schools and colleges. We find that, to account for the existence of 'particulars' – individuals within a species – Aristotle used the analogy of bronze spheres. Out of a mass of bronze you can make any number of bronze spheres. Bronze is the matter; sphere is the form which moulds it. Bronze spheres are alike in being spherical; they are different in that they are made from particular and individual lumps taken from that mass of bronze. Mankind corresponds to this analogy but with significant differences.

As a species, Man corresponds to the general notion 'Bronze Sphere'. But a particular man corresponds to 'one particular bronze sphere' – or, as it was normally put, to '*this* bronze sphere', *haec aenea sphaera*.

This is where Aristotle departed radically from Plato. Plato saw an individual man as being composed of matter from this world and of an imprint derived from the form Man in the divine mind. To understand one man, therefore, you had to understand the ideal form of Man. To understand Man your soul could draw on pre-natal memories or else on revelation. These memories and revelations may be your own or other people's; in either case the knowledge conveyed originated outside this world.

Aristotle cut out the divine mind. An individual man is not a 'particular' because of his body (his matter) alone any more than a bronze sphere is a 'particular' because of its bronze (its matter) alone. One bronze sphere is *haec aenea sphaera* in the sense that it is 'this (one particular) bronze sphere': that is, it is one particular case of the form Sphere moulding matter. The whole of 'this sphere', form *and* matter, is the particular.

So too with a particular man. Montaigne is not a 'particular' – an individual man – because of his body alone. He is this particular *man* – one-soul-in-one-body: that is, he is one particular case of the form of the species Man imposed upon matter.

Montaigne did not feel that he had the gift of explaining the elements of a subject – and questions of form and matter were, in all conscience, elementary enough. In the Renaissance, glossed editions of the *Metaphysics* explained it all from the very outset. Montaigne used the word *forme* throughout the *Essays* in ways which show that he largely accepted Aristotle's theory of individuation, but in an idiosyncratic way.

The *Essays* describe one particular man, Michel de Montaigne, but they do not treat him as one odd creature in the void. To this study of himself Montaigne links his interest in the species Man and in human moral wisdom and imperatives. Where this corner-stone of the *Essays* is concerned he is clear and unambiguous, using the appropriate simple, though technical, terms to explain what he is doing. 'You can link the whole of moral philosophy to a lowly private life just as to one made of richer stuff.' This is because (B) 'Every man bears the *forme entiere* (the whole form) of the human condition' (III. 2, p. 21).

If this assertion is not true, Montaigne's project collapses and the *Essays* make no sense. If it is true, it is arguably the most important sentence Montaigne ever wrote. Not that there is anything unusual in the assertion as such; that the whole form of the human race is to be found in every single man and woman is the teaching of Thomist theology and so, in a special sense, the teaching of Montaigne's Church. We may note the categorical nature of Montaigne's assertion. There is no tentative sceptical hesitation here. This is an issue on which he did not need to keep an open mind. He had found it to be true – with startling and unexpected consequences. And he could find it true by his chosen method of human inquiry, since Aristotle's notion of specific form does not demand any knowledge originating from outside this world.[2]

---

[2] Useful definitions may be found in Signoriello: *Lexicon peripateticum philosophico-theologicum*. Cf.s.v.*Forma*: 'Form is communicable and universal'. Aquinas' commentary on Peter Lombard's sentences is cited to prove that it is the capacity to be received in many individuals which gives form its property of universality (*atque eo quod 'in pluribus est receptibilis, rationem universalitatis habet'*); 'e.g. *humanitas*, which is the form of Man, can be common to many; hence the differences which proceed from form lead not to a diversity of individuals or to numerical diversity but to a diversity of species'. Although form is itself both *communicabilis* and *universalis*, individuation proceeds from the matter to which it is joined in any given case; 'for example, the *humanitas* in Socrates is proper to Socrates, not to any man, in that it is circumscribed by one set of material conditions not another (*ex eo quod ab hisce, et non aliis conditionibus materiae conscribitur*'. For those who accept this, there is no reason why Montaigne's own form should not be both universal *per se* yet circumscribed by its matter and so proper to him as Michel de Montaigne.

CHAPTER FIFTEEN

Fair Forms and Botched Forms

1. Aristotle and the glossators

Aristotle gave Montaigne the means of justifying his study of himself. If there were nothing but an infinite number of individual people – if the human race were nothing but infinite singulars and particulars – then nothing could be known about Man in general and no wisdom could be drawn from a study of even a great many particular cases. Aristotle overcame this difficulty by teaching (like Montaigne) that, in the case of all the particular individuals within any species, the whole form of the species is found, in its entirety, in each and every one of them.

Take two particular men – Aristotle calls them Callias and Socrates. Callias and Socrates both have the form of Man. But it is the union of the form Man within their separate bodies which makes each of them '*this* man' Callias and '*this* man' Socrates: 'The whole of this form, together with this flesh and these bones (*tota vera jam talis forma in his carnibus et ossibus*), is Callias, say, or Socrates.'

These men are different because they are moulded out of distinct lumps of matter. They remain of one species because form is indivisible – *indivisibilis est forma*. Every man has this indivisible form within his individual person.

Antonio Scaynus in his commentary on the *Metaphysics* sums it up clearly. There can be no knowledge if singulars remain singulars. But because 'form is everlasting and universal in all eternally existing species', knowledge of singulars can be had from their universal form.

It is at this point that the analogy with bronze spheres breaks down in the case of Man. If you say 'sphere' you can mean either the species Sphere or this particular sphere. 'That is because individual spheres do not have particular names by which they may be called, whereas in the human species individual men do have particular names: Socrates, for example, or Plato, and so on.'

Each particular man can be identified by a personal name. It does not prevent him from having, in his own self, the entire universal form, Man. 'If he did not, he would not be a man.' That is why a knowledge of particulars can be derived from a knowledge of species and specific forms.

But if that is true, is not the contrary true too? Montaigne saw this with blinding clarity. If he painted the whole of his being, his *estre universel*, as Michel de Montaigne, he could gain access to man as universal in the philosophical sense of that term – access, that is, to that 'universal form' which, when joined to the matter of individual bodies, makes every man and woman (in ways which are teased out in the *Essays*) into a particular human being. In other words he could find out what Man is.

The old analogies are still useful as a way of following what Montaigne was doing. If you wanted to find out about Bronze Sphere as a universal, you would not study only the sphericalness of one or more individual spheres, nor would you study only the bronze: you would study an example or two of the bronze as moulded into spheres, the unity which is spherical bronze. So, too, Montaigne studied more than his form apart or his matter apart; he studied Michel de Montaigne, a person consisting in a form espoused to a body and so enjoying his *essence* – his 'being' as a man:

> (C) It is not my deeds that I am writing down, it is me – my *essence* (II.6, p. 60).

2. Botched forms and individual forms

At this point Montaigne had to tread with care. Aristotle's teaching about forms, interpreted in ways which pleased Nominalists and terrified Realists, had given rise to quarrels so disruptive of Christian unity that the Church had intervened. On 19 December 1513 the decree *Apostolici Regiminis* was promulgated at the Fifth Lateran Council. The Aristotelian teaching that the whole of the form of a species is present in every individual of that species could mean that there was only one form shared between them all, or that all forms are identical. And since the form of Man, his *humanitas*, is soul, that could mean that there was only one kind of soul – or even only one soul – for the whole of human kind. The Fifth Lateran Council anathematised those who asserted that the intellective soul is 'one in all men' (*unicam in cunctis hominibus*).

Philosophers, Aristotelian or otherwise, were ordered to teach orthodox psychology from their chairs – an extraordinary case of theologians over-stepping limits. The Gallican Church did not accept the catholicity of Lateran V. But Montaigne was wise not to remain ambiguous on such a point.

He found ways of keeping the universality while emphasising the individuality. He himself had a botched form of Man; if he were to be improved he would have to be re-formed – moulded again. Some great men were better forms of Man. But all were forms of Man, not of beasts or angels.

> I can condemn my *forme universelle* and beg God that I be re-formed and that he should pardon my natural weakness. But it seems to me that I should no more call that repentance than that I should call repentance my displeasure at not being an Angel or Cato (III. 2, p. 32).

The point is that angels have a higher form than men, while Cato was one of the best formed men the world has seen. (Although Montaigne does not mention it, Dante thought that Cato was the natural man who could best represent God.)

3. Angels and Cato

Men who live their lives according to the order of Nature must accept that they are not souls. They are more – and less – than that.

Christianity, under the influence of Greece, had hesitated. Rome did so no longer. A man's form (his soul) is akin to an angelic spirit. Unlike an angel it has to learn to live – in this life and for eternity – with a body. In this world at least, the body makes any man akin to the beasts; yet he is not a beast, any more than he is an angel. His human individuality requires, now and forever, both body and soul. So, on those occasions when

Montaigne alludes to human beings as *formes* and *ames* (souls) it is a powerful hyperbole; he is claiming that, as far as these particular people are concerned, their forms are so excellent that the body plays a strikingly subordinate rôle in their individual personality. He himself was quite at home with his status as a man, neither beast nor ethereal spirit. This is why he rarely repents and why, at times, he nevertheless yearns for a total reformation: '(C) my conscience is content with itself – not as the conscience of an angel, not as the conscience of a horse, but as the conscience of a man' (III. 2, p. 23). Angels and horses have an easier time than a man, crawling twixt heaven and earth.

Montaigne called the Younger Cato one of the *sainctes formes*. The beauty of his virtue (which it is the duty of decent men to paint as beautiful as it was) produced transports of admiration – ecstatic wonder: 'It is not unfitting that emotion should transport us under the influence of such holy forms.' Later, Montaigne would keep the respect but moderate the transport.

Socrates too was right to accept his unjust condemnation to death, keeping unsullied 'so holy (*saincte*) an image of the human form'.

Saincte – despite the translations just given – means not holy in a Christian sense but 'worthy of pious admiration'. Montaigne was never tempted to exclaim, like a character in Erasmus nearly did, 'O Saint Socrates, pray for us'. Socrates was not perfect. He was a man who had improved his 'vicious kink' (*vicieux pli*) by reason, and whose virtue was serene and constant. It is as reasonable man that he has the edge even over Cato: Cato 'ravishes our judgment': Socrates 'wins it over'. When great-souled virtue is extolled in poetry, ecstasy is 'not unbecoming' in us readers (*ne nous messieroit pas*). Cato shows how high 'human virtue and firmness can reach'. But even in these cases it is better to be won over than to be enraptured (I. 37, p. 303; III. 12, p. 345). These 'transports' become an obstacle to Montaigne's objectives and are soon to be played down. But even when they have full play, as here, what transports the ecstatic, ravished reader is his own ordinate emotion when confronted by the highest human greatness beautifully portrayed.

4. **The soul at home**

Here we come back to our ecstasies. The form of man is his soul;
it can be quietly at home in its body or off on fantastic jaunts. As
we would expect, Montaigne insists on judging a man when he is
'at home':

> (B) Vicious souls are often incited to do good from some outside
> source; in the same way, good souls may do evil. We should judge
> them from their settled state, when they are *chez-elles* – at home –
> if ever they are so (III. 2, p. 28).

A man is at home – *apud se* in Latin – when his soul is in the
body. When it is not in the body, the word that springs to mind is
furiosus, in some sense, good or bad.

By insisting on this, Montaigne justifies his full portrayal of
his *estre universel*, his soul-at-home-in-his-body. Anything else
would be more, or less, than human.

5. **Human brotherhood**

Montaigne, studying the whole of his being, his *estre universel*,
in the light of his reading and converse, is like a philosopher
acquiring knowledge of the species Bronze Sphere by taking one
fairly imperfect example – the 'this bronze sphere' that he knows
most intimately – and comparing it with a variety of other ones,
some of which are in far better shape.

What did Montaigne and La Boëtie talk about in their glorious
intimacy? Potentially dangerous notions about the brotherhood
of man, for one thing. Such thoughts led La Boëtie to prefer
doges and senators to monarchs. These political conclusions
arose from thoughts on Aristotelian forms and moulds. La Boëtie
wrote:

> Nature, the Minister of God, the Governor of Men, has made us
> all of the same form, and, it seems, with the same mould, so that
> we can all mutually know each other as companions, or rather as
> brothers ... This good Mother Nature ... has fashioned us all on
> the same pattern, so that each one can see himself and, as it were,
> recognise himself in the other.[1]

[1] La Boëtie, *De la Servitude Volontaire*, ed. P. Bonnefon, 1892, pp. 15-17: 'La

Armed with such ideas Montaigne could sympathetically understand each and every human being, friend and foe alike. And that included both sexes once he concluded that men and women are 'cast in the same mould' (III. 5, end).

6. The greater forms

Concern with the brotherhood of man can be reductive. In Montaigne's case it was constructively so.

The greater forms can be, in varying ways, debunked and reduced to the common level; Montaigne resisted attempts to level down humanity at its highest. But great men remain great ... men. Cato's greatness was like that of soldiers sallying forth: that of Socrates was stable and constant:

> (B) He was always one and the same; he mounted to the ultimate point of vigour not by sallies but by complexion (III. 12, p. 323).

This raises the question of the temperament of Socrates. His complexion was melancholic. That was never in doubt. Yet was it the kind of melancholy which Ficino found in Aristotle's *Problems*, a special disposition towards divinely enraptured genius, or was it the kind of melancholy which Montaigne championed as his own? He preferred the melancholy which kept the soul at home in the body; according to Ficino's interpretation of the *Problems*, Socrates' melancholy sent his soul soaring aloft in ecstatic rapture and made him prone to enthusiasms brought on by his special daemon. Montaigne had to deal with that. If Socrates had a daemon, he was not simply the wisest form and pattern set before humanity; he was superhuman: a man inspired.[2]

Montaigne tackled the problem in several ways. Often he simply ignored the daemon. Socrates was 'the man most worthy to be known and to be presented to the world as an example'.

Nature, la ministre de Dieu, la Gouvernante des hommes, nous a tous faits de mesme forme et, comme il semble, à mesme moule, afin de nous entreconnoistre tous pour compagnons ou plustost pour freres. [...] Cette bonne mere Nature nous a tous figurés à mesme patron, afin que chascun se peut mirer et quasi reconnoistre l'un dans l'autre.'

[2] Cf. Ficino, *Opera Omnia*, Paris, 1641; I, p. 485, etc.

Happily we know him from the accounts of Plato and Xenophon, 'the most clear-sighted man there has ever been'. The words that are applied to the model of mankind and his character include *vulgaire* (popular) *naturel, ordinaire, commun*; he brought philosophy down from heaven and set it among men. In his defence against his accusers he used no art nor rare erudition: '(B) He did a great favour to human nature by showing how much it can do by itself' (III. 12, p. 325).

Montaigne's next remark would be surprising – even comic – if he had not prepared us for the brotherhood of man: 'Each of us is richer than he thinks' – we could all be more like Socrates if we tried.

Quite early in his quest Montaigne had tackled the daemon head on. His method, as always, was to examine himself. The daemon of Socrates was 'perhaps a certain thrust of the will' which presented itself to him without awaiting the counsel of his arguments: 'It is likely that, in a soul like his (well purified and prepared by the continual exercise of wisdom and virtue) inclinations such as these, albeit bold and undigested, were nevertheless important and worthy to be followed.' Then comes Montaigne's appeal to common experience, especially his own:

> (B) Everybody can feel in himself some image of such agitations (C) of a prompt, vehement, fortuitous opinion. It is open to me to allow them some authority – to me who allow little enough to human prudence. (B) And I have had some agitations – (C) equally weak in reason yet violent in persuasion or dissuasion and which were more ordinary in the case of Socrates – (B) by which I have allowed myself to be carried away so usefully and so successfully, that they could have been judged to comport something of divine inspiration (I. 11, end).

With that tortuous and reworked sentence Montaigne made Socrates a purer individual than himself but not, as it were, a creature of a different species.

As for the statement that these vehement agitations 'could have been judged' to have some connexion with divine inspiration, it does not contain even the shadow of a suggestion that they ought to be so judged; Montaigne is explaining how even men like Socrates, Plato and Xenophon could not unreasonably make the mistake which they did and so take inner convictions for divine promptings.

CHAPTER SIXTEEN

The Body

1. Wondrously corporeal

Man is body and soul. Platonising Christianity gave the body a low place in the union. Ascetics strove to avoid the 'contagion' of the body; philosophers and theologians advised how to tame the body; saints, like philosophers, practised dying in ecstatic trances during which, as far as it was permitted to do so, the soul left the body behind. But the glummer Platonisers did not have it all their own way. St Francis of Assisi dubbed his stubborn old body Brother Ass. As for the Aristotelians, they held that there is a natural union between body and soul. Some condemned this particular conception of the union of these two elements of man but others developed theories which were not dissimilar. For St Bonaventura there was a *colligantia naturalis* – 'natural mutual bond' between the perfect soul and the perfectible body.

In Christian philosophy Man was often regarded as a union of two main elements. These were variously called body and soul, body and spirit or matter and form. It was also normal, at the same time, to follow St Paul and see man as consisting of three elements in a rising hierarchy of body, soul and spirit. This was a marked departure from the classical trilogy of body, spirit and soul. (All of these senses – including the classical ones – can be found in Renaissance writers.) Montaigne seems content with the simpler concept in which man has two 'master parts': body and soul (or body and spirit).

It was widely assumed that the soul (or spirit) could have a good effect on the body, but that the body could have only a polluting effect on the soul. Montaigne rejected that on the grounds of his own experience: 'it is always Man we have to deal with, Man, whose condition is wondrously corporeal (*merveilleusement corporelle* (III. 8, p. 186).

Erasmus, despite marked Platonising tendencies, had already protested against age-old metaphors for the body which made it no more than the soul's tool, dwelling-place or prison. One of the speakers in his colloquy, *The Religious Banquet*, raised the question quite aggressively: 'Whilst we are amply feeding our souls we must not overlook their *collegae*' (their 'fellows', or 'partners'). When asked who these *collegae* were, he replied: 'Why, our bodies. They are partners of our souls aren't they? I prefer that term to tool or dwelling-place or prison' (*Opera*, 1703-06, I. 680A).

Montaigne went further: the body and soul should be like a happily married couple. For him, as for Sebond, the Christian marriage is a loving, stable union of unequals, each of whom helps the other, each contributing something unique. Man's traditional superiority to woman does not distort this loving union. Mutual love and obligation bring priceless gifts to both. The body and soul remain 'married' until death – and will find each other again in the general resurrection. Death is 'the great divorce' (C.S. Lewis chose that as the title for a book). Paul declared that men should love their wives 'as their own bodies', and Bonaventura drew the conclusion that bodies should be loved as wives (*In Sententias* 3, 4). Montaigne was in good company.

2.   Debts to Sebond

Sebond made Montaigne see marriage as an image of the mutual love binding superior soul to lesser body; Sebond drew his inspiration from Raimond Lull. Lull, Sebond and Montaigne all came from the same part of Europe; was there a tradition of such teaching in south-west France, centred perhaps on Toulouse?

We are all *merveilleusement corporels*; the wonder and the vigour of that assertion bear the authentic ring of a personal discovery. Yet it was, in part at least, the flowering of a seed planted by Sebond. In the *Theologia naturalis* Sebond explained that the soul loved both God and its body:

> ... because God coupled the soul to the body and the body to the soul, and bound the body to the soul and made a natural marriage between them.

The soul knew that the body was made for it.

Montaigne turned this passage into French very freely, showing the direction in which his mind was already working: the bond linking body and soul is called 'marvellous' when nothing in the text requires it:

> Now God attached the soul by a marvellous bond, and the body to it, so closely that he made from them a unique partnership and, as it were, a natural marriage.[1]

Sebond (in Montaigne's version) insisted on the close partnership of body and soul and on their 'happy marriage'. Both gained from this. The body is 'enriched', the soul 'embellished'. The powers which the soul gains from its lesser partner are called 'corporeal, carnal and organic' – not in contempt but because they 'are attached to our body, our flesh and our organs.' They 'work through our members'; their 'form and vigour' depend on 'the state and health of those organs' (ch. 105, p. 112r).

The debt to Sebond went deeper. Sebond may have prompted Montaigne to study and love himself as an essential step on the way to truth and the love of God. Using language and concepts derived from Aristotle and scholasticism, Sebond maintained that an individual 'must first love himself *sicut hunc hominem, et non tanquam hominem* (as 'this man', not as Man in general). Montaigne translated this with vigorous simplicity: individual man must love himself 'as John or Peter, not as Man' (*comme Jean, ou Pierre, et non comme homme*). As Tom, Dick or Harry we would say; 'as Michel de Montaigne' is what he says in the *Essays*.[2]

In the end Montaigne became more positive than Sebond about the joys of the body lightened by the spirit, but he never abandoned completely the man who pointed the way to so fruitful a conclusion.

Other influences supported Montaigne in his acceptance of the

---

[1] *Theologia naturalis*, chapter 155 (p. 255): ' ... quia copulavit animam cum corpore, et corpus cum anima, et alligavit corpus animae, et fecit quoddam naturale matrimonium ... ' Montaigne (p. 163r of his translation) renders this as: 'Or Dieu l'a attachée au corps d'un lien merveilleux, et le corps à elle si estroictement, qu'il en a dressé une societé singuliere et comme un naturel marriage.'

[2] *Theologie naturelle*, chapter 145, p. 153v; *Theologia naturalis*, p. 238.

body, including the mediaeval concept *naturalia non sunt turpia*, 'what is natural is not vile'. He was also influenced by Cicero in Book 4 of *On the Ends of Good and Evil*. Erasmus helped too; he never tired of preaching the dignity of the matrimonial embrace: 'No part of the body is dishonourable; God created all things good and beautiful' (*Opera omnia*, 1703-06; I. 718D).

But most fruitful of all was Sebond's advice near the beginning of his treatise: 'Let a man begin by knowing himself and his nature if he wishes to find out truth about himself.' ... Man is 'outside himself' (*hors de luy*). Let him 'come back to himself and return home ... Let him be brought back and led back home' (*Theologie naturelle* 5v-6r). Sebond does not mean by those words exactly what Montaigne does. But the identity of expression is striking.

Such lessons, suitably adapted, Montaigne never forgot. For him they were yet another way of warning ordinary men against most kinds of ecstasy.

3. Platonists, Averroists, Realists, Nominalists ... and Ascetics

Montaigne avoided tenchicalities. He did not seek quarrels with out-and-out Platonists, with rationalist followers of the Arabian philosopher Averroës, nor with Realists or Nominalists. He owes something to all of them. His debts to Aristotelian scholarship are particularly clear. What he has to say about the composite nature of individual man as body plus soul, for example, fits quite snugly into some of the more influential interpretations of *Metaphysics* 1035b current in his day.[3]

---

[3] Fonseca develops at length the Aristotelian opinions resumed in his Index as *Naturas universales esse suis singularibus*. That is the doctrine underlying Montaigne's assertion that 'chascun porte en soy la forme entiere de l'humaine condition' – which is, indeed, a straight-forward application of it to the human race, each singular (individual person) of which carries within himself the whole form of the human species, *humanitas*. Montaigne at times seems to write as a 'Realist' – as when he asked ironically in the 'Apologia for Sebond': Do you think that God has used up 'toutes ses formes et toutes ses idées en cet ouvrage.' (*Essais*, II. 12, EM, p. 257). One of the parts of Fonseca most relevant to Montaigne is his commentary on *Metaphysics* 1035b (VII. 10. 15), *Homo verò et equus* (Fonseca, III, p. 345), a passage of central importance for Aristotle's anti-platonic doctrine of forms and, I believe, in its Latin version, the basis of

But where does all this leave those Christian saints who do rise above the limitations of their bodies? The full force of this question does not seem to have struck Montaigne until he came to write his final comments on the Bordeaux copy. Had friendly theologians or Roman censors raised the matter with him? If so his reply is coherent and cogent: ordinary men are, indeed, body and soul conjoined and ought to remain so. God's grace may modify this truth, enabling a few souls to treat their bodies' necessities with benign neglect. But even they do not lose all contact with humanity nor humanity with them. They can be appreciated imaginatively by that vast majority who are not touched by special grace. Even *l'homme moyen sensuel* may catch a momentary glimpse of the joy that is granted to a constant few.

The chapter on the Younger Cato begins with a disclaimer: Montaigne does not judge all men by his own limitations. In the final version he strengthened it, taking quite a few words to do so. He himself was 'engaged', he said, 'to one form'. He did not, 'like everybody else', bind others to that form; he was more inclined to acknowledge differences than similarities. Take the case of genuine celibates: although not a sexually continent man himself, Montaigne recognised the reality of the continence of Feuillants and Capuchins: imagination could even help him to put himself in their place for a while. This enabled him to see that great human beings should be judged apart, not from 'common examples' (I. 37, p. 300).

This is a modification of the main tendency of the *Essays*. Socrates, Cato, Epaminondas and others lived virtuous lives

Montaigne's assumptions. Nevertheless Montaigne avoids technicalities and, above all, philosophical contentiousness. What he writes at this point does not require acceptance of the Platonic doctrine of forms, though it does apparently assume the reality of form-in-matter, as in Aristotle. It is however reconcilable with the other key passage of the *Metaphysics* 1033a (VII. 8. 6): 'The completed whole, *this* form, in *these* flesh and bones, is Callias or Socrates, different because of their matter but the same in species, since form is indivisible' (Translated from Bessarion's Latin version).

Fonseca's opinions seem to be close to Montaigne's own assumptions; but Montaigne could also be close to Antonio Scaynus who, having faced the fact that no knowledge could be obtained from singulars alone, as such, believes knowledge to be possible because of the everlasting universal form existing in each particular individual within a species. That is true, he adds, even if universals do not exist outside the mind (*Paraphrases de Prima Philosophia Aristotelis*, Rome, 1587, pp. 117, 287f.).

which, however elevated, are admired in so far as they were anchored in their humanity. Yet true Christian ascetics virtually ignore even some of the necessary appetites of their bodies and so do not cultivate the humanising marriage of body and soul. How can this be? Other major additions do not resolve such tensions until the final pages of the *Essays*. The answer lies in wrong and right attitudes towards ecstasy and in a more complex interpretation of the way in which the 'entire form' of humanity exists in each particular man.

CHAPTER SEVENTEEN

Wisdom

1. Socrates triumphant

Montaigne had many heroes: Alexander the Great, the Younger Cato, Epaminondas, Socrates. All were to be admired, but none was to be followed in all things. Even the greatest of them are eventually shown to have been men with failings. As far as sheer greatness was concerned, Alexander won the prize. His manhood could even stand comparison with the human nature of Christ:

> It is full of reason and piety to take examples from the *humanité* of Christ. He ended his life at the age of thirty-three.

Montaigne adds that 'the greatest man who was simply a man, Alexander', died at the same age (I. 20, p. 104).

The saints as such have no place as examples in the *Essays*, since their holiness, achieved under special grace, takes them out of the natural 'condition' of Man; nevertheless their human aspects and their problems do hover into focus when necessary. In the same way arguments may be advanced to support the Christian religion, despite the fact that Montaigne's own religious faith was based not on argument but on grace. However, detailed theological reasoning would have taken Montaigne beyond the boundaries of the kind of wisdom which he had set himself to seek.

Contemporary writings were criticised, Montaigne tells us, 'for being purely human and philosophical, with no admixture of Theology'. He himself condemned the critics: it is better to keep philosophy and theology apart; 'divine instruction holds its rank better when apart, as Queen or Governor'. He condemned the opposite fault: it is far too common for theologians to write like humanists (I. 56, p. 415).

Once theology and Christian saints are left aside, the great names of antiquity have the field almost to themselves. When it comes to wisdom, no one rivals Socrates. But his melancholic ecstasies are a drawback; they are acknowledged, only to be regretted. All hint of the divine disappears. When Socrates 'was seen standing one day and night in view of all the Grecian army', it was because he was 'surprised and caught up by some deep thought'. The language remains that of high rapture – *ecstase; surpris et ravi* – but Socrates is no longer shown as praiseworthily practising death, his mind departing from the body in search of spiritual truth. Instead he is seen as the wisest man ever, deep in unimaginable thought. That was not what Socrates was admired for. For two thousand years Socrates' claims to ecstatic revelation had been gratefully accepted as valid. The truth of his teachings was vouched for by these revelatory ecstasies. But Montaigne admired Socrates for mundane virtues – for his moderation; for his hardiness in war; for his patience in face of hunger, poverty and a nagging wife; for his constancy in the ordinary affairs of life. The kind of greatness Socrates had did not stop him enjoying a drink with friends or from playing five-stones with children. He was the supreme example of every sort of ordinary, ordinate human perfection – not because his soul aimed high but because it knew how to keep within human limits.

This would have seemed an odd thing to say of Socrates if you thought of him as Ficino, Erasmus or Rabelais had done.[1]

---

[1] Montaigne's portrait of Socrates as a man abounding in wisdom within the context of a full, ordinary life was a common one (cf. *Insignum aliquot virorum Icones*, Lyons, J. de Tournes, 1559, pp. 68f). Others besides Montaigne were also questioning the assertion that Socrates' ecstasies were a sign of religious favour. Cf. the Coîmbra Jesuits' commentary on Aristotle's *De Anima*, Cologne, 1603, col. 514: 'Alcibiades in the *Symposium* relates that Socrates, "deep in thought, once stood still, in one place, in the midst of the army, for one whole day and night until sunrise." Since it is not likely that such abstractions from the senses happen because of a miracle, it must be conceded that ecstasy can be produced by a faculty of nature'. It is pointed out, on the authority of Fracastorius, (*lib. 2. de Intellectione*), that melancholics are particularly prone to these natural ecstasies. Such ecstasies can be classified as a 'natural privilege' but are not to be confused with those specially privileged ecstasies produced by divine power.

2. Socrates criticised

In the *Essays* Montaigne subjects even this paragon to discreet
criticism in the light of his own experience. As he prepared to
bring the *Essays* to a close, Montaigne stressed the moral beauty
of those who know how to live a full life 'naturally'; unusual
phenomena, including ecstasies such as those of Socrates,
haunted his mind. 'The wildest form of illness', he had written,
'is to despise our being (*nostre estre*). If anyone wants to set his
soul apart, to free it from the contagion of the body, let him do so
boldly (if he can) when his body is feeling ill.'

Montaigne was earnestly playing with words and concepts.
'Contagion' is what Platonising mystics attribute to the body,
even when healthy. Montaigne does not. He restricts 'contagion'
to illness. The soul might understandably find a sick body
'contagious' and so strive to leave it, but, apart from those 'less
distracted' and 'spritely enthusiasms' mentioned earlier, the soul
should share in all the pleasures of its healthy body, teach it
moderation and *s'y plaire conjugalement*, 'delight in it as if it were
wedded to it as a husband' (III. 13, p. 423).

Socrates did not do that all the time, so even he, Philosophy's
own teacher, comes in for criticism.

3. Me

We have been told what Socrates thought. Now we are told what
'I' think.

Montaigne believed in progress of a sort – we may be lesser
men than the ancients, but we are standing on their shoulders.
Once the *moy* has come to the fore Socrates is duly criticised for
failing to see something that Montaigne (with the help of
Socrates) can now see more clearly. That 'something' is the
happy wisdom of avoiding ecstasy and keeping the pleasurable
marriage of body and soul in full and continuous activity until
the moment of death. This marriage is something to linger over
gratefully: 'You have to study, savour and chew over the
sweetness of it if you are to render condign gratitude to him who
vouchsafes it to you.' In this way your soul can 'measure how
much she owes to God for your being at peace with your
conscience and other internal passions; for having your body in
its natural disposition, enjoying ordinately and competently

those sweet and flattering functions by which God, through his grace, makes up for the pains with which his justice chastises us' (III. 13, p. 425).

Not to associate the spirit (or soul) with all bodily pleasures is to experience them *stupidement* (dully). Montaigne even had himself woken up so that he could enjoy falling asleep again.

Death, in the sense of the pain of dying, no longer obsessed Montaigne. His concussion when a soldier seems to have cured him of that fear; his soul had been temporarily wrenched from his body, and he had felt nothing (II. 6). The case he finally makes is not in defence of any kind of preparation for death but of a positive affirmation of the goodness of life, of life as it really is, with a soul living in a body as it really is – a body with its right to enjoy its necessary pleasures in its own good time. 'As for me, I love life and cultivate it as it has pleased God to vouchsafe it.' Seneca, Cicero, Plutarch, Socrates and Genesis – are all marshalled in support of such wisdom.

Philosophy reluctantly recognised that no bodily pleasure exceeds that of a sexual climax – the body's own ecstasy. Montaigne did not regret sexual pleasure, he increasingly dwelt on its 'necessity'. He did not wish '(B) that children were produced *stupidement* with our fingers or our heels, (C) but rather, speaking with reverence, that we could also do it voluptuously with our fingers and our heels as well'. Plaints about such pleasure are '(B) ungrateful and (C) iniquitous'. These pleasures have, after all, been granted to man by God or by his agent, Nature (whom La Boëtie called *la ministre* of God).

(B) I accept with a good heart (C) and gratefully (B) what Nature has done for me, I welcome it and congratulate myself over it. You do wrong to that great and all-powerful Giver to refuse his gift, to nullify it or disfigure it. (C) *Tout bon il a fait tout bon* – himself entirely Good, he has made all things good.

Cicero is cited saying the same: 'All things which are in accordance with Nature are worthy of esteem' (III. 13, p. 426).[2]

[2] Montaigne's attitudes were to become widely preached by Christian writers. Cf. *Les Triomphes de la Religion Chrestienne* by Father Boucher, the Queen's Franciscan preacher, Paris, 1628, p. 762; see also the Capuchin father Ives' *Morales Chrestiennes*, Paris, 1648: mankind must accept its corporeality; to complain that we are not angelic intelligences 'is to fall into a noteworthy ingratitude for the gifts of God ... ' (p. 127; see also pp. 131ff.).

Quite traditionally Montaigne interlaced God and Nature, Biblical and classical. The classical elements are, on the whole, duly docketed in the editions; the liturgical and Scriptural ones, less reliably so. The 'Good who has made all things well' is the God of Genesis, the New Testament and liturgy: he is the Giver of all good gifts who saw that all he made was good.

Philosophy is condemned whenever she forgets man's corporality, but Socrates is largely excused from responsibility for her errors. Montaigne personalises Philosophy, making her a disciple who has forgotten her lessons. Socrates, her master, had taught her differently. All those astringent and ascetic philosophers who decry the body, calling it brutal or bestial, are condemned, not least in the margins of the Bordeaux copy; it is 'childish' of Philosophy to say that it is a wildly inappropriate 'match to wed the divine to the earthly', or to claim that 'sexual pleasure is a brutish quality'. It is not. All we have we owe to the Giver – and that includes *volupté*. Not to be grateful is iniquitous.

Montaigne advocated ordinate behaviour. As in the case of his championing of constancy, temperance or moderation, he went back to the roots in Plato and, especially, in the ethics of Aristotle: virtuous men are those who react with ordinate affections to the proper objects of desire, appreciating things at their just value. Over and over again Montaigne sings the praises of 'order' in human life: all the philosophers – the Peripatetics, Stoics and so on – urged the rightness of an ordinate life, guided by reason; but they could be inordinate about the need to be ordinate, taking it to absurd lengths which led to a parody of ordinate reactions. A philosopher should be grateful and enjoy lying with his wife; he should not simply take a spiritual pleasure in doing an appropriate job with her, aimed at a useful end. It is absurd and gross for a philosopher to claim 'that the only enjoyment he gets from a beautiful young wife' is one which by-passes the body – namely the pleasure his conscience enjoys from performing an ordinate action – 'like', said Montaigne with a laugh, 'pulling on his boots for a useful ride'.

'Socrates, Philosophy's preceptor and ours', taught no such fantastic nonsense. Because the pleasures of the soul have more variety, constancy and dignity than those of the body, he put the pleasures of the soul in the higher place, but not in the only one. Temperance – the soul's wise gift to the body – is no enemy of pleasure (III. 13, pp. 427-8).

That sounds the height of Renaissance wisdom. Yet even this Montaigne is about to dispute with Socrates, 'the great Teacher of philosophy and of us all'.

4. Nature and natural marriage

If Montaigne's method of investigation was to work, it had to lead him from 'this man' ('me') to 'you and me': to Man. This is what happens as the *Essays* draw to a close: the *je* and the *me* which have been dominating the syntax give way to *nous*. And this 'we' embraces all mankind – Socrates included.

'Nature is a gentle guide, yet no more gentle than wise and just' – Cicero had said it centuries before: *Natura dux optima*, Nature is the best guide. Montaigne tried to follow her footsteps. The main schools of philosophy are in verbal agreement: the Academics who follow Plato, like the Peripatetics who follow Aristotle, all say that the sovereign good is 'to live according to Nature'. As for the Stoics, they tell you 'to agree with Nature,' which amounts to the same thing. (The end of the *Essays* owes many debts to Cicero; not all are acknowledged. This one, from *Tusculans* 5.28.82, is not.)

The trouble is that it is easier to follow in the footsteps of Nature without the philosophers than with them! They claim to teach what the path of Nature is; in practice they confound her traces. The worst are those who do violence to the nature of man, instructing us to tear our bodies from our souls. One of Montaigne's reactions against such false and sophistical philosophies was his concern for 'primitivism'. Primitive man as Montaigne conceived him did not wrench his soul from his body in the name of some false higher wisdom; for Montaigne, admiration for simple men went together with a distrust of philosophical ecstasy. A person who wishes to discover his *forme maistresse* within his complex being as man – discover, that is, the personal, individual, permament strand in the transient, variegated flux of his experience and sensations – may well be wary of civilised veneers, wary too of anything which takes his 'being' apart or which claims to take him 'out of himself', even if 'above himself'.

CHAPTER EIGHTEEN

Wedded Bliss

1. Divorce reform

In the end it is the turn of Socrates to be found wanting for his assertion that the soul's pleasures are to be preferred on account of their *dignité*: '(B) Is it not an error to judge that some activities, simply because they are necessary, *sont moins dignes* – have less dignity?' Surely such a 'marriage of pleasure and necessity' is 'a most becoming one'. What is the point of 'dismembering a structure' such as man, whose parts are 'interwoven with so closely-knit and brotherly a congruity'? We should be doing the opposite: tying our two main parts more closely together by their *mutuels offices*, the duties which each owes to the other (III. 13, p. 428).

The background to Montaigne's final wisdom is partly classical; it includes Cicero's treatises *De officiis* (*On Duties*) and *De finibus* (*On the Ends of Good and Evil*). Cicero was rare in giving central importance to the body: 'How', he asked, 'did you suddenly come to discard first the body, then all those things which are in accordance with nature though they are out of our power, and, finally, even duty, *officium*?' (*De finibus* 5.11.26).

In Christian doctrine the Holy Spirit is the Giver of life; the spirit of man partakes of this enlivening power. For Montaigne, the duty of man's spirit is indeed to 'awaken and quicken' (*vivifier*) the sluggish body; the body's task is 'to arrest the spirit in its lightness, to pin it down'. Montaigne insists that pleasure is the driving force in the whole of human life – even for the saints and the ascetics. To sustain this, he had Christian authority in reserve: he could not champion the marriage of body and soul without wandering into regions where philosophy and theology overlap.

Classical philosophy did not normally respect the body in the way Christians should. A religion which gives the body a place in the world to come is fundamentally at variance with those who teach that souls yearn to quit their bodies for all eternity. Nevertheless, Montaigne ingeniously found support for his Christian Epicureanism in a severe philosopher and an even severer saint, quoting as a challenge unattributed passages from Seneca and the *City of God*, where Augustine condemns the Manicheans who held the body to be evil (III. 13, p. 428).

In the French sandwiched between these two unusually heavy slabs of Latin prose, Socrates' notion that the spirit's pleasures have more *dignité* is closely pressed in argument; Montaigne's experience of his own humanity had taught him that no part is unworthy of cultivation. Some activities are more worthy: none is unworthy:

> (B) There is no part *indigne* in this present which God has given to us; we must account for it down to the last hair. It is not a merely formal commission to man to conduct himself according to his condition as man, it is expressly stated, inborn (*naifve*) (C) most fundamental (B) and the Creator gave it to us seriously and severely.

A Lutheran or *Réformé* making such dogmatic assertions would have had specific Biblical proof-texts in mind. As a post-Tridentine Roman Catholic layman, Montaigne did not. For what Cicero called the *conditio humana* Montaigne had already, in his chapter on presumption, harked back to the relevant Christian fundamentals, especially to the resurrection of the body: 'The body occupies a large part in our being (*nostre estre*); it holds a high rank.' It is for that very reason that ecstasy, with its detachment from the body, is not an ideal for most of common humanity:

> (A) Those who wish to take our two principal pieces apart and to sequester one from the other are wrong. We must, on the contrary, couple and join them closely together. We must command the soul not to withdraw to its quarters, not to entertain itself apart, not to despise and abandon the body.

(It could only do that, anyway, by some sort of counterfeit monkey-parody, some *singerie contrefaicte*.) The spirit should

rally to the body, embrace it, cherish it, keep it, control it, counsel
it, set it upright and bring it back when it goes astray – it should
marry it in other words and serve it as a husband, so that their
actions may not seem diverse and contrary but harmonious and
uniform (II. 17, p. 419).

Montaigne's almost unique source of inspiration where such
ideas are concerned was the *Natural Theology* of Sebond, helped
out, perhaps, by St John Chrysostom. Theologically he clung to
the doctrine of the resurrection of the body; philosophically he
accepted – in so far as he found him to be worth it – the one
philosopher his church had made peculiarly her own: Aristotle.

Individual man is form and matter, soul and body, married
together. 'Christians have been specifically taught about this
bond', which links man's two principal parts in loving wedlock.

> They know that divine justice embraces this fellowship and
> society of body and soul, going so far as to make the body able to
> receive everlasting rewards. They know that God watches the
> whole of man in action, willing that he should, in his entirety,
> receive punishment and reward according to his merits (II. 17,
> p. 419).

Among the ancient Greeks only the Aristotelians are allowed to
have glimpsed this truth about the human condition:

> (C) The Peripatetic Sect – the most civilised of all sects –
> attributed to wisdom this one care: to provide for the common
> good of the two associate parts [of a man] and to procure it.

Montaigne was doubtless thinking of the *Nicomachaean Ethics*
(cf. 7.14.8). All other schools of antiquity lean, we are told, too
far one way or the other.

2. Archimedes' ecstasy

Montaigne's respect for Aristotle leaves room for Plato too. The
soul needs 'food' as the body does; that is elementary Platonism.
But Montaigne added that Man has enough time in this life to
give both body and soul the food they need. Throughout the
Essays Montaigne delighted in belittling human pride. When
insisting that experience shows that man's pride is never more
silly than when he neglects his body and claims to be ecstatic, he

gave his delight full play: even what men take to be major intellectual achievements do not matter all that much. 'Ask that man over there' what his head is so chock full of that he regrets spending time on a good meal: 'You will find that none of the food on your table is so tasteless' as his soul's pabulum. His reasoning, and what scholastic philosophy called his 'intentions', are not even worth your modest goat-meat stew. Montaigne, the wise and balanced melancholic, is trailing his coat before the partisans of another school of melancholy, for he goes on to add that the body's enjoyment of its necessities should be neither denied nor postponed – not even if you are a Greek philosopher whose discovery the whole world names after you. The example he gives is a blow aimed at felling those with whom he disagreed:

> Even if it were Archimedes' raptures, what does it matter? (III. 13, p. 429).

Archimedes does not figure here by accident. Melanchthon's treatise *On the Soul* helps us to recover the force of Montaigne's amused aggressiveness. In that treatise Archimedes' discoveries are cited (as they often were) as the greatest of all examples of revelatory ecstasies made to melancholic geniuses. Melanchthon is explaining – need it be said? – Aristotle's *Problems* 30.1. For Melanchthon these ecstasies are encouraged by balanced melancholy modified by blood – by Montaigne's temperament! Such melancholy made a man 'more ardent, tenacious, *vehementissimus*' (very inclined to mental transports).

Melanchthon pointed out that we can see poets who are 'as though moved by divine inspiration'. Those inspired men whom scholars called 'artificers' show the same forces at work:

> The same applies to other excellent creative men when they fall into cogitations because of a major impulse of the mind. Archimedes did not realise that his city had been captured, nor even notice soldiers bursting into his house. What could be more melancholic than his leaping from the bath and running naked through the forum yelling *Eureka*, when he discovered the method of detecting how much silver had been mixed with gold? (Melanchthon, *Opera* III, Basle 1541, pp. 66-8).

Marsiglio Ficino had already said the same, linking – also in praise not in blame – Plato's vehement ecstasies, Socrates' catalepsies and Archimedes' 'divine' rapture. All were, on Aristotle's authority, melancholics of genius (*Opera*, 1641, I, pp. 280-1).

Montaigne was not impressed. Even cogitations like those of Archimedes can wait their turn. They need no overriding precedence over the body's few undemandingly pleasurable 'necessities'. Generations had been taught that Archimedes discovered his principle through ecstatic inspiration associated with his complexion. Montaigne, elsewhere in the *Essays*, cites Plato and Aristotle on such ecstasies, but nowhere is it suggested that such inspiration is desirable for the wise – or even possible without madness. Archimedes' soul was concerned with *amusemens* (ways of spending time) and *imaginations* (similitudes conceived in the mind). They can take their place in the queue. Against the standards of eternity his famous principle does not amount to much. There is not the slightest hint that he was actually inspired. Quite the reverse: *amusemens* and *imaginations* do not need attendant, heaven-sent daemons.

3. Eternity

During a lull in his attack, Montaigne placed eternity before his reader. Mankind is divided into two. There is the vulgar mass, which includes Socrates, Plato, Archimedes, Cato, you and me, all made in the same mould; all common humanity. The only other category of mankind is tiny; it is reserved exclusively for celibate Christian mystics. They – alone now – are referred to as souls (*ames*) not as souls-and-bodies; they alone have souls which may rightly, and with impunity, neglect their bodies, thought not (since they are human) do without them completely. They form the standard against which human presumption is to be judged:

> (B) Here, I am not touching upon – nor am I mixing up with scrapings from the human pot such as we are and with the vain desires and cogitations which amuse us – those souls, worthy of veneration, which are elevated by ardour of devotion and piety to a constant and conscientious meditation of divine things (III. 13, p. 429).

Here we find the ecstasy which Plato wrote about and which Christians know about: that 'vehement' movement of the soul by which a saintly contemplative ignores the body while his soul enjoys a foretaste of future blessedness. Even these venerable souls are Epicureans, like the rest of us, but they enjoy pleasures of which we know nothing. They act as if they were not souls married to their bodies but souls practising the divorce of death.

> (C) Anticipating, by dint of a lively, vehement hope, the use of that food which is everlasting, the ultimate end and final stay of the desires of Christians, the only constant and incorruptible pleasure, they despise lingering over our fluid, ambiguous necessary satisfactions and easily hand over to the body the care and use of sensual, temporal food (III. 13, p. 429).

'Necessary satisfactions' (*necessiteuses commoditez*) has its full Aristotelian sense of pleasure derived from essential bodily functions. These *necessaria* include food and sex; they fall within the domain of temperance, which does not attempt to eliminate them but to moderate them (*Nicomachaean Ethics* 7.4.2). As Montaigne puts it: '(C) Temperance is not the plague of pleasure but its seasoning' (III. 13, p. 423).

A Christian Epicurean enjoying a foretaste of everlasting bliss hardly notices his body and its necessary demands – Erasmus had made the same point in the *Praise of Folly*, though his contemplatives are more literally ecstatic. But for the rest of us, including Socrates who remained amorously susceptible unto the last, these *necessiteuses commoditez* mean a great deal; and rightly so.

Montaigne had said much the same thing when writing on solitude. But this time a vital warning is underlined: these contemplatives are an élite. You had better not try to ape them. Your bodily necessities will have their revenge if you do.[1]

---

[1] The resurrection of the body is a credal certainty for Montaigne, but 'foretastes of heavenly bliss', when vouchsafed to the privileged few, are experienced only in the soul, which in its rapture leaves the body to look after itself. This is quite orthodox. On such matters Montaigne may be compared with Erasmus: both call on authoritative teachings of St Paul in I Corinthians 2, citing verse 9 to make their point. Montaigne is very dogmatic about the gulf separating catholic teaching about the joys of the elect from the erroneous human reasonings of Plato. In the 'Apologia for Sebond' he alludes to Plutarch's treatise 'On the face appearing in the circle of the Moon', in which mention is made of the 'fields of Dis' – the aerial domain in which the souls of the classical dead are purged of the 'contagion of their bodies'. (In Montaigne, as in Amyot's French

4. Special privileges for Christian voluptuaries

In his chapter on prayer Montaigne had protested against the
trivialisation of the Scriptures. As completely as any
Sorbonagre, he reserved the study of Holy Writ to those whose
vocation it was to pursue such studies: '(C) it is not an
occupation for everybody but of people vowed to it, called to it by
God' (I. 56, pp. 412-13).

Similarly, but very, very exceptionally, some are called to be
contemplative ascetics: '(B) *c'est un estude privilegé*', a
privileged endeavour.

Even here, where Christianity comes to the fore, Montaigne's
debt to Cicero is a real one. In a treatise much concerned with
ecstasy, Cicero spoke of 'a rare kind of men who are called away
from the body and are enraptured to a knowledge of things
divine, *cura omni studioque*, with application and total zeal' (*De
divinatione* 1.49.111). Such ideas had long been taken into
Christianity.

----

translation of Plutarch, this domain is called the 'verger de Pluton', Pluto's
orchard.) Montaigne condemned Plato's 'decyphering' of such arcane matters on
the arresting grounds that even Plato's explanations and comparisons were too
earthbound, too corporeal, for divine reality. He lumps them together with the
grossly sensual view of heaven attributed to Mahomet. For Montaigne, the joys
of paradise infinitely surpass the powers of human speech and human
'imagination' – the power to picture them. They have no root whatsoever in
bodily analogies of temporal pleasures:

(C) All the pleasures of mortals are mortal. (A) If recognising parents, children,
friends can touch and titillate us in the next world, and if we grasp at such a
pleasure, then we still remain within notions of fitness which are earthbound,
finite. We cannot condignly conceive those high, divine promises if we are able to
conceive them at all. To imagine them condignly, we must imagine them
unimaginable, unutterable, incomprehensible, (C) and entirely different from
our own wretched experiences. (A) Eye cannot see, says St Paul, nor can there
rise up into the heart of man, what God has prepared for his own (II. 12, p. 248ff).

The purifications to which Plato would subject human souls after death would
change human beings into something different: 'It would not be ourselves ...
Something else would receive these rewards.' Unaided human reason cannot
reach certainty about the afterlife; nor is even God's own revealed truth
enough by itself, since reason will pervert revelation as soon as it 'leaves the
path traced and trodden by the Church'. Such doctrines were the very stuff of
authoritarian humanist catholicism in the late Renaissance and Counter-
reformation. For the texts alluded to directly or indirectly by Montaigne, cf.
Plutarch, *Moralia* 943C (Amyot, II, p. 626); Plato, *Gorgias* ad fin.; *Republic* 10.
For Erasmus, cf. the closing pages of the *Praise of Folly*.

This *studium* (*estude* in the masculine gender) is a special grace leading to busy application and zealous study. *Un estude privilegé* is a boon available to a few; it is never for the masses. Ecstasies which give man a foretaste of bliss are beyond man's greatest efforts.[2]

The *Essays* show that Montaigne was fully aware of the paradoxical power of his Christian Epicureanism with its acceptance of pleasure – even for the saints. He can be assumed to have known that he was fundamentally changing an idea which Ficino expounded in his own treatise *On Pleasure*. Ficino attacked the contention, attributed to Aristippus and Eudoxus of Archytas in ancient times, that bodily pleasures are greater than those of the mind (or soul). By reaction Ficino made the pleasures of the ecstatic spirit the only ones that really mattered. All the themes of Montaigne's praise of privileged Christian voluptuaries enjoying in advance spiritual food are to be found in Ficino – except the vital point that they are rare.

Like Montaigne at the start of *De l'experience*, Ficino cited *Metaphysics* 1.1: 'All men naturally desire knowledge', with an appetite bothersome when thwarted, pleasurable when satisfied. But he drew conclusions from it which are not Montaigne's:

> There is one thing naturally cognate to all men, one thing sought by them all, one thing, finally, which is the greatest joy. It consists entirely in true contemplation, which, as Plato said, is the true food of the soul, filling the soul with ineffable pleasure. Because of this, different people seek different pleasures for the body but, in the case of the mind, one and the same joy is loved by all (*Opera*, 1641, I, p. 1031, col. 2 of *De voluptate*).

Montaigne was more orthodox than Ficino. By restricting the soul's *pabulum*, which Plato wrote about, to the food enjoyed in anticipation by a few Christian souls living in constant ecstasy under special grace, he subverted much of Ficino's Platonising ethics. For Montaigne ordinary people – all the rest of us, Socrates included – are right to lend half an ear to the teachings of Aristippus and Eudoxus. They were wrong at one extreme, but it is equally wrong to rush to the other: bodily pleasures are not greater than those of the soul, but they are worthy ones which the

[2] For the rare nature of privileged ecstasy, cf. my *Ecstasy and the Praise of Folly*, 1980, pp. 182ff.

soul's pleasures must not be allowed to crowd out. There must be
room for both; Man was created that way.

Montaigne was drawing yet another, not unexpected,
conclusion from the chain of argument started by *Metaphysics*
1.1. To those who declared that *All men naturally desire
knowledge* means (as Ficino thought) that all men, in actual
fact, naturally desire to contemplate God as a way of
obtaining knowledge, a standard Christian reply was that the
kind of knowledge which Aristotle wrote about in the opening
sentence of his treatise is supra-natural – to be obtained 'only
by God's grace and gift' (*Metaphysics,* ed. Pedro Fonseca, 1599,
I, col. 60).

Montaigne insisted that such a 'privileged endeavour' was
outside the natural order which applied to most of mankind and
so outside the scope of the *Essays* and their wisdom. In all
matters of religion there is need of grace. Where unaided human
religious fantasies are concerned, 'no opinion is too odd'. True
religion 'is beyond human reasonings; it is all the more excusable
for anyone to get lost in them, if he is not extraordinarily
enlightened through divine favour' (I. 23, p. 140).

Since we have all been made in the same mould, since, that is,
each one of us bears within himself the entire form of Man, we
can understand human error only too well. But how can we ever
understand those saintly contemplatives whose whole experience
depends on supernatural grace?

5.   People like us

Montaigne had already answered that query. Despite his own
lack of chastity and despite his attachment to a particular form
of (mere) Man, he could glimpse in imagination the reality of the
lives of Feuillants and Capuchins. He believed that their
devotion to celibate chastity was real and effective; but the way
not to understand them is to try, without special grace, to follow
their example.

Since words and idioms change their meaning, Montaigne is
often misunderstood about this *estude privilegé.* He wrote, quite
reasonably, that the contemplatives whom he honoured were not
like most men; they were following a privileged path of zealous
devotion:

(B) C'est un estude privilegé. (C) Entre nous ce sont deux choses que j'ay tousjours veües de singulier accord: les opinions supercelestes et les moeurs sousterraines.

(B) It is a privileged endeavour. (C) Among us there are two things which I have always seen to accord together particularly well: supercelestial opinions and subterranean morals (III. 13, p. 429).

It is not uncommon to find that translated and interpreted as though it were a bitter gibe, a sneer, demolishing what has just been said, aimed at Christians – especially the clergy – for using sublime spirituality as a cloak for lechery. It is taken to mean:

> *Between you and me*, I have always found two things to be in singular harmony: supercelestial opinions and subterranean morals.

Such an interpretation is to be found in the work of excellent scholars; it nevertheless does unnecessary violence to the coherence of Montaigne's argument. It is read into his text, not found in it. Coming as it does at the climax of the *Essays*, such a misunderstanding takes on an almost legendary importance. It is cited all over the place. The very grossness of the error makes for its force – like the Emperor's new clothes. And yet, in context, the phrase *entre nous* does not convey a sneer nor even a hint of bitterness. Those words do not convey a judgment on lecherous priests and monks nor, indeed, on anyone at all other than the whole of mankind – apart from a handful of privileged contemplatives. Montaigne is contrasting 'those venerable souls' who enjoy a foretaste of eternal bliss by feeding on the solid, pleasurable, spiritual *pabulum* vouchsafed to privileged contemplatives, with all the rest of 'us scrapings of the human pot' (*la marmaille d'hommes que nous sommes*), who have to come to terms with our bodily necessities or else suffer on the rebound.

All Christians, by definition, are the objects of divine grace. But the rôle of the grace vouchsafed to ordinary Christians is to enable them partly to overcome the effects of sin and to be Christians despite their shortcomings. Privileged grace does more. It raises a chosen few above humanity to angelic purity. But for Montaigne what applies to that elect has no relevance to 'us'. *Entre nous* – among people like you, me, or, say,

Archimedes – even such ecstasies as we may fall into or provoke ourselves into do more harm than good; they may confirm us in mere opinion and have no lasting value, no constancy. 'Among us' ecstasy most definitely does not make men into angels; it may do quite the reverse, bringing us back with a bump below humanity, not simply down to earth, but way beneath it.

In the first version of the chapter Montaigne had written less provocatively:

> (B) Our endeavours (*estudes*) are all wordly ones, and among men of this world the most natural ones are the most just (EM 3, p. 429 variant).

We, as creatures of the world, are limited to *estudes mondains* – worldly affairs, not other-worldly ones. That is firm enough. The final version is firmer still: people like us should not 'strive' (as Keble's hymn puts it) 'to wind ourselves too high for mortal man'. We will come a cropper if we do.

But there is a bolder emphasis than may at first appear. Montaigne was writing for a public who knew what Aristotle's *necessaria* were. He wrote as a member of a church whose ecstatic contemplatives were, for the most part, a celibate elect.

6.   Socratic ecstasy and Christian coenobites

In the last few sentences of the *Essays* the language of ecstasy lies thick on the page. There is talk of *ecstases* and *daemoneries*, of the spirit which tries to break its fellowship with the body (*se dissocier du corps*); of those who wish to be 'outside themselves' (*hors d'eux*) – the standard definition of ecstasy – and to 'escape from their humanity'.

All that is wrong. The body has its necessities; the mass of mankind must give due attention to both of the parts that make up the human condition. There is time enough for both, in all conscience. Our spirit has all the time in the world to *faire ses besongnes*, 'to do its jobs' – an amusing phrase which likens the pleasure to be derived from even Archimedes' spiritual cogitations to one of the principal *necessaria*: sexual intercourse, *la besongne*.

This humorous body language is an essential part of the meaning of these final sentences; *naturalia* really are not *turpia*.

Montaigne, never prone to mince words, brings this home simply, with the help of the great Aesop:

> (B) Aesop (C) that great man (B) saw his master pissing as he walked along. 'What', he said, 'do we have to shit as we run?' (III. 13, p. 429).[3]

Defecation, as the saintly Melanchthon pointed out, is one of the pleasurable *necessaria*. So Montaigne can insist that even the pleasures of fecal evacuation and micturition may rightly claim their fair share of our time. The case certainly needed making: Rabelais (who never accepted the body as Montaigne did) has his pupils regularly going to the lavatory in the company of their tutor, so that they can concentrate on purging their minds of error at the same time as they absentmindedly purge their bodies of impurities.[4]

Montaigne opposes such attitudes. People want to cultivate a higher spiritual life at the expense of their bodies:

> (B) That is *folie*. Instead of transforming themselves into angels

[3] Montaigne insists on Aesop's greatness – as a man. That is a way of undermining a standard legend, allegedly based on Socrates, which made Aesop the chosen vehicle of 'daemonic' ecstasies, during which the whole of moral philosophy was revealed to him while still a slave. (Cf. Sebastian Foxius, *Phaedo, sive de immortalitate animae*, Basle, 1555, pp. 60B—61B.) The humanising of Aesop is in keeping with the *Essays* as a whole. Montaigne consistently rejects the belief that learned men are privately inspired: 'My father, warmed by the new ardour with which King Francis I embraced learning … sought the acquaintance of learned men, receiving them at home like *personnes saintes* who had some private inspiration from divine wisdom.' Montaigne's father, lacking formal education, treated them as 'oracles', whereas Montaigne himself 'quite liked' learned men, but did not 'worship' them. (The key phrase is *'quelque particuliere aspiration de sagesse divine'*; Montaigne returns to it a few pages later and adapts it to the context of the faith of Christians: *'par foy et par une inspiration particuliere de la grace divine'* (*Apologie de R. Sebond* II. 12, beginning, E.M. pp. 141 and 143).) The change from *sagesse* to *grace* suggests that what men acquire even from grace is little enough in comparison with divine wisdom. That was a theme of Christian 'folly' since Origen. As for Aesop, he was a great, wise, good but 'unenlightened' man, in no ways 'inspired'.

[4] See Melanchthon on Cicero's *De officiis* (Paris, 1543, p. 30, s.v. *Temperantia et modestia*): 'It is especially seemly not only to do nothing against Nature but to do with delight whatever Nature requires. For example there is nothing wrong with shitting, but it is wrong to shit in public as Diogenes did' (Melanchthon uses the blunt word *cacare*).

they transform themselves into beasts. Instead of winding high
they plunge low.

By now, readers know that this *folie* is not mere silliness but
madness – the madness which depressed the genius of Tasso to
bestial insanity and which, at best, made Archimedes dash
insanely about the forum, as he overvalued his interesting little
tidbit of a discovery.

Folie is always a danger; melancholy can change from being
the spur of genius to being the cause of madness. Robert Burton
sums up the lesson in his inimitable language: 'I may not deny
that there is some folly approved, a divine fury, a holy madness,
a spiritual drunkenness in the saints of God themselves.' But
that is not all. Burton's conclusion is the same as the one that
Montaigne reached: 'we commonly mistake and go beyond our
commission; we reel to the opposite part; we are not capable of it'
(*Anatomy of Melancholy*, Preface, pp. 77-9).

And, after quoting from a letter in which Erasmus defended the
ecstasy praised by his character 'Folly', Burton asserted that
there is 'a divine melancholy' when authentic, 'but as it is abused,
a mere dotage, madness' (3.4.1.2., p. 343).

7.　The vita beata

Who are these people who vainly attempt to turn themselves into
something more than Man? Those who lack the privilege but
who nevertheless seek ecstasies and try to ignore their bodies.
Yet Montaigne hints at more. These people want to 'transform
themselves into angels'. For centuries it had been traditional to
use the term 'angelic life' in a particular way: the angelic life is
the celibate life; in Christian culture it was particularly applied
to celibate contemplatives.

Ecstatic bliss normally figures in treatises as the blessed (or
happy) life. Montaigne knew Seneca's treatise *De vita beata* and
drew on it for some views on ecstasy which he did not accept.
This prompted me to read Renaissance treatises on the subject,
which have proved helpful in understanding what Montaigne
was talking about. A useful work, which enables us to recapture
something of the world of assumptions which Montaigne was
challenging, is the *De vita beata* of Agostino Dato.

Most men, we are told, can enjoy happy and honourable

marriages, while moderating their marital intercourse which, for Dato (as for others), evoked Hippocrates' description of sex as 'part of that dreadful illness epilepsy'. But some are able to live a life 'above humanity', despising all human temptations; all their *studium* is a striving towards truth. 'Their couch is sad but chaste.' Men who were classed as striving above humanity include the Greek philosophers, the Jewish Essenes, the priests of Egypt who 'among many other things abstained from wives'. Best of all, eclipsing all the others, are those who 'in our time lead the religious life of catholic monasticism (*catholicae religionis coenobitas*)'. These people, 'in some way, do doff the weakness of their humanity and imitate the life of the angels. Preferring celibacy to matrimony, they separate their mind from their senses better than even Socrates did and, since they are more truly enraptured by the higher ecstasy of the soul, they *die* better than false philosophers do – if true and solid philosophy (not the painted, feigned variety) is, indeed, a *meditatio mortis*, a preparation for death.'

Dato admits that this sort of man is very rare: 'Only a few can be found in the whole world.' They enjoy unbelievable pleasure (*incredibilis quaedam voluptas*) – far more than can be experienced by others. But clearly neither Dato nor Montaigne expected the average 'celibate' priest to be much of a saint; he would be all the better for not trying to force himself to quit his body and revel in rapture. Let him acknowledge his bodily necessities and stay sane.[5]

With such standard doctrines Montaigne more or less agreed, though even for privileged contemplatives he played down the element of 'practising dying' with the soul leaving the body behind. But he added a proviso so fundamental that it changed everything: he placed a total barrier between privileged Christian contemplatives and all other would-be ecstatics. Precisely because Christian teachings on ecstasy are indebted to Socrates and Plato, Montaigne – like Agostino Dato or like any

---

[5] Augustinus Datus (Senensis): *Opera*, Sienna, 1503, *De Vita beata*, pp. cclxxii v.f. For Dato, quite orthodoxly, catholic ascetics 'in some way doff the weakness of humanity'. That is a step towards ecstasy: These ecstatic ascetics are few indeed – '*vix pauci toto orbe reperiuntur*' – but they enjoy *incredibilis voluptas*. 'The life of such men is so much more blessed than that of others, that the others are absent from true blessedness' (cf. Erasmus towards the end of the *Praise of Folly*).

other Christian who tackled such a question seriously – had to
state, unambiguously and finally, where he placed pagans like
Socrates and Plato. Where do they stand in relation to those
privileged Christian coenobites who enjoy a constant foretaste of
heavenly bliss? We are left in no doubt. For Montaigne the
ecstasies of Socrates, like those of Plato, are mere
embarrassments – a proof not of higher spirituality but of
pathetic humanity:

> (C) Those transcendant humours frighten me like high,
> inaccessible places. Nothing is more difficult for me to swallow in
> the life of Socrates than his ecstasies and daemoneries: nothing so
> human in Plato as the reason people give for calling him 'divine'
> (III. 13, p. 430).

In the Renaissance Plato's divine status was attested by the
philosopher himself: he was said to have claimed 'frequently to
have enjoyed the supreme Good in contemplation, his soul
having actually left his body'. Ficino is adamant where Plato's
claims are concerned (*Opera* I, 280f.). Towards the end of the
sixteenth century the Jesuits of Coîmbra expounded these ideas
persuasively in their edition of Aristotle's *De anima* (III, art. 3,
p. 513). Such influential commonplaces of Platonising Christians
are the errors that Montaigne sought to overthrow.[6]

[6] The entire section of the commentary of the Jesuits of Coîmbra on the *De
Anima* of Aristotle, devoted as it is to Ficinian ecstasy and to that *Prisca
Theologia* studied by D.P. Walker, makes an excellent backcloth to the
understanding of Montaigne at the final stages of the *Essays*. With its help one
can see more clearly what Montaigne is supporting and advocating, and,
especiallly, what he is by-passing, undermining or overthrowing. On the sole
authority of *Divina sapientia Secundum Aegyptios* (II. 4) Plato is honoured, in
the Commentary, with frequent and privileged ecstasies, reminiscent of St Paul's
unique rapture, during which Plato (like Paul) had a revelation of immortality
'which cannot be expressed in speech nor perceived with the ears nor
comprehended by thought'. Such claims for Plato or Socrates are dismissed by
Montaigne as human fantasies. The Jesuits of Coîmbra (col. 515) believe that
ecstasies such as those of Socrates and Plato were *ex naturae privilegio* (in no
ways 'divine', though in a sense, privileged, but with a natural privilege only) –
and that they were induced by melancholy; 'Melancholics are more prone to
ecstasy' (as the side-note emphasises): the text of the Commentary explains that
'melancholics, as Fracastorius published in Book Two of his *De intellectione*, are
inclined to abound in thought and so are held to be prone, in this manner, to
being caught away from their senses'. Montaigne restricts the 'privilege' of high
ecstasy to the supernatural, not natural, sphere and does not link the privileged
ecstasies of the elect themselves with states induced by melancholy.

Where most people are concerned, Montaigne distrusts ecstatic melancholy: we may note that it is the *humours* that provoke these transcendental fantasies which 'frighten' him. They are precisely those melancholy humours which upset his own complexion when he first returned to live in the solitude of his estates and which he subsequently learned to hold at arm's length. Wise melancholics keep the soul 'at home' as Socrates told men to do – and did himself most of the time; they do not, as Socrates occasionally did, send it off chasing opinions or spiritual delusions.

8. Astonishment

The ecstasy of amazement, however, falls into a special category. Wise men obey the laws of the land and conform to the order of Nature. God made the rules governing such ordinate behaviour; he alone, in his providence, may suspend them. When he does so, we have a miracle. Faced by a true miracle, ecstatic amazement is, in fact, the ordinate response.

In the margins of the chapter devoted to advocating conservatism in matters of politics, Montaigne copiously reminded his readers how Christ's victory over 'death and sin' had run its course within a framework of political legality. Throughout the ages, rather than subvert the state, God has preferred to allow the '(C) innocent blood of the elect, his favoured ones, to run' under unjust magistrates. To overthrow the state (as Montaigne's religious enemies were doing) is forbidden to mankind. God may sometimes suspend this general rule: man must not.

(C) If divine Providence has sometimes passed beyond the rules to which we are bound by necessity, it is not for us to dispense with those rules (I. 23, p. 155).

Such divine interventions 'are blows of his divine hand'. We must not imitate them but greet them with ecstatic amazement (*non pas imiter, mais admirer*); they are 'inordinate' miracles – outside the order of nature (*extraordinaires*); they are 'express, particular' cases of 'the kind of miracle which Providence offers us as witness of almighty power', and they are above our order of being, above human strength. It is – as always in Montaigne –

lunacy to mimic such things in purely human contexts: '(C) madness and impiety' to try to reproduce this kind of miracle, 'which we are not meant to follow but to contemplate with amazement. They are acts of his Person, not ours' (I. 23, p. 155).

Even true miracles such as these are neither sought after nor yearned for by Montaigne. If he had the choice he would prefer the kind of life where God did not break in with such amazing disturbances. The divine never touches human life without upsetting that natural order in which man is most at home.

At all events, such miracles have nothing to do with melancholy genius or a man's complexion. They are acts of God.

9. The whole being of man

Nothing shows up the human weakness of Alexander the Great more clearly than his 'fantasies' about his divine status. Montaigne placed Alexander's manhood side by side with Christ's, but not his deluded 'divinity'. Alexander had nothing divine about him, though he thought he had. Self-idolatry, like all idolatry, is toppled by Montaigne as an all-too-human folly.

To reach such conclusions and apply them to all men required a revolution in Montaigne's attitude to genius. He had once been ready to react with ecstatic amazement before the human beauty of heroic virtue portrayed in poetry. His chapter on outstanding men – Homer, Alexander the Great and Epaminondas – places them '(A) as it were above the human condition', and there is talk of 'miraculous' virtue. Surprise is expressed that Homer '(A) who created so many gods, has not himself been deified'; so much that he achieved was '(A) against the order of Nature (*contre l'ordre de la Nature*)'.

But that was only a stage on Montaigne's journey of discovery. In the margins of the Bordeaux copy it is all countered, and the humanity of such persons is trenchantly asserted: they are great men; '(C) no form nor fortune of Man' exceeds them. And Alcibiades is preferred to the lot of them – as a man, not venerable (*sainct*), but a civil, moderate gentleman: a *gualant homme* (II. 36, p. 573). Glorifying virtue in poetry will produce a kind of ecstatic amazement in the reader or hearer, but there will be nothing divine about it.

God enjoys his Being. That basic tenet of monotheistic

speculation underlies Montaigne's blunt assertion that the way to resemble God is to be like him on the human level:

> (B) It is a perfection, absolute and as though divine, to know how loyally to enjoy one's being (III. 13, p. 430).

The being of man, his *estre*, is what makes each individual human person a particular example of the human race. As the Franciscan Boucher explained to the next generation in his *Triomphes de la Religion Chrestienne* (1628, p. 766), the rôle of the *forme essentielle* is to give specific and natural being to the matter of which it is the proper form. The soul (as *forme*) unites with a body and makes a person – gives it *l'estre de l'espece humaine*, the state-of-being of a member of the species Man. The human *estre* cannot exist without the soul and body together. The 'being' of a man or woman demands this union of them both. It is a scholastic commonplace that *forma dat esse rei*, that form gives 'being' to a substance by 'informing' it.

It is within this *estre*, this state-of-being as individual man, as body informed with soul, that Montaigne seeks a human perfection akin to God's. If we enjoy our *estre* we are at least like God in that: he enjoys his. As far as most of us are concerned, there is no need to try to split our 'being' into its two component parts.

This thought had a new urgency for Montaigne, partly because of his reflexions on human sexuality – additions in the margin of his chapter on Virgil bind that chapter even more closely to the end of *De l'experience*. Those who call sex bestial are roundly condemned: '(C) Are we not brute-beasts to call bestial the act which makes us?' No other creature despises his being; yet 'we men' consider our very being to be vitiated (III. 5, p. 118).

Montaigne is not talking of sin when he talks in this way of the *vice* of our *estre*. He is condemning those who regret that God made man as soul-and-body and belittling Philosophy for 'preaching' that there is something wild about '(C) marrying the divine and the earthly, the rational and the irrational' in Man (III. 13, p. 427). His contention was soon to be commonplace, if it were not so already. Jean Boucher saw this union as a 'special mark of Divine Wisdom; joining by this means Heaven and Earth within each man who, on one side, shares qualities with the angels: on the other communicating with the beasts of the earth ... The order of the universe requires this' (*Triomphes de la Religion Chrestienne*, p. 762).

The human condition is this necessary union of body conjoined to soul. The Church taught what Montaigne presupposes: *anima mea non est ego*, 'my soul is not me' (is not the whole of man); Plato wrongly said that it was. Not understanding this, we men have recourse to various ecstasies – *sortons hors de nous*. But it is no good: however high your throne, 'you sit down on your arse'.

Montaigne's quest is over. He has studied the particular being who is himself: a botched form of Man moulding his bodily matter. His intellectual journey took him from death to life, from self to all humanity. His conclusion is not simply how he, Michel de Montaigne, should live, but how men and women in general should try to live:

> (B) The most beautiful lives, to my taste, are those which frame themselves to the common model, (C) the human model, with order but (B) without miracles and *sans extravagance* (III. 13, end).

Thus the last words in the book (before a brief special plea is made for tolerance towards old men) are *sans extravagance*. The noun *extravagance* suggests wandering about outside the natural paths allotted to Man. Randle Cotgrave, in his *Dictionarie of the French and English Tongues* (1611 etc.), includes in the meanings of *extravagance* 'a giddie, unsteadie, fantasticall action'. Such, for Montaigne, were most men's ecstasies.

As he had written in the earliest version of the apologia for Sebond, 'all *voyes extravaguantes*' – all roads, that is, which wander off away from the normal and the usual – '*me faschent*, irritate me' (II. 12, p. 305). In the end even Socrates was not allowed to be an exception to the rule; indeed Montaigne found Socrates' ecstasies and daemoneries especially *fascheuses* (III. 13, p. 430).

Ecstasies and daemoneries are but vain attempts to escape from the human condition; in essentials they show contempt for the life of man. Yet 'the opinion which despises our life is ridiculous. After all, it is our being and our all'. Contempt for his condition is an illness peculiar to man alone: 'No other creature hates and despises itself.' Yet it is quite vain to wish to be anything other than what we are: 'Anyone who desires to be changed from man to angel effects nothing for himself whatsoever' (II. 3, p. 28).

Of course, there is, in the background, always the proviso repeated at the end of the book and spelled out in the apologia for Sebond:

This discourse only touches on our common order and is not sacrilegious enough to want to embrace those divine, supernatural and extraordinary beauties which can sometimes be seen shining among us like stars beneath a bodily and earthly veil (II. 12, p. 202).

But it does include virtue as philosophy knows it and even religion, in that ordinary men may be carried beyond what is appropriate to people of their sort: 'The archer who shoots past the target misses as much as the one who falls short' (I. 30, p. 258).

Montaigne believed that such moderation was supported not merely by ancient philosophers but 'by God's word' – or, rather, 'by God's voice' as he changed it to later – speaking through St Paul in Romans 12:3. (He could do this because he followed the Latin Vulgate, not the Greek.) He was so struck by it that he inscribed it on his library wall: 'Be not wiser than is becoming, but be soberly wise' (I. 30, p 257).[7]

10. Poetry has the last word

At the end of his *Essays* Montaigne chose to cite Horace's prayer to keep his sanity and to be granted an old age which retained the joys of the lyre:

Frui paratis et valido mihi,
  Latoe, dones, et, precor, integra
    cum mente, nec turpem senectam
      degere, nec cythara carentem.

Vouchsafe, O Son of Latona, that I may enjoy in good health the

---

[7] Romans 12:3 (Vulgate): *Ne plus sapite quam oporteat: sed sapite ad sobrietatem.* Erasmus had already shown that the meaning Montaigne was to get out of the Latin is not in conformity with the Greek (which is concerned not with a classical-sounding 'moderation' in learning but with a prudently sober estimate of one's own unimportance).

things I have prepared, but with, I pray, my mind intact, not
sinking into squalid senility nor lacking the lyre.

(Odes 1.31.17-20)

Being carried away by the arts is the only *furor* welcomed to the
last. It may be a *folie*, but it avoids something worse: *sottise*,
stupidity (III. 9, p. 270). Apart from that: no *extravagance*, no
spiritual gadding about.

Miracles are not denied (though without the Church's
guidance you cannot recognise one when you see one); at all
events they are best kept away from the lives of ordinary people.
Such things are not ordinate, and the life man needs is an
ordinate one. He had said the same in *Du repentir*: a man should
live according to the natural order; in youth and in old age he
himself had lived *avec ordre, selon moy* – 'ordinately' according
to his own standards. As Boucher put it: the very order of the
world requires Man to be what he is.

Only one thing can spoil all this: senile dementia. Burton
helps to explain why the *Essays* end with Horace's plea for
sanity. Increased melancholy is the danger. Old age 'being cold
and dry, and of the same quality as melancholy is, must needs
cause it'.

Therefore Melanchthon avers out of Aristotle as an undoubted
truth that old men familiarly dote, because of black choler, which
is then superabundant in them: and Rhasis, that Arabian
Physician, calls it a necessary and inseparable accident to all old
and decrepit persons (*Anatomy of Melancholy*, p. 183).

Maintain your being to the end, by keeping body and soul
together – that was the advice of Cicero in his treatise *On Old
Age*, a work that any elderly humanist was sure to read again as
death approached:

The best end of life is one that comes *integra cum mente* – when
the mind is intact and the senses unimpaired, and when Nature
herself loosens asunder the work which she had put together (*De
senectute* 20-72).

In his edition of Cicero, Aldus Manutius commented that the
phrase *integra cum mente* meant, 'before, lacking your senses,
you become deranged'. And, he added (a lesson Montaigne had

learned by watching his peasants face to face with death): 'meanwhile, keep body and soul, both, sufficiently fed, and pray not to lose your faculties. Shall wise men fear what even uneducated young rustics know how to despise?'

CHAPTER NINETEEN

Genius among Men

1. The higher forms again

Socrates taught that right and wrong begin 'at home'. For the Renaissance this was proverbial wisdom. When Montaigne decided to keep his soul 'at home' – to keep it at home in his body – he brought home with it every aspect of his life, including his experience as a soldier fighting for his king and his religion, his wide reading, all his knowledge of men and women, good and bad, ancient and modern, lord and peasant, Catholic and *Réformé*, natural and civilised. He also brought home for consideration and inquiry his sexuality and all the traditional causes of ecstasies. The result was a revolution in thought arising from his perception of an underlying unity within the all but infinite variety of the human species. He did not descend into particulars from the general: his confidence grew until he dared rise to the general from one particular person: from 'me' to Man.[1]

Montaigne believed in the uniformity of nature. But he did not accept the doctrine of the natural equality and identity of endowment of all human forms. In an extreme version of this doctrine, certain Aristotelian theologians and philosophers claimed that, so far as their natural qualities were concerned, there was no difference between the soul of Judas Iscariot and the human soul of Jesus of Nazareth. As forms of Man they were identical in endowment and capacity. Such doctrines horrified

[1] For a useful contemporary discussion of the meaning, scope and limitations of the doctrine *Ab universalibus ad singularia progredi oportere*, see Archangel Mercanarius, *Dilucidationes obscuriorum locorum philosophiae naturalis Aristotelis*, Leipzig, 1590, pp. 11ff.

many. Yet if individual persons do differ in their various
endowments, how does that come about within the single species
which is Man? Some explained it in terms of bodily variation;
some by the injection of the divine or the diabolical into human
life; some thought in terms of the superhuman and the
subhuman: Socrates, Seneca, Homer, Caesar – to jumble some
names together – might be thought of as rising above their
species, ceasing to be (mere) Man. Similarly with the great
examples of evil. Renaissance playwrights, for example, work
upon the animality of the Nebuchadnezzars and the
Tamberlanes, portraying them as men who sank below the level
of their species.

Montaigne abandoned such opinions, but he eventually placed
phenomena such as Siamese twins within a special category. He
did so with the help of a Platonic notion (studied by A.O.
Lovejoy in *The Great Chain of Being*). There are, it was said, no
missing links in the vast 'chain' of creation: the very fertility of
God's creative powers required him to create every genus which
it was possible to create, every one of them constituting a link in
the chain of forms which stretches from that of the highest
creature in the highest heaven to that of the lowest creature to be
found anywhere. It was this theory that led Montaigne to wonder
whether Siamese twins might be individual cases of otherwise
unknown 'links', corresponding to generic forms (perhaps known
only to God) from which they, in some unexplained way, derive
their 'monstrous' characteristics:

> (C) What we call monsters are not so for God, who sees the infinite
> number of forms which he has included within the immensity of
> his creation; it is to be believed that the figure which astonishes us
> relates to, and derives from, some other figure of the same genus
> unknown to man. God is all-wise; nothing comes from him which
> is not good, common and regular: but we cannot see the
> disposition or the relationship (II. 30, p. 515).

Cicero is cited in support of this: 'A man is not amazed by something which happens often, even if he does not know why it
occurs; but when anything happens which he has never seen
before, he believes it to be a portent' (*De divinatione* 2.21).
Montaigne insists that ecstatic amazement has no place in a
wise man's reaction to a new phenomenon such as a 'monster':
we are too ready to say that something is 'against nature' when it

is merely 'against custom' (II. 30, end).[2]

This special status given to 'monsters' as rare natural cases related to unknown forms did not affect Montaigne's approach to the genus Man. Nor would he admit good daemons, let alone evil devils, within the limits of his human inquiry. For him, men remain men. Moralists might call lust 'animal'. Yet the coarse brutal slaking of sexual desires which some men revelled in he found to be only metaphorically brutal or bestial; it was all too human. Brutes are not as brutal or as bestial as man when it comes to cruel sexuality. The only way in which man may really sink below the species Man is by becoming mad.[3]

What, then, are we to make of those 'forms' he had earlier called 'holy', great and venerable? Are they particular cases of rare or unknown genera? Certainly not.

Montaigne's acceptance of qualitative differences between human forms is what one would expect from him as a Renaissance Roman Catholic of a particular philosophical bent. Theologians and philosophers traditionally disagreed about this – both between themselves and among themselves. The Franciscan preacher Jean Boucher is again a good and succint guide, so I follow him; philosophers and glossators say the same thing, often more technically. According to Boucher, 'Aristotle and his disciples believe that all forms of Man are equally endowed by Nature with the same powers. For them, what makes for the differences between men are the varying degrees of organisation or disorganisation within the bodies to which their souls are joined'. To this may be added differences of climate and – particularly important – the different humours or temperaments of various men. Boucher explains that differences between individuals 'proceed from the dominant humour: we can see that melancholics are more ingenious; phlegmatics gross and heavy; cholerics agile and quick, also light in understanding;

---

[2] For a very brief naturalistic explanation of the kind of ecstasies which interested Montaigne, including astonishment in face of the unknown, cf. Fracastorius, *De sympathia et antipathia rerum*, Lyons, 1550, cap. 20: *De admiratione, & Ecstasi, & risu*, pp. 179f.

[3] This was quite a common position to adopt; cf. D. Lambin's edition of Horace's *Opera* (Paris, 1604, on *Odes*, I. 31, s.v. *Integra cum mente*): through madness, a human being loses his *humanitas* and ceases to be a man; that is because, as Aristotle taught in the *Nicomachean Ethics*, the *mens* is the best part of man and so *amentia* is the gravest and most troublesome of states.

the sanguine more happy and pleasant and of agreeable company'. But many theologians go beyond this, insisting that the human forms themselves vary in degrees of endowment. Just as there are degrees of white which remain within the species Whiteness, so, for them, 'all rational souls remain of the same species', despite inequalities. 'A soul which is, by nature, more perfect than another, still remains within its specific nature, that is, it does not abandon its *species* to climb into a higher one; nor can a soul actually descend to a lower one ...'

In other words, for those who think as Boucher does and as Montaigne did before him, each and every man and woman, however good or evil, remains within the species Man. Nobody is superhuman. Nobody is subhuman – even the bestial madman does not have a 'bestial' soul. All souls of men and women are human, but they are not equally endowed.[4]

The *Essays* show that Montaigne was also aware of differences caused by bodily endowments, climate (both literally and in the sense of locally-based cultures) and various complexions – not least the melancholic. But he accepted his Church's teaching that the individual forms of Man also vary in natural perfection. Each man bears within himself 'the whole form of the human condition' – not only is he completely Man, but all the potentiality of Man is in him. Yet his own dominant form (what Montaigne calls his *forme maistresse*) is necessarily limited, so

---

[4] See R.-P. Boucher, *Les Triomphes de la religion chrestienne*, Paris, 1628, p. 771, Question 34, entitled, 'De cette esgale presence essentielle de l'Ame je viens à une autre en vous demandant si toutes les Ames sont esgales és degrez de perfection naturelle'. The explanation draws upon Peter Lombard (lib. 2. dist. 32) and the Commentaries of Bonaventura and others. This inequality of souls (or forms) can be explained in terms of the varying limitations of the bodies individually chosen by God for them and would be probably inexplicable if the souls were created independently of their bodies. Boucher stresses that inequality of form does not result in changes of species ('car une Ame plus parfaicte qu'une autre demeure tousjours en sa nature specifique, ne sortant point de son espece pour monter à une plus haute, n'y pour descendre à une plus basse'; p. 772). When Boucher talks strictly of men in terms of angelic or bestial tendencies it is as a comparison:' ... quelques unes subtiles *comme* des Anges, & d'autres grossières & stupides *comme* bestes' (p. 774). It is doubtful whether Montaigne accepted that even madmen were, *sensu stricto*, beasts not men. There is no suggestion in Montaigne of the soul of a madman actually sinking to a lower species even though, as body-plus-soul, he was acting as a beast. The concept that varying degrees of perfection are to be found in human forms is foreign to Aristotle and to scholastics like Aquinas; it was expounded by Duns Scotus and had many partisans in the Renaissance.

he must not mistake his *forme maistresse* for the *maistresse forme* of Nature. His *forme maistresse* is subject to all the limitations of body and temperament and is endowed by Nature with its own degree of perfection or imperfection.

Montaigne acknowledged the excellence of great men. When defending Cato and Plutarch he condemned those who judge everything by their own narrow standards – by what they are able to do or wish to do. 'Everybody believes that the *maistresse forme* of Nature is within himself, making that the touchstone and compass of all other forms.' This is wrong and Montaigne will have none of it. Yet, in the end, after much hesitation, he succeeded in keeping even the greatest forms of human kind well within the species Man.

Montaigne's admiration for the great had been real enough for him to explain his reactions in terms of the ecstasy of amazement. But while he remained 'stunned' and 'astonished' by the 'venerable forms' no moral progress was possible: he had to be able to judge them. Otherwise a major group of men rose above humanity and so were closed to his methods of investigation. Moral progress became possible once he laid aside ecstatic wonder. Then he could say that he 'fixes his gaze on great men' and '(B) judges what makes them rise so high'. Once he had identified the cause, he went on to claim '(C) to some extent to perceive the seeds of it' within himself. If that was so, it became possible and legitimate for him to judge himself against these great men – and to judge them against himself.

This is the key. He now considers these men as men, different from himself only in degree. The greatness of Cato grew from 'seeds' which exist in all men. The same applies to the 'extreme baseness' of some human souls: it does not 'astonish' him and he finds no difficulty in believing that fully human beings can be so base (II. 32, pp. 531-2).

Control of ecstatic *admiratio* (astonishment) in face of all but the truly divine became part of Montaigne's considered wisdom (Cf. II. 30, end). Thus, in the end, Socrates becomes not a saintly exception to be venerated but a model for mankind – always excepting his 'ecstasies and daemoneries' for which he had long been admired as divine, as though he had risen above the species Man. It is interesting to see how Montaigne reached this conviction. In his chapter on empty vanity, for example, Montaigne considered Socrates' preference for death rather than exile. It puzzled him, since he could not square it with mere humanity. In such 'heavenly' lives as that of Socrates he could honour some aspects but could not feel emotionally involved. At that stage, moreover, he felt that 'some lives are so elevated and so *extraordinaire*' – so outside the natural order – that he could not really honour them, since he could not even conceive of them. Socrates claimed to be a citizen of the world; yet there he was fearing exile from his homeland! How can such contradictions in a great man be reconciled? (III. 9, p. 241). Montaigne eventually cut the knot by insisting on the humanity of this greatest of men. Once we are dealing with a man, however great, inconsistencies cease to surprise: men are like that.

2. Sallies and constancy

The old heroes were ecstatic in their bravery. Montaigne – even when all had been considered and weighed – did not deny the existence of many sorts of natural ecstasy: they existed and he distrusted them. Already in the first version of his chapter on virtue, Montaigne had reached this conclusion by his chosen method of looking into himself: 'I find from experience', he wrote, 'that there is a difference between [ecstatic] leaps and sallies of the soul and a settled, constant habit.' Seneca had dared to believe that the Stoic sage surpassed the divine, since God already has the property of impassibility, but the sage acquires it! Montaigne dismissed such nonsense. There is nothing impassible or constant in man. In the end Montaigne was unimpressed by claims that some men are superhuman: 'It can even happen to us – to us who are but misbegotten men; our souls are awakened by the speech or actions of others and we shoot them far above their ordinary state. This kind of passion thrusts and agitates the soul, ravishing it somewhat outside itself' (II. 29, p. 504). Because of this, quite ordinary men can know directly, from their own experience, something of the ecstatic virtues of the heroes of other times and of our own. All of us, including them, are and remain human. The divine has no place in Montaigne's account of the process by which the soul of heroes or philosophers is driven *hors de luy* – ecstatically 'outside' its normal state.

What others can do, we can share in, at least to some extent:

(C) Ordinate conduct, moderation, constancy apart, I believe that anything at all can be done, even by a man who, taken overall, is lacking and deficient (II. 29, p. 505).

3.   Inspiration, or unfair arguments?

In the early days, Montaigne noted that Plato's title *divine* enjoyed 'universal consent; nobody has tried to contest it', unlike the same title boastfully attributed to Pietro Aretino – a common enough author 'who in no wise approaches that ancient divinity' (I. 51, end). Yet before the end of the *Essays* Montaigne had done what 'nobody' did; he had contested Plato's right to that title: the very claim to be divine was a pathetic indication of the man's humanity.

In the margins of the Bordeaux copy Montaigne wrote dismissively about the way in which Plato and Socrates called on inspiration to help them out of difficulties. To support a weak argument, Plato had asserted that even the wicked know how to distinguish good people from bad, '(C) through some divine inspiration ... '. Montaigne's comment is arrestingly blunt: '(C) that person and his pedagogue are marvellous and bold workmen' when it comes to introducing 'divine operations and inspiration, anywhere and everywhere when human strength gives out!' (II. 16, p. 404).

4.   Judging revelations

It may well have been Montaigne's bad experience of the medical profession that led him to be ironical about all but specially privileged revelations vouchsafed to God's chosen few. Whenever medical experts based their remedies on divine revelations – as they often did – Montaigne kept his counsel and took his medicine! As for the proofs which 'authors say they have acquired from some daemon or other,' he said with detachment, 'I am quite happy to accept them (I never touch miracles) ... '. He saw such claims as dishonest ways out of hopeless situations. His choice of examples tells us much about his own preoccupations: among the infinite data which doctors would have to digest if 'their art' were to have value, he cites only one illness (epilepsy); among the infinite variety of complexions, only one (melancholy); among the infinite variations of the heavens, only one (the conjunction of Venus with Saturn – the planet which presided over all sorts of melancholy).

With such reflexions he toppled the gods of medicine from their pedestals. (If you wanted to know about melancholy would you go to them?) It is a fact that the medical art went back to very few great names. Herein lay its weakness: that three 'inspired' witnesses and three 'inspired' doctors should set up as professors to the whole human race is not reasonable (II. 37, p. 608). Hippocrates and Galen are two of these 'professors'. Another could well be Plato or Aristotle – both were authorities in medicine. Montaigne's amusement at those who claim to get their proofs from daemons may imply a laugh at the followers of the daemonic Aristotle, but would also apply to Platonising doctors, who had their daemons to inspire them. Hippocrates was thought to have been inspired. A Renaissance doctor like Cardano believed himself to be inspired too.

Ficino can be classed with 'Plato and his pedagogue' as one who had recourse to the divine when reason ran out. Ficino read the whole of Platonic *mania* into the thirtieth of Aristotle's *Problems*. The relevant passage of Ficino's commentary – the basis of so much Renaissance thought on ecstasy – represents just what Montaigne overthrew when he brought all men, except those privileged by special grace, firmly back into the human species. Ficino wrote:

> We must give reasons for the assertions of Democritus, Plato and Aristotle that some melancholics at times excel everyone else in their genius, so that they seem divine rather than human. Democritus, Plato and Aristotle definitely assert this, but they hardly seem to explain adequately why.

So Ficino proceeded to do so under inspiration – *monstrante Deo*, 'with God showing him the way' (*Opera*, 1641, I, p. 485). How can we argue with people who make their authorities superhuman and then explain what they mean by private inspiration direct from God!

Once Montaigne saw this, his whole attitude to revelation and ecstasy changed. Take the divinity away from Plato and Aristotle, reject Ficino's claim to divine guidance, and it is only a tiny step to doubt that the *Problems* were authentic anyway. One more step, and it does not matter whether they are or not:

they contain such stupidities.

Montaigne was reading the *Problems* when preparing the 1588 edition of the *Essays*. He was struck by the ease with which natural philosophers find causes for everything. He took an example from the *Problems* themselves: Why do we say 'bless you' when somebody sneezes? Well, '(B) we produce three sorts of wind; the one that comes out from below is too dirty; the one from the mouth, the belch of gluttons. The third is sneezing. As that comes blamelessly from the head we give it this honourable welcome. Don't laugh at such subtlety! It derives (they say) from Aristotle' (III. 6, beginning).

Again: lame women are more enjoyable to lie with. Why? Montaigne might hazard the guess that their irregular movements increase the pleasure of *la besongne*. But, he added, '(B) I have just learned that ancient authority has decided the matter'. He went on to give a dead-pan account deriving indirectly from *Problems* 10.25: the vaginas of such women are more forceful because they take the nourishment which the crippled thighs and legs are deprived of. He breaks off to make the comment: 'At this rate, what can't we reason about!' (III. 11, p. 319).[5]

5. Imagination and ecstasies

Montaigne had tried out for himself what it was like to lie with a lame woman. He found that imagination can make you believe you have exceptional sexual pleasures from crippled women,

[5] Montaigne's theme goes back indirectly to *Problemata* 10, 25 or 26, but it is misleading to state that his allusion to ancient explanations of the sexual potentialities of lame women are actually expounded there. Standard treatments of this theme are, as in Aristotle himself, man-centred, connected with the practice of the Amazons who crippled their future studs. They explain why crippled men, not crippled women, are more sexually desirable. Cf. the best-known text on this subject: Erasmus, *Adagia* 2.9.49, *Claudus optime virum agit*. But Montaigne is talking of women not men. For this, cf. Junius who, in his exposition of an adage *Cucumere vescens chlamydem texito*, has an explanation relevant to women, partly derived from Ermolao Barbaro (whom he accused Caelius Richerius Rhodiginus of plagiarising): cf. *Adagia id est Proverbiorum ... omnium quae apud Graecos, Latinos, Hebraeos, Arabas, &c. in usu fuerunt*, 1643, p. 663; Rhodiginus, *Antiquae lectiones*, Book 4, chap. 5, *Cur claudi salaciores*. See also Septalius on *Problemata*, 1632, pp. 97 and 294. On sneezing, cf. J.Guastavinius' *Commentarii in priores decem problematicum sectiones*, Lyons, 1608, p. 342.

even when you do not really do so; but imagination can also help you to glimpse the nature of real ecstasies, which are above the sustained experience of ordinary men. By 'imagination' Montaigne implies a force of disturbing power, enabling man to picture both absent realities and pure fantasies. The Roman medical writer Celsus, like Augustine later, vouched for ecstatic effects which may in fact be explained in terms of the power of imagination on soul and body. Montaigne recalls that the mysterious wounds of king Dagobert and the stigmata of St Francis might be accounted for in this way (I. 21, p. 123). The same examples and the same conclusions can be found in Cornelius Agrippa and Robert Burton.[6]

Montaigne weighed all forms of ecstasy, including sexual and philosophical ones, against his personal experiences. In special cases, imagination may make the soul's pictures into bodily realities. He had no doubt that, where ordinary men are concerned, imagination may even help to picture for a moment the spiritual states which privileged ecstatics experience with constancy.

Montaigne is always worth careful attention when he discusses imagination and fantasy (both subject to melancholy disturbances). He was '(A) one of those who felt the force of imagination very strongly'. As he wrote when discussing his melancholy tendencies, if he had not learned to tame his imagination '(A) he would have been in continual fear and frenzy' (I. 21, beginning: I. 20, p. 108).

Frenzies and ecstasies may be induced by imagination, and what passes for inspiration may be unexplained good luck. Montaigne did not consider such impulses to be divine, but he did not consider them negligible either. The amused tolerance which led him to take medicines based on allegedly revealed recipes worked elsewhere too: '(A) Not only in medicine but in several of the more certain arts fortune plays a great part. Why should we

---

[6] Cf. *Anatomy of Melancholy*. Pt. 1, Sect. 2. Mem. 3. Subs. 2 (Dent edition, I, pp. 253f): 'On the force of imagination': 'Especially it rageth in melancholy persons … ' who may be 'witch-ridden'. 'Fracastorius *lib*.3. de *intellect.* refers all ecstasies to this force of imagination … Dagobertus' and St Francis' scars and wounds, like Christ's (if at least any such were), Agrippa supposeth to have happened by force of imagination.' And so on. Fracastorius' approach to melancholy and ecstasy, with its rigorous exclusion of divine interventions, is a good yardstick for judging what Montaigne has to say.

not attribute to good luck (*bonheur*) those poetic sallies which catch an author away and ravish him outside himself?' *Orateurs* (prose-writers and public speakers) feel these 'extraordinary movements and agitations too'. Painters may even be in an ecstasy of amazement before their own paintings (I. 24, p. 162).

When writing about artistic creation – especially of poetry but also of excellent ancient prose – Montaigne regularly kept the language, though not the substance, of Platonic ecstasy: it was not in the earlier versions of the *Essays* but in the margin of the Bordeaux copy that he wrote: '(C) Poetry is an art (said Plato) light, flighty, daemonic' (III. 9, p. 270). When talking of poetry his most typical words are *fureur* and its cognates. But despite terms like 'daemonic', the supernatural is eliminated. What seems like poetic inspiration can be explained by other means: by luck, by imagination, by the demands of deep reflexions and profound thinking.

In the same way that artists feel themselves inspired, so mad inspirations from outside – *fureurs estrangeres* – are said to make leaders choose unlikely courses which then turn out right. Even in the early days, Montaigne was sceptical: 'Ancient Captains, in order to lend plausibility to their bolder decisions', told their men they had been led to such conclusions 'by some inspiration or other, some sign or prognostic' (I. 24, p. 163).

What may have brought Montaigne to place more and more distance between his wisely ordinate man and any form of ecstasy was the credence widely but unwisely given to the accusations of witnesses in cases of witchcraft. These witnesses were themselves amazed by the strange events they claimed to have witnessed. It is one thing to appear to be ecstatically amazed as a poet, author, painter – or even as a great statesman or general who cannot account for his lucky intuitions: it is quite another thing to treat the convictions of dazed witnesses in a court of law as matters of life and death for wretched old women. Divine truth or divine relevation is one thing: astonished opinion is another.

It is right that we should take 'God's own word' about witches when he deigns to reveal it, for it provides 'certain and irrefragable examples'. But that does not mean that we should take the word of a man who is '(B) amazed by his own narration – necessarily amazed if he is not out of his senses'. We should only act on such evidence if God gives his *approbation surnaturelle* – a miraculous sign of approval – which will not be often. 'The privilege which it pleased God to grant to some of the testimonies we have must not be cheapened.' Men lie. They take their opinions for revealed truths. Yet, when all is said and done, '(B) it is putting a high price on your conjectures to roast a man alive' (III. 11, pp. 315-17).

The trouble arises from the power of imagination – the very thing wise melancholics learn to distrust.[7]

Montaigne seems to have reached the same conclusion as Jerome Mercurialis in the section on mania in his *Medicina Practica* (1601): melancholy madness is a form of alienation (as all authorities maintain), but it alienates the imagination, not the mind. In which case it has nothing at all to do with the manias Plato wrote about. Once this is accepted as true, the theories of Ficino based on the thirtieth of Aristotle's *Problems* fall to the ground, in so far as they apply to the natural ecstasies

---

[7] Montaigne discusses witchcraft in relationship to law; in medieval and Renaissance times the liberal view – that witches are deceived, only doing in imagination what they think they do corporeally – derived authority from Canon Law (26, qu. 5, *Episcopi*). The 'delusions' by which they are 'seduced' are classed there as the works of devils. 26, qu. 5 gave difficulties to keen prosecutors when witches were charged with going bodily to their sabbaths. Cf. the *Lucerna inquisitorum haereticorum pravitatis* of Bernardus Comensis in *Tractatus juris civilis*, 1584, Bodley, at L.Z.16, Art. Seld., p. 348v; the same point is raised by Bartholomaeus Spineus in *Quaestio de Strigibus*, ibid., p. 356r.f. Such works show that Montaigne was challenging deeply-entrenched legal authority. And yet, as Burton rightly insists, many medical authorities attributed all cases of alleged witchcraft entirely to melancholy delusions: 'Wierus, Baptist Porta, Ulrich Molitor, Edwicus, do refer all that witches are said to do, to imagination alone, and this humour of melancholy' (*Anatomy of Melancholy*, Part I, Sect. 2. Mem. 1. Subs. 6). Montaigne never gives the devil any rôle to play in the delusions of witches. He was not alone in that. Cf. Burton (*Anatomy*, Part I, Sect. 2. Mem. 1. Subs. 3, p. 202): 'Many deny witches at all, or if there be any, they can do no harm; of this opinion is Wierus, lib. 3. cap. 53, *de praestig. daem*., Austin Lerchmeyer, a Dutch writer, Biarmannus, Ewichius, Euwaldus, our countryman Scott ... They laugh at such stories; but on the contrary are most lawyers, divines, physicians, philosophers, Austin ... ' (Montaigne is prepared to believe 'Austin' – St Augustine – but not the others!) Cardano, as cited by Reginald Scott in the *Discoverie of Witchcraft* (p. 16), attributed belief in witchcraft to three causes: 'the imagination of the melancholike, ... the constancie of them that are corrupt therewith, and the deceipt [deceiving] of the Judges.' J. Wier gives an important place to devils, but sees witches as being much the same as deluded ecstatics (*Cinq livres de l'Imposture et tromperies des diables*, Paris, 1569, p. 137vf. Montaigne's interest in sex-changes may be connected with similar preoccupations; Wier discusses them also at this point).

of unprivileged mankind.[8]

This brings natural man back to his own resources. Even Platonic ecstasies are discounted as unstable poor relations of privileged Christian ones; there is nothing divine about them. If the language of *furor* and *mania* continues to be used, it is as metaphor. Montaigne based none of his philosophical judgments on *mania* and only one on divine enthusiasm.

All judgments made from external appearances alone '(C) are marvellously uncertain and doubtful. No witness is more reliable than each man may be to himself', provided that we judge ourselves when we are 'at home' – that is, when we are in the state diametrically opposed to ecstasy or the philosophical practising of dying (II. 16, p. 339).

6.   Geniuses are men

An entire culture had explained the achievements of genius in terms of melancholy ecstasies. Yet Montaigne concludes that in order to be wise it is not desirable to go beyond the ordinate. And nobody (as far as human wisdom can tell) is worked upon by spiritual forces raising Man above humanity – except ascetic contemplatives. Only these privileged contemplatives complicate the picture. Philosophy does indeed admit that they – and they alone – represent the highest reach of all. In other cases philosophy advocates not ecstatic *furor* but tranquillity of mind.

This explains why Montaigne, partly under Stoic influence, wrote that Philosophy herself had once been taught by divine enthusiasm from the true God, and so made to realise that the highest wisdom of all does not consist in philosophical calm. In this way Montaigne brought the divine madness of Platonising Christianity into harmony with the dominant Aristotelianism of an essentially scholastic moral theology. The complicating factor was the second Person of the Trinity, Holy

---

[8] Hieronymus Mercurialis, *Medicina Practica*, Frankfurt, 1601; cap. xvi, *De mania*, p. 70: 'Mania is a *mentis alienatio* or a continuous ecstasy, without fever or inflammation ... It is called an alienation of the mind as distinct from melancholy, in which it is the imagination which is alienated, not the mind ... From the above description it is obvious that this sick *furor* is far different from the *furor* which Plato talks about in the *Timaeus*.'

Truth, *la saincte Verité* who dragged Philosophy beyond her
natural sphere of calm serenity, of *ataraxia* and *tranquillitas
animi*. Truth compelled Philosophy to admit that, for the very
few, there is a higher state than the one that she can reach: that
of Christian Folly.

(C) It was a pure enthusiasm – breathed into the spirit of
Philosophy and wrenched from her, against her normal teachings,
by *la saincte Verité* – that the tranquil state of our soul, the quiet
state, the sanest state that Philosophy can obtain for the soul,
is not the soul's best state. Our waking is more drowsy than our
sleeping; our wisdom, less wise than our folly; our dreams, worth
more than our discourse; the worse place we can take is *en nous*,
within ourselves (II. 12, p. 319).

As a natural philosopher, Montaigne is only concerned with the
lesser state, the one that owes nothing to direct inspiration from
Truth. At all events it is right for the souls of the mass of
mankind to stay within the limits of natural philosophy and to
resist the temptations of that highest state revealed by Truth.
Whatever may be right for the 'few', it is wrong for 'us' to aspire
to being *hors de nous* in what can only be a foolish parody of true
ecstasy. The divine madness of the few is the bestial madness of
all the others. We avoid that fate by enjoying our 'being' in its
natural condition. That is why ordinary humans have been
granted compensations, including the God-given pleasures of the
body – pleasures which great and busy men like Socrates,
Alexander and Caesar found time to enjoy. Such pleasures –
which strengthen the soul, not weaken it – are 'natural and,
consequently, necessary and just' (III. 13, p. 419).

Montaigne urges the wise to accept the human condition in
terms consecrated by traditional piety: they should enjoy
everything that God has granted them and render 'condign
thanks' to God for every pleasure. *Graces condignes* are ordinate
thanksgivings, proportionate to the bounty of each particular
gift. Typically, Montaigne insists that for a man to offer up
condign thanks he must 'savour and ruminate' the gifts of bodily
pleasures, associating his soul with them, '(B) not so that it
should become drunk on them, but so that it should take
pleasure in them – not losing itself but finding itself in them' (III.
13, p. 425).

This advice applies especially to those like Montaigne, whose conscience and passions are at peace and who accept their bodies with buoyant gratitude. Such men have a soul which 'measures' how much it owes to God, 'enjoying ordinately and appropriately those pleasures which God vouchsafes, in compensation for the pains he so justly sends upon mankind' (III. 13, p. 425).

Philosophy, unaided, can obtain no higher state for the human soul.

Montaigne conquered melancholy with melancholy. In a sense he had always done so. Young love can be a form of ecstasy; so when he was struck with grief over the death of La Boëtie (a grief which was powerful and just, he tell us, '(B) on account of my complexion') he sought out a *vehemente diversion*, a mind-departing distraction, by deliberately making himself fall in love by art and industry – something rendered easier by his age (III. 4, p. 63). That might be all right in youth, but it seemed less and less wise as time went on. For there is a wiser melancholy, wiser than all the melancholic ecstasies of natural man. It is the reverse of vehement, being inclined, rather, to stolidity. It keeps the soul at home and weighs all things in the quiet intimacy of that 'privat roome' at the back of the shop. Unlike ecstatic melancholy, it keeps madness well away.

Yet even that is not enough; the best of complexions may become too rigid. Complexions affect the very form, or soul, of men: '(B) We ought not to nail ourselves so strongly to our humours and complexions ... To keep yourself attached and bound, of necessity, to one single way of life is to be, but not to live. The fairest souls are those that have most variety and suppleness' (III. 3, beginning). He himself found that he passed easily from moroseness to joy, from bouts of melancholy humour to accesses of choler. That was, for him, more proof of human inconstancy.

Mad melancholics like Molière's Alceste cherish their rigidities and seek out dark corners in rural solitudes. Not so the wise: they keep up their commerce with friends, women, books. The solitude that Montaigne advocated was never a local one. It always emphatically remained a matter of the mind withdrawing, not from people nor from the body, but from an excessive engagement in outside affairs.

It took Montaigne a lifetime to reach his conclusions, since he worked from particulars not universals. An attractive humanist of an earlier generation, Celio Calcagnini, reminded his readers that young men can be knowledgeable when knowledge consists in universals; but they can hardly be wise; wisdom depends on particulars and so on a long acquaintance with the experiences that life can offer (*Opera*, 1544, p. 118; cf. *Nicomachaean Ethics*, VI, 8, 5-8).

Montaigne's wisdom brought him, by roundabout paths, from one particular, himself, to the whole of human kind.

Concordance of references

The references are arranged as they appeared above, under chapter and section. The first reference is to the *Edition municipale,* i.e. to *Les Essais de Michel de Montaigne publiés d'après l'exemplaire de Bordeaux, avec les variantes manuscrites & les leçons des plus anciennes impressions, des notes, des notices et un lexique, par Fortunat Strowski,* Bordeaux, 1906 (vol.I), 1909 (vol.II), 1919 (vol.III). The translations are given on the basis of this edition.

The second reference, V/S, is to the Villey/Saulnier edition: *Les Essais de Michel de Montaigne; édition conforme au texte de l'exemplaire de Bordeaux, avec les additions de l'édition posthume ..., par Pierre Villey, rééditée sous la direction et avec une préface de V-L. Saulnier,* Presses Universitaires de France, 1965.

The third reference, Platt., is to Plattard's edition: *Michel de Montaigne: Essais: texte établi et présenté par Jean Plattard,* Société 'Les belles lettres', 1947. Page numbers only are given, the volume being indicated by the chapter number of the *Essays.*

The penultimate reference, Pl., is to the Pléiade edition: *Montaigne. Oeuvres complètes. Textes établis par Albert Thibaudet et Maurice Rat; Introduction et notes par Maurice Rat,* 1962.

The final reference, S., is to my translation of *The Complete Essays* (both hardback and paperback editions).

1.1 Curiosity
II.12, p. 259 (V/S p. 525; Platt. p. 282; Pl. p. 506). S.588.
III.11, p. 316, (V/S p. 1032; Platt. p. 132; Pl. p. 1009). S.1168.

2.5 Montaigne's earlier writings
Estienne de La Boëtie, *Oeuvres Complètes,* ed. Paul Bonnefon, Bordeaux & Paris, 1892, p. 159.

2.6 The hunt for wisdom
II.10, p. 103 (V/S p. 409; Platt. p. 112; Pl. p. 388). S.459.
I.56, p. 408 (V/S p. 318, Platt. p. 245; Pl. p. 303). S.318.

2.7 Wider doubt
III.12, p. 322 (V/S p. 1037; Platt. p. 138; Pl. p. 1013). S.1173.

3.1 The earliest hints of melancholy
I.26, p. 227 (V/S p. 174; Platt. p. 50; Pl. p. 17). S.196.

3.2 Fashionable melancholy and sanguine melancholy
I.26, p. 227 (V/S p.174; Platt. p. 50; Pl. p.174). S.196.
II.17, p. 421 (V/S p. 641; Platt. p. 61; Pl. p. 624). S.729.
I.2, p. 9 (V/S p. 11; Platt. p. 9; Pl. p. 15). S.7.

3.3 True melancholia
I.26, p. 211 (V/S p. 162; Platt. p. 32; Pl. p. 162). S.182.

3.6 Montaigne's sanguine melancholy
II.1, p. 320 (V/S p. 568; Platt. p. 350; Pl. p. 551). S.640-641.

4.1 Poetic madness, or a lunatic's chains?
II.12, p. 32 (V/S p. 568; Platt. p. 350; Pl. p. 552). S.640-641.
II.12, p. 212 (V/S p. 492; Platt. p. 232; Pl. p. 471). S.548.
II.12, p. 212 (V/S p. 492; Platt. p. 233; Pl. p. 472). S.548.

4.2 Drunkenness and Platonic mania
II.2, p. 21 (V/S p. 347; Platt. p. 28; Pl. p. 330). S.390.
II.2, p. 21 (V/S p. 347; Platt. p. 29; Pl. p. 330). S.390.
II.2, p. 11 (V/S p. 340; Platt. p. 18; Pl. p. 322). S.381-382.

5.1 Privileged ecstasy
II.12, p. 149 (V/S p. 445; Platt. pp. 160-1; Pl. p. 422). S.496.
II.3, p. 37 (V/S p. 360; Platt. p. 46; Pl. p. 342). S.405.
II.12, p. 143 (V/S p. 440; Platt. p. 154; Pl. p. 417). S.439f.
II.12, p. 149 (V/S p. 445; Platt. pp. 160-1; Pl. p. 422). S.496.

5.2 Grace
II.12, p. 151 (V/S p. 446; Platt. p. 163; Pl. p. 424). S.498-499.
II.12, p. 152 (V/S p. 447; Platt. p. 164; Pl. p. 425). S.499.
III.2, pp. 32-5 (V/S pp. 813-15; Platt. pp. 40-3; Pl. pp. 791-3). S.916-919.
III.2, p. 37 (V/S p. 816; Platt. p. 45; Pl. p. 795). S.920.

6.1 Sexual ecstasy
III.5, p. 137 (V/S p. 892; Platt. p. 156; Pl. p. 870). S.1009.
I.28, p. 243 (V/S p. 186; Platt. p. 66; Pl. p. 185). S.210.

6.2 Sexual climaxes
III.5, p. 73 (V/S p. 844; Platt. p. 85; Pl. p. 281). S.952.
III.5, p. 74 (V/S p. 844; Platt. p. 85; Pl. p. 281). S.952.
III.5, p. 139 (V/S p. 893; Platt. p. 157; Pl. p. 872). S.1011.

III.5, p. 143 (V/S p. 896; Platt. p. 162; Pl. p. 875). S.1014-15.
III.5, p. 94 (V/S p. 859; Platt. p. 108; Pl. p. 837). S.970.
III.5, p. 118 (V/S p. 877; Platt. p. 135; Pl. p. 856). S.991.
III.5, pp. 137-8 (V/S p. 892; Platt. p. 156; Pl. p. 871). S.1009f.
III.5, p. 138 (V/S p. 893; Platt. p.157; Pl. p. 871). S.1010.

6.3 Poetic ecstasy
II.12, p. 208 (V/S p. 489; Platt. p. 228; Pl. p. 469). S.544f.
III.3, p. 46 (V/S p. 823; Platt. p. 54; Pl. p. 801). S.927.
II.2, p. 20 (V/S p. 347; Platt. p. 28; Pl. p. 329). S.390.

7.1 Melancholy retreat
I.26, p. 212 (V/S p. 164; Platt. p. 34; Pl. p. 163). S.184.
II.8, p. 69 (V/S p. 385; Platt. p. 78; Pl. p. 364). S.442f.
II.8, p. 79 (V/S p. 392; Platt. p. 89; Pl. p. 372). S.440f.

7.2 Bravery and pedantry
I.39, p. 314 (V/S p. 241; Platt. p. 140; Pl. p. 235). S.271.

7.3 A place of one's own
I.39, p. 315 (V/S p. 242; Platt. p. 142; Pl. p. 236). S.271.
I.39, p. 312 (V/S p. 240; Platt. p. 139; Pl. p. 234). S.269.
I.39, p. 313 (V/S p. 241; Platt. p. 140; Pl. p. 235). S.270.

8.1 Amorous zeal
I.56, p. 414 (V/S p. 321; Platt. p. 251; Pl. p. 307). S.360.
II.11, p. 131 (V/S p. 430; Platt. p. 141; Pl. p. 409). S.481.

8.2 Religious zeal
II.11, pp. 120, 127, 130, 133 (V/S pp. 422, 427, 429, 431; Platt. pp.
129, 137, 140, 143; Pl. pp. 400, 406, 408, 410). S.473, 480-482.
II.19, p. 463 (V/S p. 672; Platt. p. 104; Pl. p. 654). S.763.
II.30, p. 258 (V/S p. 197; Platt. p. 81; Pl. p. 195). S.223.

9.1 Change and decay
I.26, p. 187 (V/S p. 146; Platt. p. 7; Pl. p. 144). S.164.

9.2 Platonic forms
II.12, p. 366 (V/S p. 601; Platt. p. 399; Pl. p. 586). S.680.

9.3 How to know individuals
II.1, p. 8 (V/S p. 337; Platt. p.15; Pl. p. 320). S.379.

10.1 The footloose soul
III.2, p. 21 (V/S p. 805; Platt. p. 29; Pl. p. 782). S.908.
II.12, pp. 366-7 (V/S p. 601; Platt. p. 399; Pl. p. 586). S.680.
I.46, p. 359 (V/S p. 279; Platt. p. 192; Pl. p. 269). S.312

11.1 Experience
III.13 (1st sentence of *De l'experience*).
III.13, p. 360 (V/S p. 1065; Platt. p. 179; Pl. p. 1041). S.1207.
I.47, p. 368 (V/S p. 286; Platt. p. 203; Pl. p. 276). S.320.
III.13, p. 361 (V/S p. 1065; Platt. p. 180; Pl. p. 1042). S.1207
III.13, p. 363 (V/S p. 1067; Platt. p. 183; Pl. p. 1044). S.1210.
III.13, p. 363 (V/S p. 1067; Platt. p. 183; Pl. p. 1044). S.1210.
III.13, p. 375 (V/S pp. 1075-6; Platt. p. 195; Pl. p. 1053). S.1221.

11.2 Words
III.13, p. 366 (V/S p. 1069; Platt. p. 186; Pl. p. 1046). S.1213.
I.26, pp. 221-5 (V/S pp. 170-4; Platt. pp. 44-9; Pl. pp. 170-4). S.189ff.
I.40, p. 325 (V/S p. 251; Platt. p. 154; Pl. p. 245). S.281.

11.3 The end of Man
III.13, p. 364 (V/S p. 1068; Platt. p. 184; Pl. p. 1045). S.1210.

12.1 Satisfaction for the soul
I.39, p. 318 (V/S p. 245; Platt. p. 146; Pl. p. 239). S.275.

12.2 Asceticism
I.39, p. 319 (V/S p. 245; Platt. p. 146; Pl. pp. 239-40). S.275.

13.1 Authority
I.56, p. 408 (V/S p. 317; Platt. p. 245; Pl. p. 303). S.355.
I.56, p. 408 (V/S p. 318; Platt. p. 245; Pl. p. 303). S.355.
II.2, p. 18 (V/S p. 345; Platt. p. 26; Pl. p. 328). S.388.

13.2 The body and the Church
III.8, p. 186 (V/S p. 930; Platt. p. 210; Pl. p. 909). S.1084.
III.13, p. 420 (V/S p. 1108; Platt. p. 244; Pl. p. 1089). S.1259.

14.1 Physics or metaphysics?
II.10, p. 102 (V/S p. 409; Platt. p. 112; Pl. p. 388). S.459.
For Montaigne's indifference to natural philosophy, see II.12, p. 322
(V/S p. 570; Platt. p. 352; Pl. p. 553). S.642f.
III.13, p. 365 (V/S p. 1069; Platt. p. 185; Pl. pp. 1045-6). S.1212f.
III.13, p. 371 (V/S p. 1072; Platt. p. 190; Pl. p. 1050). S.1217.

14.2 Forma mentis
I.50, p. 387 (V/S p. 302; Platt. p. 224; Pl. p. 290). S.338.
III.2, p. 29 (V/S p. 811; Platt. p. 37; Pl. p. 789). S.914.

14.3 Honesty
III.2, p. 21 (V/S p. 805; Platt. p. 29; Pl. p. 782). S.908.
I.9, p. 40 (V/S p. 36; Platt. p. 45; Pl. p. 37). S.35.
II.18, p. 456 (V/S p. 666; Platt. p. 97; Pl. p. 649). S.757.

III.11, p. 318 (V/S p. 1033; Platt. p. 134; Pl. p. 1011). S.1170
III.9, p. 265 (V/S p. 991; Platt. p. 73; Pl. p. 969). S.1121.

14.4 The whole form of mankind
III.2, p. 21 (V/S p. 805; Platt. p. 29; Pl. p. 782). S.908

15.1 Aristotle and the glossators
II.6, p. 60 (V/S p. 379; Platt. p. 71; Pl. p. 359). S.426.

15.2 Botched forms and individual forms
III.2, p. 32 (V/S p. 813; Platt. p. 40; Pl. p. 791). S.916.

15.3 Angels and Cato
III.2, p. 23 (V/S p. 806; Platt. p. 30; Pl. p. 784). S.909.
I.37, p. 303 (V/S p. 231; Platt. p.127; Pl. p. 227). S.259.
III.12, p. 345 (V/S p. 1054; Platt. p. l64; Pl. p. 1031). S.1194.

15.4 The soul at home
III.2, p. 28 (V/S p. 810; Platt. p. 36; Pl. p. 788). S.913.

15.6 The greater forms
III.12, p. 323 (V/S p. 1037; Platt. p. 139; Pl. p. 1014). S.1174.
III.12, p. 325 (V/S p. 1038; Platt. p. 140; Pl. p. 1015). S.1175.

16.1 Wondrously corporeal
III.8, p. 186 (V/S p. 930; Platt. p. 210; Pl. p. 909). S.1054.

16.3 Platonists, Averroists, Realists, Nominalists ...and Ascetics
I.37, pp. 299-300 (V/S p. 229; Platt. p. 124; Pl. p. 225). S.257f.

17.1 Socrates triumphant
I.20, p. 104 (V/S p. 85; Platt. p. 114; Pl. p. 83). S.93f.
I.56, p. 415 (V/S p. 323; Platt. p. 252; Pl. p. 308). S.361.

17.2 Socrates criticised
III.13, p. 423 (V/S p. 1110; Platt. p. 247; Pl. p. 1091). S.1261f.

17.3 Me
III.13, p. 425 (V/S p. 1112; Platt. p. 249; Pl. p. 1092). S.1263.
III.13, p. 426 (V/S p. 1113; Platt. p. 251; Pl. p. 1093). S.1264.
III.13, pp. 427-8 (V/S p. 1113; Platt. p. 252; Pl. p. 1094). S.1265.

18.1 Divorce reform
III.13, p. 428 (V/S p. 1114; Platt. p. 252; Pl. p. 1094). S.1266.
III.13, p. 428 (V/S p. 1114; Platt. p. 252; Pl. p. 1095). S.1266
II.17, p. 419 (V/S p. 639; Platt. p. 58; Pl. p. 622). S.727.
II.17, p. 419 (V/S p. 639; Platt. p. 58; Pl. p. 623). S.727.

18.2 Archimedes' ecstasy
III.13, p. 429 (V/S p. 1114; Platt. p. 253; Pl. p. 1095). S.1267.

18.3 Eternity
III.13, p. 429 (V/S p. 1114; Platt. p. 254; Pl. p. 1095). S.1267.
III.13, p. 423 (V/S p. 1110; Platt. p. 247; Pl. p. 1091). S.1267.

18.4 Special privileges for Christian voluptuaries
I.56, pp. 412-13 (V/S p. 321; Platt. pp. 412-13; Pl. p. 306). S.358f.
III.12, p. 429 (V/S p. 1114; Platt. p. 254; Pl. p. 1095). S.1267.
I.23, p. 140 (V/S p. 111; Platt. p. 153; Pl. p. 109). S.125.

18.5 People like us
III.13, p. 429 (V/S p. 1115; Platt. p. 254; Pl. p. 1095). S.1267.
III.13, p. 429 (EM variant) (V/S p. 1115; Platt. p. 254; Pl. p. 1095). S.1267.

18.6 Socratic ecstasy and Christian coenobites
III.13, p. 429 (V/S p. 1115; Platt. p. 254; Pl. p. 1095). S.1268.
III.13, p. 430 (V/S p. 1115; Platt. p. 254; Pl. p. 1096). S.1267; (also for 18.7).

18.8 Astonishment
I.23, p. 169 (V/S p. 121; Platt. p. 168; Pl. p. 120). S.136.
I.23, p. 155 (V/S p. 121; Platt. p. 169; Pl. p. 120). S.137.

18.9 The whole being of man
II.36, p. 573 (V/S p. 757; Platt. p. 225; Pl. p. 735). S.856f.
III.13, p. 430 (V/S p. 1115; Platt. p. 255; Pl. p. 1096). S.1268.
III.5, p. 118 (V/S p. 878; Platt. p. 135; Pl. p. 856). S.993.
III.13, p. 427 (V/S p. 1113; Platt. p. 251; Pl. p. 1094). S.1265.
II.12, p. 305 (V/S p. 558; Platt. p. 334; Pl. p. 541). S.629.
III.13, p. 430 (V/S p. 1115; Platt. p. 254; Pl. p. 1096). S.1265.
II.3, p. 28 (V/S p. 354; Platt. p. 36; Pl. p. 334). S.397.
II.12, p. 202 (V/S p. 485; Platt. p. 221; Pl. p. 464). (For 'sacrilege' the text of 1588 read 'temeraire'.) S.540.
I.30, p. 258 (V/S p. 198; Platt. pp. 81-2; Pl. p. 195). S.223.
I.30, p. 257 (V/S p. 197; Platt. p. 81; Pl. p. 195). (For 'biaiz s'accommode la *voix* divine' the text of 1588 read 'biaiz se peut accommoder la parolle divine'.) S.223.

19.1 The higher forms again
II.30, p. 515 (V/S p. 713; Platt. p. 161; Pl. p. 691). S.808.
II.32, pp. 531-2 (V/S p. 725; Platt. p. 180; Pl. p. 703). S.821.
III.9, p. 241 (V/S p. 973; Platt. p. 47; Pl. p. 951). S.1101.

19.2 Sallies and constancy
II.29, p. 504 (V/S p. 705; Platt. p. 149; Pl. p. 683). S.799.

II.29, p. 505 (V/S p. 705; Platt. p. 150; Pl. p. 683). S.799.

19.3 *Inspiration, or unfair arguments?*
II.16, p. 404 (V/S p. 629; Platt. p. 44; Pl. p. 613). S.344.

19.4 *Judging revelations*
II.37, p. 608 (V/S p. 783; Platt. p. 262; Pl. p. 763). S.883.
III.11, p. 319 (V/S p. 1034; Platt. p. 135; Pl. p. 1012). S.1171.

19.5 *Imagination and ecstasies*
I.21, p. 123 (V/S p. 99; Platt. p. 134; Pl. p. 97). S.111.
I.20, p. 108 (V/S p. 88; Platt. p. 118; Pl. p. 86). S.97.
I.24, p. 162 (V/S p. 127; Platt. p. 177; Pl. p. 126). S.143f.
III.9, p. 270 (V/S p. 994; Platt. p. 78; Pl. p. 973). S.1125.
I.24, p. 163 (V/S p. 128; Platt. p. 178; Pl. p. 127). S.144.
III.11, pp. 315-17 (V/S pp. 1031-2; Platt. pp. 130-3; Pl. pp. 1008-9).
S.1166.
II.16, p. 399 (V/S p. 626; Platt. p. 38; Pl. p. 609). S.711.

19.6 *Geniuses are men*
II.12, p. 319 (V/S p. 568; Platt. p. 349; Pl. p. 568). S.640.
II.12, p. 320 (V/S pp. 568; Platt. p. 350; Pl. p. 552). S.640.
III.13, p. 419 (V/S p. 1108; Platt. p. 243; Pl. p. 1088). S.1258.
III.13, p. 425 (V/S p. 1112; Platt. p. 249; Pl. p. 1092). S.1263.
III.4, p. 63 (V/S p. 835; Platt. p. 73; Pl. p. 813). S.941.

Two Latin versions of Aristotle, *Problemata* 30.1 (abridged)

1. The version of Theodore Gaza

Cur homines, qui ingenio claruerunt, vel in studiis philosophiae, vel in Republica administranda, vel in carmine pangendo, vel in artibus exercendis, melancholicos omnes fuisse videmus? & alios ita, ut etiam vitiis atraebilis infestarentur ceu inter heroas de Hercule fertur? hic enim ea ipsa fuisse natura putatur; & morbum commitialem sacrum ab illo, & Herculeum prisci nominavêre. Puerorum quoque motio mentis idem hoc explicat & eruptio ulcerum quę mortem interdum antecedit. Id enim plerisque atra bile consistit. Et Lysandro Lacędemonio proximè ante obitum genus id ulcerum emersit. Adde Ajacem, & Bellerophontem, quorum alter penitus ad insaniam prorupit, alter loca persequebatur deserta. Unde illud Homeri:

> Ast hic quando etiam gravior diis omnibus errat,
> In campos solus latos: ínque avia rura,
> Ipse suum cor edens, hominum vestigia vitans.

Quinetiam plerósque alios ex heroum ordine morbo eodem laborasse compertum est. Annis verò posterioribus Empedoclem, Socratem, Platonem & alios complures viros insignes hoc fuisse habitu novimus, atque etiam partem ordinis poëtarum ampliorem. Nam & multos id genus hominum morbi ob ejusmodi habitum corporis exercent, & aliqui suapte natura in eos ipsos affectus perspicuè vergunt: omnes tamen ferè, ut dictum jam est, natura hujusmodi extitere. Ergo causam primùm exemplo haud sanè incommodo vini capiemus. Vinum enim immodicum tales maximè homines reddere videtur, quales melancholicos esse affirmamus, morésque varios id condit, cùm bibitur, ut iracundos, humanos, misericordes, audaces, quorum nihil mel, aut aqua, aut lac, aut ejusmodi aliquid efficere potest. Intelligi planè quàm varios reddat homines licet, si quis potantes ipsum animamvertat, ut gradatim evariat. Ubi enim vinum hominem frigentem taciturnúmque à sobrietate accepit, paulo liberaliori poculo refovet, excitátque id verba: tum largiori potu verborum uberem, eloquentem, fidentémque reddit: posthac processu potandi ampliori, audacem propensúmque facit ad agendum: deinde pleniùs amplificato in contumeliam & petulantiam vertit: mox ad insaniam propemodum accendit: postremò, nimio ex potu resoluit, stultúmque agit, in modum eorum qui à pueris morbo laborant comitiali, aut etiam eorum qui vitiis atrae bilis majorem in modum continentur ... Si modum (atrabilis) excedit, hominem facit attonitum, aut obtorquentem, aut anxium, aut formidolosum: sed si admodum incalescit, securitatem animi, cantilenásque parit, & mentis alienationem, & ulcerum eruptionem, & alia pleraque generis ejusdem. Parti igitur hominum maximé victu quotidiano redundans, mores nihilò immutat, sed morbum melancholicum tantummodo creat. At quibus habitu natura tali constiterit, mox his multa & varia morum genera exoriuntur, prout scilicet alius aliam habitus intemperiem sortitus est. Exempli gratia, in quibus multa & frigida bilis est atra, hi stolidi sunt, & ignavi: in quibus permulta & calida, ii perciti, & ingeniosi, amasii, propensi ad omnem excandescentiam, & cupiditatem, nonnulli etiam loquaciores. Multi etiam propterea quòd ille calor sedimentis in vicino est, morbis vesaniae implicantur, aut instinctu lymphatico infervescunt, ex quo sibyllae efficiuntur, & bacchae, & omnes qui divino spiraculo instigari creduntur, cùm scilicet id non morbo, sed naturali intemperie accidit. Maracus civis Syracusanus poëta etiam praestantior erat dum mente alienaretur. At quibus minùs ille calor remissus ad medioritatem sit, ii prorsus melancholici quidem, sed longè prudentiores: & quanquam aliqua in parte minùs excedant, multis tamen in rebus caeteris sunt omnibus praestantiores, alij in studiis literarum, alii in artibus, alii in Republica ... Homines melancholici varii inaequalésque propterea sunt, quia vis atrẹbilis varia & inequalis est: quippe quẹ vehementer, tum frigida tum calida reddi eadem possit. Et quoniam vim eandem morum obtinet instituendorum, (mores enim calidum condit, & frigidum omnium maximè, quae nostro in corpore habentur,) idcirco nos morum qualitate afficit quadam, informátque ut vinum, quod prout plus minúsve corpori intermistum infusúmque est, varios reddit. Flatuosum utrumque est, & vinum, & atra bilis. Cúmque sit, ut portio quoque aliqua temperata illius inaequabilis ordinis habeatur, flatúsque modo quodam acquiratur integrè, habitúsque respondere calidior frigidiórque possint ob exuperantiam qualitatis, hinc efficitur porrò, ut melancholici omnes non per morbum sed per naturam sint ingenio singulari.

From *Aristotelis Opera Omnia*, ed. Duval, Paris, 1629, f., vol. 4, pp. 815-19. (In some earlier versions there are minor variants in this text, as, for example, *hujuscemodi* for *hujusmodi*; cf. *Problemata Aristotelis cum duplici translatione antiqua verò & nova. s. Theodori Gazẹ cum expositione Petri Apone*, Venice, 1505, page E3vf. The older version given in this volume is interesting, but remote from Montaigne: it is the translation of Bartholomew of Messana, which usually accompanies the commentary of Peter d'Abano: see R.J. Durling, *A Catalogue of Sixteenth-Century Printed Books in the National Library of Medicine*, Bethesda, Maryland, 1967, p. 36, entry no. 286.)

2. The version of L. Septalius

Cur omnes, qui egregii fuerunt, vel in Philosophia, vel in civilibus, vel in poësi, vel in artibus videntur esse melancholici, & ita quidem, ut infestentur etiam à morbis, qui sunt ab atra bile, ceu fertur ab heroicis de iis, quae sunt circa Herculem? Etenim ille visus est factus hujus naturae, ut & propterea morbum comitialem ab illo denominabant antiqui Herculeum, & sacrum morbum. Et quae pueris contingit mentis commotio, hoc explicat, ut & eruptio ulcerum in coeta, quae mortem antecedit: id enim plerúmque ex nigra bile evenit. Contigit autem & Lysandro Laconi ante mortem fieri ulcera haec. Quin & praeterea quae contigerunt circa Ajacem, & Bellerophontem, quorum alter maniacus factus est omninò, alter loca prosequebatur deserta. Unde illud Homeri.

> *Ast hic quando etiam Diis gravior omnibus errat,*
> *In campos solus latos; inque avia rura.*
> *Ipse suum cor edens hominum vestigia vitans.*

Et alii ex Heroïbus simile quid passi sunt. Et posteriorum Empedocles, Plato, & Socrates, & alii plures notorum; & praeterea eorum, qui in poësi se exercuerunt plurimi. Multis siquidem talium fiunt morbi ab huiusmodi temperamento corporis. His autem inesse natura demonstrat ad has passiones repens. Oportet igitur causam sumere, primò ab exemplo argumentantes. Vinum etenim immodicum maximè tales reddere videtur, quales melancholicos esse affirmamus, & varios mores producit epotum, puta iracundos, humanos, misericordes, truculentos. Atqui neque mel, neque lac, neque aquam, neque aliquid similium videbit quispiam varios adeò facere, si quis observaverit, ut mutat bibentes à priori statu. Assumptum enim à frigentibus hominibus unde sobrii, & taciturni erant, paulò plus, potest loquaciores facere. Adhuc autem plus faciendos, & audentes ad aggrediendas actiones etiam timidos. Quin praeterea uberiùs epotum contumeliosos, deinde maniacos; si verò valdè in bibendo excedatur, dissoluit, & facit stupidos, sicut ex pueris laborantes morbo comitiali, aut laborantes vehementi melancholia ... Si verò superabundaverit in corpore, apoplexiam aut stupores, aut torporem facit, aut timorem: quando autem magis incalescit alacritates, mentis commotiones, & ulcerum exacerbationes, & alia similia. Multis igitur à quotidiano cibo facta diversitatem morum non producit, sed morbum solùm aliquem melancholicum. Quibus autem à natura consistat temperamentum, tale confestim isti secundùm mores fiunt omni genere morum variabiles pro alio, atque alio temperamento, verbi gratia; Quibuscunque quidem multa, & frigida inest, stolidi sunt, & inepti; quibus autem multa, & calida, maniaci, industrii, amasii, & propensi ad iram, & concupiscentiam, nonnulli etiam verbosi magis. Multi enim quòd calor is est prope locum mentis, morbis afficiunter maniacis, & lymphaticis. Unde Sybillae, & Bacchides: & numine afflati fiunt omnes, ubi morbo tales non fiant, sed naturali temperie: Malacus Syracusanus praestantior etiam erat poëta, dum mente alienaretur. At quibus caliditas magna ad mediocritatem reducitur, ii melancholici quidem sunt, sed prudentiores tamen, & minus admirandi; ad multa autem differentes in aliis. Siquidem ex iis, alii ad disciplinas, alii ad artes, alii ad gubernandam Rempublicam idonei redduntur. ... Quia facultas atrae bilis varia, & inaequalis est, homines melancholici varii inaequalésque sunt, quòd vehementer tum frigida, tùm calida eadem reddi possit, & quoniam vim habet formandorum (mores enim calidum format, & frigidum omnium maximè, quae nostro in corpore habentur) ideò nos, ut vinum, prout magis, minúsque corpori commixtum, facit nos tales, & tales secundùm mores; flatulentum enim utrunque & vinum, & atra bilis. Quoniam autem contingit & benè temperatam esse, & inaequalitatem obtinere, & benè quodammodò se habere, & ubi oportet calidiorem esse, & iterum frigidam, aut è contra, ob hos excessus, quos subit, efficitur, ut melancholici non per morbum, sed per naturam, excellant ingenio.

From *Ludovici Septalii Patricii Mediolanensis, Protophysici Regii in Mediolanensi Dominio, & Politicae Scientiae in patria Professoris, in Aristotelis Problemata Commentaria ab eo latine facta* ... Lyons, Claudius Landry, 1632, pp. 345-8. (Some discreet, and usual, changes in spelling and punctuation, in the interests of clarity.)

The passage cited has at the head a marginal note reading, 'Viri egregii in aliqua scientia, arte, aut facultate cur magna ex parte melanchonici'.

Select Bibliography

1. Texts

The best basic text remains that of Fortunat Strowski: *Les Essais de Michel de Montaigne, publiés d'après l'exemplaire de Bordeaux, avec les variantes manuscrites & les leçons des plus anciennes impressions, des notes, des notices et un lexique*, 5 volumes, Bordeaux, 1906-1933. (In the course of the work François Gebelin and Pierre Villey joined in the task of editing and annotating.) This text is normally called *L'Edition municipale* or *L'Edition critique*.

An excellent substitute for everyday use is the edition of Pierre Villey, re-edited by V.-L. Saulnier: *Les Essais de Michel de Montaigne. Edition conforme au texte de l'exemplaire de Bordeaux avec les additions de l'édition posthume* (etc.) 2 volumes, Presses Universitaires de France, Paris, 1965 (3rd edition, 1978). This text is known as Villey/Saulnier.

2. Concordance

Since the completion of this study, a *Concordance des Essais de Montaigne* has been established by R.E. Leake, assisted by D.B. and A.E. Leake (2 volumes, Droz, Geneva, 1981). It will save readers hours of not always fruitless search for a quotation or *locus*. It gives references which can be traced in the Villey/Saulnier edition and then (with the help of a table of page equivalents) in the *Edition municipale*, the *Pléiade* and the *Garnier* editions. It does not include the handy edition of Plattard for the Société 'Les belles lettres'.

3. Bibliographies

(a) For older works consult:

Plattard, J., *Etat présent des études sur Montaigne*, Paris, Les Belles Lettres, 1935

Tannenbaum, S.A., *Michel Eyquem de Montaigne*: A Concise Bibliography, New York, 1942

Cioranesco, A., *Bibliographie de la littérature française au XVIe siècle*, Paris, 1959

Giraud, J., *Manuel bibliographique littéraire* (*1921-35*), Paris, 1939; (*1936-45*), Paris, 1956

(b) For current and more recent works consult:

Bulletin de la Société des Amis de Montaigne

Bibliothèque d'Humanisme et Renaissance

Studi Francesi

Bibliographie internationale de l'Humanisme et Renaissance, Droz, Geneva, 1965 – in progress

Klapp O., *Bibliographie der französischen Literaturwissenschaft*, Frankfurt A/M., 1960 (in progress)

Rancoeur, R. (editor): *Bibliographie de la littérature française du moyen âge à nos jours*, Paris, 1962 (in progress); based on running bibliographies appearing in the *Revue d'Histoire littéraire de la France* (q.v.)

4. Further reading

(a) Basic studies

Three standard interpretations of Montaigne are conveniently summed up in three studies:

(i)   Pierre Villey: *Les Sources et Evolution des Essais de Montaigne* (2nd edition, Hachette, Paris, 1933). An impressive study, especially of sources and datings.

(ii) Hugo Friedrich: *Montaigne* (A Francke R.G. Verlag, Berne, 1949 (revised 1967); French translation by Robert Rovini, Gallimard, Paris, 1968. Useful, but weak on religion and the influence of Platonic and Aristotelian philosophy.

(iii) R.A. Sayce: *The Essays of Montaigne. A critical exploration.* Weidenfeld and Nicolson, London, 1972. Dr Sayce was at his best when treating the complexities of Montaigne's text.

The bases of all modern studies of Melancholia are:

(i)   Panofsky, E., and Saxl, F., *Dürers 'Melancholia I'*, Berlin and Leipsig, 1923

(ii) Klibansky, R., Panofsky, E., and Saxl, F.: *Saturn and Melancholy*, London, 1964.

A new interpretation of Montaigne is that of Antoine Compagnon: *Nous, Michel de Montaigne* (Editions du Seuil, Paris, 1980). It is the first published study I know which gives a large place to Montaigne's debt towards scholastic traditions; the work assumes the validity of some curious critical approaches but is well worth reading.

(b) Life of Montaigne

The two standard works, both excellent, are Donald M. Frame: *Montaigne: A Biography* (New York 1965) and Roger Trinquet, *Le Jeunesse de Montaigne* (Nizet, Paris, 1972).

(c) General

Works of particular interest to the subjects treated in this book are marked with an asterisk, but are not, otherwise, necessarily more important than the others.

A useful introduction to the kind of questions raised here is the last book of the late Dame Frances A. Yates, *The Occult Philosophy in the Elizabethan Age*, London, Boston and Henley, 1979.

Abel, G., *Stoizismus und frühe Neuzeit. Zur Entstehungsgeschichte modernen Denkens im Felde von Ethik und Politik*, Berlin, 1978

*Agrippa, H.C., *De Vanitate omnium scientiarum et excellentia Verbi Dei*, in *Opera*, 2 volumes, Lyons, 1531

A Lapide, Cornelius; S.J., *In Omnes Divi Pauli Epistolas Commentaria*; editio ultima aucta et recognita, Lyons, 1660

Allen, D.C., 'The degeneration of man and Renaissance pessimism', in *Studies in Philology* 35 (1938)

*Allen, D.C., *Doubt's Boundless Sea: Skepticism and faith in the Renaissance*, Baltimore, 1964

*Andrews, M., *Montaigne and Poetry* (unpublished Ph.D. thesis; University of London, Senate House, London WC1) 1973

Aneau, B., *Picta Poësis*, Lyons, 1568

*Anglo. S., '*Melancholia and witchcraft; the debate between Wier, Bodin and Scot*', in *Folie et Déraison á la Renaissance, 1973*, Brussels, 1976

*Antonioli, R., 'Aspects du monde occulte chez Ronsard' in *Lumières de la Pléiade, IXe stage Internationale d'Etudes Humanistes à Tours*, Paris, 1966, 224ff

*Aristotle, *De Anima*, ed. by the Jesuits of Coïmbra, Cologne, 1603

*Aristotle, *Metaphysica*, trans. by Bessarion; commentary by J. Arguropoulos; edited by J. Lefèvre d'Etaples (Faber), Paris, 1515

*Aristotle, *Metaphysica*, commentaries by P. Fonesca, Rome, 1577

*Aristotle, *Paraphrasis in xiiii libros de prima philosophia, Antonio Scayno auctore*, with text, trans. Bessarion, Rome, 1587

*Aristotle, *Problemata*, with two Latin translations, an 'Antiqua' (by Bartholomew of Messana) and a modern (by Theodore Gaza), Paris, 1520. See Appendix A

Aulotte, R., *Amyot et Plutarque: la tradition des 'Moralia' au XVIes*, Geneva, 1965

*Babb, L., *The Elizabethan Malady: a study of melancholia in English literature from 1580 to 1640*, East Lancing (Michigan) 1951

*Babb, L., *Sanity in Bedlam: a study of Robert Burton's Anatomy of*

Melancholy, East Lancing (Michigan) 1959

Baraz, M., *L'Etre et la connaissance selon Montaigne*, Paris, 1968

*Bernardus, *Comensis: Lucerna inquisitorum haereticorum pravitatis*, in *Tractatus juris civilis* (q.v.)

*Bernoulli, R., 'La mise à l'index des *Essais* de Montaigne', *Bulletin de la Société des Amis de Montaigne* 4, 8 (1966) 4f

Blinkenberg, A., 'Quel sens Montaigne a-t-il voulu donner au mot *Essais* dans le titre de son oeuvre?' *BSAM* 3, 29 (1964) 22f

Boas, G., *The 'Happy Beast' in French Thought of the Seventeenth Century*, Baltimore, 1933

Boase, A.M., *The Fortunes of Montaigne: a history of the Essays in France, 1580-1669*, London, 1935

Boase, A.M., 'Montaigne et les Sorcières,' in *Culture et politique en France à l'époque de l'humanisme*, ed. F. Simone, Turin, 1974

Boase, A.M., 'The early history of the *Essai* title in France and England', in *Studies presented to H. W. Lawton*, Manchester, 1968

*Bodin, J., *De la demonomanie des sorciers*, Paris, 1580

Boisset, J. (with Stegman, A.), *Aspects du libertinisme au XVIe siècle*, Paris, 1974

*Bolgar, R.R. (ed.), *Classical Influences on European Culture, 1500-1700*, Cambridge, 1976

*Boucher (Révérend-Père; de l'ordre de Saint-François), *Les Triomphes de la religion chrestienne*, Paris, 1628

Bouwsma, W.J., *The Two Faces of Humanism: Stoicism and Augustinianism in Renaissance thought*, in H. Oberman (ed.), *Itinerarium Italicum for P. O. Kristeller*, Leiden, 1975, 5ff

*Bowen, B., *The Age of Bluff: paradox and ambiguity in Rabelais and Montaigne*, Urbana, 1972

Bowen, B., 'Cornelius Agrippa's *De Vanitate*: Polemic of Paradox', in *Bibliothèque d'Humanisme et Renaissance* 34 (1972) 249f

Bowman, F.P., *Montaigne: Essays*, London, 1965

*Bright, T., *A Treatise on Melancholy*, London, 1586

Brown, F.S., *Religious and Political Conservatism in the 'Essais' of Montaigne*, Geneva, 1963

Brunschvigg, L., *Descartes et Pascal, lecteurs de Montaigne*, New York, 1944

*Brunyate, M., 'Montaigne and Medicine', in K. Cameron, *Montaigne and his Age*, Exeter, 1981

Burke, P., *Montaigne*, Oxford, 1981

*Burton, R., *The Anatomy of Melancholy*, ed. with an Introduction by H. Jackson, London, Melbourne and Toronto (Dent); Totowa, N.J., (Rowman and Littlefield) 1972 (and subsequent editions)

*Calanna, Petrus, *Philosophia Seniorum Sacerdotia & Platonica*, Palermo, 1599

Cameron, K., *Montaigne et l'humour*, Paris, 1966.

Cameron, K. (editor), *Montaigne and his Age*, Exeter, 1981

*Carreras Y Artau, T. and J., *Historia della filosofia española: filosofia cristiana de los siglos XIII al XV*, 2 vols, Madrid, 1939-1943

*Casaubon, M., *A Treatise concerning Enthusiasm, as it is an effect of Nature: But is mistaken by many for either Divine Inspiration or diabolical Possession*, London, 1655

*Castelli, E. et al., *L'Umanesimo e 'La Follia' – scritti di E. Castelli: M. Bonicatti, P. Mesnard; R. Giorgi; I.L. Zupnick: E. Grassi; A. Chastel; F. Secret; R. Klein*, Rome, 1971

*Castor, G., *Pléiade Poetics*. A study of 16th-century thought and terminology, Cambridge, 1964

Cave, T., 'Copia and Cornucopia', in Sharratt, P., *French Renaissance Studies*, (q.v).

Cave, T., *The Cornucopian Text: problems of writing in the French Renaissance*, Oxford, 1979

*Céard, J., *La Nature et les prodiges*, Geneva, 1978

*Cicero, *De Officiis*, with commentaries of Erasmus, Xytus Betuleius, Amerbach, F. Maturantius, C. Calcagnini; Paris, 1562

Clark, C., 'Montaigne and the Imagery of Political Discourse', in *French Studies* 24 (1970) 33ff.

Clark, C., *The Web of Metaphor: studies in the imagery of Montaigne's Essais*, Lexington (Kentucky), 1978

Clark, D.L., *Rhetoric and Poetry in the Renaissance*, New York, 1922

*Colerus, Jacobus, *De immortalitate animae*, Paris, 1591

*Coppin, J., *Montaigne, traducteur de Raymond Sebon*, Lille, 1925

Crahay, R., 'Controverses religieuses à propos de la *Republique* de Jean Bodin', in Peronnet, M. (ed.), *La Controverse Religieuse, XVIe-XIXe Siècles*, Montpellier, 1980, 57f.

Dagens, J., *Bérulle et les Origines de la restauration catholique* (1575-1611), Bruges, 1952

*Datus, A. (*Senensis*), *Opera*, ed. G. Datus, Sienna, 1503

Davis, N.Z. *Society and Culture in Early Modern France*, London, 1975

De Caprariis, V., *Propaganda e pensiero politico in Francia durante le guerre di religione* I (1559-1572), Naples, 1959

Dédéyan, Ch., *Montaigne chez ses amis anglo-saxons*, Paris, 1944

Delègue, Y., 'Du paradoxe chez Montaigne', in *Cahiers de l'Association Internationale des Etudes Françaises* 14 (1962), 241f.

Demerson, G., 'Un Mythe des libertins spirituels: le prophète Elie', in *Aspects*, ed. Boisset (q.v.)

Donaldson-Evans, L., 'Montaigne and Poetry', in *Neophilologus* 58 (1974) 360f.

*Draper, J.W., *The Humors and Shakespeare's Characters*, Durham (N. Carolina), 1945

Dréano, M., *La Religion de Montaigne* (2nd ed., revised) Paris, 1969

Dréano, M., *La Renommée de Montaigne en France (1677-1802)*, 2nd ed., 1961

*Ellrodt, R., *Genèse de la conscience moderne*, Paris, now printing.

Erasmus, D., *Opera Omnia*, ed. Leclerc, Leiden, 1703-06

*Ficino, M., *Opera Omnia*, Paris, 1641
*Foxius, S., *Phaedo, sive de immortalitate animae*, Basle, 1555
*Fracastorius, H., *De Sympathia et Antipathia Rerum*, Venice, 1546
*Fracastorius, H., *Opera Omnia*, Venice, 1555; also consulted, edition of Lyons, 1591
Frame, D.M., *Montaigne in France, 1812-1852*, New York, 1940
*Frame, D.M., *Montaigne's discovery of Man: the humanizing of a humanist*, New York, 1955
*Frame, D.M., *Montaigne's 'Essais': a study*, New Jersey, 1969
Frame, D.M., (with McKinley, N.B.), *Columbia Montaigne Conference Papers*, Lexington (Kentucky), 1981

Garapon, R., 'Quand Montaigne a-t-il écrit les *Essais* du livre III?', in *Mélanges Frappier*, Geneva, 1970, i, 321f.
Gaullieur, E., *Histoire de la Réformation à Bordeaux et dans le ressort du Parlement de Guyenne, 1523-1563*, Paris, 1884
Gilson, E., *Jean Duns Scot: introduction à ses positions fondamentales,* Paris, 1952
Glauser, A., *Montaigne paradoxal*, Paris, 1972
Gray, F., *Le Style de Montaigne*, Paris, 1958
Gray, F., 'The Unity of Montaigne in the *Essais*', in *Modern Language Quarterly* 22 (1961) 79f.
*Guastavinius, J., *Commentarii in priores decem problematicum sectiones*, Lyons, 1608
*Guazzo, Brother F-M., *Compendium Maleficarum*, ed. M. Summers, trans. E.A. Ashwin, London, 1929 (reprint 1970)

*Hallie, P.P., *The Scar of Montaigne: an essay in personal philosophy*, Connecticut, 1966
*Harris, C.R.S., *Duns Scotus*: vol. I 'The Place of Duns Scotus in Medieval Thought'; vol. II 'The Philosophical Doctrines of Duns Scotus'; New York, 1959
*Harrison, G.B. (ed.), The *Melancholike Humours* (of Nicolas Breton, 1600) *Edited with an essay on Elizabethan Melancholy*, London, 1929
Heger, H., *Die Melancholie bei den Französischen Lyriken des Spätmittelalters*, Bonn, 1967
Holyoake, S.J., 'The Idea of *judgement* in Montaigne', in *Modern Language Review* 63 (1968) 340f.
*Horace, *Opera*, ed. D. Lambinus, Paris, 1604

Icones, insignum aliquot virorum, Lyons, J. de Tournes, 1559
Ilsley, M.H., *A Daughter of the Renaissance: Marie le Jars de Gournay: her life and works*, The Hague, 1973
*Ives, *le Père* of Paris, *Morales chrestiennes*, Paris, 1648

Janssen, H.J.J., *Montaigne fidéiste*, Nijmegen and Utrecht, 1930

Jardine, L., *Francis Bacon: Discovery and the Art of Discourse*, Cambridge, 1974

Jehasse, J., *La Renaissance de la critique. L'Essor de l'humanisme érudit de 1560 à 1614*, St.-Etienne, 1976

Joukovsky, F., *Montaigne et le problème du temps*, Paris, 1972

*Keller, L., '*Solo e pensoso: Seul et pensif*: Mélancolie pétrarquienne et mélancholie petrarquiste', in *Studi Francesi* 17 (1973)

*Kellermann, F., 'Montaigne's Socrates', in *Romanic Review* 45 (1954) 170f.

*Kellermann, F., 'The *Essais* and Socrates', in *Symposium* 10 (1956) 204f.

Kleiber, C.C.L., *De Raimundo quem vocant de Sabunde vita et scriptis*, Berlin, 1856

*Klibansky, R.; Panofsky, E.; Saxl, F., *Saturn and Melancholy*, London, 1964 (see also Panofsky, E. and Saxl, F.)

Knights, L.C., *Drama and Society in the Age of Jonson*, London, 1937

Knox, R., *Enthusiasm*, London, 1950

*Kramer, H. with Sprenger, J., *Malleus Maleficarum*, translated by M. Summers, Arrow ed., London, 1971

Kritzman, L.D., *Destruction/Découverte: le fonctionnement de la rhétorique dans les Essais de Montaigne*, Lexington (Kentucky), 1980

*Kuhn, R., *Demon at Noontide; 'ennui' in Western literature*, New York, 1970

La Boëtie, E. de, *Discours de la servitude volontaire, suivi du Mémoire touchant l'édit de janvier, 1562*. ed. P. Bonnefon, Paris, 1922

*La Boëtie, E. de, *Discours de la Servitude Volontaire*, ed. M. Rat, Paris, 1963

La Charité, R., *The Concept of Judgment in Montaigne*, The Hague, 1968

La Charité, R. (ed.), *O un amy. Essays on Montaigne in Honor of Donald M. Frame*, Lexington (Kentucky), 1977

*Laski, M., *Ecstasy*, London, 1961

*Laski, M., *Everyday Ecstasy*, London, 1980

*Lefebvre, J., *Les Fols et la Folie*, Paris, 1968

Leff, F., *Medieval Thought*, Harmondsworth, 1958

Lienhard, M., (ed.); *Croyants et Sceptiques au XVIe siècle*; Strasbourg, 1981 (*Société savante d'Alsace et des Régions de l'Est* no.30)

Limbrick, E., 'Montaigne et S. Augustin', in *Bibliothèque d'Humanisme et Renaissance* 34 (1972) 49f

*Limbrick, E., 'Montaigne and Socrates', in *Renaissance and Reformation/Renaissance et Réformation* 9 (1973) 46ff.

Limbrick, E., 'Hermétisme religieux au XVIe siècle: le Pimandre de

François de Foix de Candale', in *Renaissance and Reformation/Renaissance et Réforme*, N.S. vol. 5, no. 1 (1981) 1ff.

*Limbrick, E., 'Was Montaigne really a Pyrrhonian?', in *Bibliothèque d'Humanisme et Renaissance* 39 (1977)

Lovejoy, A.O., *Essays in the History of Ideas*, Johns Hopkins, 1948

Lovejoy, A.O., *The Great Chain of Being. A Study of the History of an Idea* (1936) Harper Torchbooks, New York, 1960 (with subsequent reprintings)

Lubac, H. de, *Exégèse médiévale. Les Quatre sens de l'Ecriture*, Paris, 1959-64

*Lyons, B.G., *Voices of Melancholy: studies in literary treatments of melancholy in Renaissance England*, London, 1971

*Maclean, I., *Woman Triumphant. Feminism in French Literature, 1610-1652*, Oxford, 1977

*McConica, J., 'Humanism and Aristotle in Tudor Oxford', in *English Historical Review* 94, no. 371 (April 1979) 291ff.

*McFarlane, I.D., 'Montaigne and the concept of imagination', in *The French Renaissance: essays presented to A.M. Boase*, London, 1968

McFarlane, I.D., *Buchanan*, London, 1981

McGowan, M., *Montaigne's Deceits: the art of persuasian in the Essais*, London, 1974

McKinley, M.B., see Frame, D.M.

*Mercenarius, A., *Dilucidationes obscuriorum locorum philosophiae naturalis Aristotelis*, Leipzig, 1590

*Mercurialis, H., *Medicina Practica*, Frankfurt, 1602

Metschies, M., *Zitat und Zitierkurst in Montaignes Essais'*, Geneva and Paris, 1966

Michel, P., *Montaigne*, Bordeaux, 1969

*Moles, E., 'Pascal's use of *abêtir*', in *French Studies* 19 (1965) 379f.

*Montaltus, Hieronymus, *De homine sano*, Frankfurt, 1591

Moore, W.G., 'Montaigne's notion of experience', in *The French Mind: studies in honour of G. Rudler*, Oxford, 1952

Moore, W.G., 'Lucretius and Montaigne', in *Yale French Studies*, 38 (1967) 109f

*Mornay, P. de., *True Knowledge of Man's Owne Selfe*, trans. A. Munday, London, 1602

Moule, C.F.D. (ed.), *Miracles*, London, 1965

Muller, A., *Montaigne*, in the series *Les Ecrivains devant Dieu*, Bruges and Paris, 1965

Naudeau, O., *La Pensée de Montaigne*, Geneva, 1972

*Nutton, V., 'Medicine in the age of Montaigne', in *Montaigne and His Age*, ed. K. Cameron, Exeter, 1981

*Oberman, H.A. *Forerunners of the Reformation. The Shape of late Medieval Thought*, New York, 1966

*Oberman, H.A. 'From Occam to Luther', in *Concilium* 7, no. 3., Sept. 1967

*Oberman, H.A., '*Simul gemitus et raptus*: Luther and mysticism', in *The Reformation in Medieval Perspective*, ed. Stephen E. Ozment, Chicago, 1971

*Oberman, H.A. *Werden und Wertung der Reformation* (2nd ed, Tübingen, 1979) Translated and adapted as *Masters of the Reformation: the emergence of a new intellectual climate in Europe*, Cambridge, 1981

*Panofsky, E and Saxl, F., *Dürers 'Melencolia I'. Eine quellen und typengeschichliche Untersuchung*, Leipsig and Berlin, 1923 (see also Klibansky, R.). This is the basic work on the question of the *Melancholia* deriving from *Problemata* 30,1

*Peter of Abano, *Super Aristotelem* (i.e. on *Problemata*), Mantua, 1475

Phillips, M. Mann, *The Adages of Erasmus*, Cambridge, 1964

Phillips, M. Mann, 'From the *Ciceronianus* [of Erasmus] to Montaigne', in Bolgar, Q.V.

*Pizzorusso, A., 'Montaigne e la delimitazione del 'umano', in *Belfagor* 25 (1970) 277f.

Plattard, J., *L'Etat présent des études sur Montaigne*, Paris, 1935

Plattard, J., 'Le Système de Copernic dans la littérature française du XVIes', in *Revue du Seizième Siècle* 1 (1913) 220f.

Plutarch, *Les Oeuvres morales et meslées*, trans. J. Amyot. Reprint of 1st ed. (Paris, 1572) in *French Renaissance Classics*, Mouton, the Hague; Johnson Reprint Corporation, New York; S.R. Publishers, Wakefield (Yorkshire), 1971

*Popkin, R.H., *The History of Skepticism from Erasmus to Descartes*, 2nd ed., revised, Assen, 1964

*Porter, R., 'The Rage of Party: A Glorious Revolution in English Psychiatry?', typewritten, polycopied paper for the talk and discussion at the Wellcome Institute for the History of Medicine, London, 24 February, 1982

Preus, J.S., *From Shadow to Promise*, Harvard University Press, 1969

Regosin, R.L., *The Matter of My Book: Montaigne's Essais as the Book of the Self*, U. of California Press, Berkley (Calif.), 1977

*Reynolds, E., *A Treatise of the Passions and Faculties of the Soul of Man*, London, 1640

*Rice, E., *The Renaissance Idea of Wisdom*, Cambridge (Mass.), 1958

Sales, Françoise de, saint, *Oeuvres*
    (1) ed. A. Ravier and R. Devos, *Pléiade*, Paris, 1969
    (2), 1669 ed. Paris, F. Léonard, both volumes, 1669

*Sanchez, F. (of Toulouse), *Quod nihil scitur*, Lyons, 1581

Saunders, J.L., *Justus Lipsius. The Philosophy of Renaissance Stoicism*. New York, 1955

Sayce, R.A., 'L'Ordre des *Essais* de Montaigne', in *French Studies* 8 (1954) 1f.

Saxl, F., see Panofsky, E.

*Schmitt, C.B., 'Giulio Castellani (1528-1586): a sixteenth-century opponent of Scepticism', in *Journal of the History of Philosophy* 5, no. 1 (1967) 15ff.

*Schmitt, C.B., *Cicero scepticus: a study of the influence of the Academica in the Renaissance*, The Hague, 1972

*Schmitt, C.B., 'The recovery and assimilation of ancient scepticism in the Renaissance', in *Rivista Critica di Storia della Filosofia* 4 (1972) 363f.

*Sclafert, C., *L'Ame religieuse de Montaigne*, Paris, 1957

*Scot, R., *The Discoverie of Witchcraft*, London, 1584

Screech, M.A. 'An aspect of Montaigne's aesthetics', in *Bibliothèque d'Humanisme et Renaissance* 24 (1962)

*Screech, M.A., 'Medicine and literature; aspects of Rabelais and Montaigne (with a glance at the Law)', in Sharrat, P. (ed.), *French Renaissance Studies*, q.v.

*Screech, M.A., 'Commonplaces ... ' In Bolgar, R. (ed.), *Classical Influences on European Culture, 1500-1700*, Cambridge, 1976

Screech, M.A., *Rabelais*, London and Cornell U.P., 1980

*Screech, M.A., *Ecstasy and the Praise of Folly*, London, 1980

Screech, M.A., 'The "Mad" Christ of Erasmus and the legal duties of his brethren', to appear in *Essays in Early French Literature Presented to Barbara M. Craig*, ed. N.J. Lacey and J.C. Nash, York (South Carolina), 1982

*Sebond, R. de, *Theologie naturelle*, trans. Michel de Montaigne, Paris, 1581

*Sebond, R. de, *Theologia naturalis*, various editions consulted including Strasbourg 1496; Strasbourg 1501; Paris 1509; Lyons 1540; and Venice 1581

Sharratt, P. (ed.), *French Renaissance Studies, 1540-70; Humanism and the Encyclopedia*, Edinburgh, 1976

Simone, F., *Culture et politique en France à l'époque de la Renaissance*, Turin, 1974

*Skultans, V., *English Madness. Ideas on Insanity: 1580-1890*, London, 1979

*Smith, M.C., *Montaigne and the Roman Censors* (Etudes de Philologie ed d'Histoire), Geneva 1981

Spenser, T., 'Turks and Trojans in the Renaissance', in *Modern Language Review* 47 (1952) 331ff.

*Spinaeus, B., *Quaestio de Strigibus*, in *Tractatus juris civilis* (q.v.)

*Springer, J. with Kramer J., *Malleus Maleficarum*, see s.v. Kramer, J.

*Starobinski, J., 'Histoire du traitement de la mélancholie dès origines à 1900', in *Acta Psychosomatica*, Basle, 1960

*Starobinski, J., 'L'Encre de la mélancholie', in *La Nouvelle Revue Française* 123 (1963) 410f.

Starobinski, J., 'Montaigne et la dénonciation du mensonge', in *Dialectica* 22 (1968) 120f

Stegmann, A. 'Montaigne critico del pensiero unmanistico', in *Studi e Ricerche di Storia della Filosofia* 36, Turin, 1960 (see also Boisset, J.)

Stein, P., *Regulae Juris. From Juristic Rules to Legal Maxims*, Edinburgh, 1966

Strowski, F., *Montaigne* (2nd ed., Paris, 1931)

Tavera, J., *L'Idée d'humanité dans Montaigne*, 1932

Telle, E.V., 'A propos du mot *essai* chez Montaigne', in *Bibliothèque d'Humanisme et Renaissance* 30 (1968) 225f.

*Temkin, O., *The Falling Sickness*, Baltimore, 1974

*Thomas, K., *Religion and the Decline of Magic*, London, 1971

Tractatus juris civilis, Paris, 1584. Copy in Bodleian Library, at L.Z. 16, Art. Seld.

*Traverso, Edilio, *Montaigne e Aristotele*, Florence, 1974

Trevor-Roper, H.R., *The European Witch-craze of the Sixteenth and Seventeenth Centuries*, Harmondsworth, 1969

Trinkaus, C., *In Our Image and Likeness*, London, 1970

Trinquet, R., 'Les deux sources de la morale et de la religion chez Montaigne', *BSAM* 4 (1968) 24f.

Valleriola, F., *Enarrationes Medicinales*, Lyons, 1554

Villey, P., *Les Essais de Michel de Montaigne*, Paris, 1967

*Waddington, R.B., 'Socrates in Montaigne's *Traicté de la phisionomie*', in *Modern Language Quarterly* 41 (1980) 328f.

*Walker, D.P., *Spiritual and Demonic Magic from Ficino to Campanella*, London, 1958

Walker, D.P., *The Decline of Hell*, London, 1964

*Walker, D.P., *The Ancient Theology*, London, 1972

*Walker, D.P., *Unclean Spirits: possession and exorcism in France and England in the late sixteenth and seventeenth centuries*, London, 1981

*Walkington, T., *Optick Glasse of Humors: the Touchstone of a Golden Temperature*, London, 1607

Watson, A., *Roman Private Law around 200 B.C.*, Edinburgh, 1971

*Welsford, E., *The Fool*, London, 1935

*Wenzel, S., *The Sin of Sloth: 'Acedia' in medieval thought and literature*, Chapel Hill (North Carolina), 1967

*Wierus, J., *De praestigiis daemonum, et incantationibus ac veneficiis*, Basle, 1564; French translation by Grévin, *Cinq livres de l'imposture et tromperie des diables, des enchantements & sorcelleries*, Paris, 1569. It is useful to consult editions of *De praestigiis* from 1568 onwards, which contain an additional Sixth Book.

*Williams, G.H., *The Radical Reformation*, Philadelphia, 1962

Yates, F.A. *John Florio: the life of an Italian in Shakespeare's England*, Cambridge, 1934

*Yates, F.A., *The French Academies of the Sixteenth Century*, London, 1947

Yates, F.A., *The Valois Tapestries*, London, 1959; 2nd ed., 1975

Yates, F.A., *The Art of Memory*, London, 1966

*Yates, F.A., *The Occult Philosophy in the Elizabethan Age*, London, 1979

*Zanta, M., *La Renaissance du Stoïcisme en XVIe siècle*, Paris, 1914

Short additional bibliography

A. Legros, *Essais sur poutres. Inscriptions et peintures de la tour de Montaigne*, Klincksieck, Paris, 1999 (now printing). A fascinating study of how Montaigne decorated his tower and the light which inscriptions and paintings throw on to the *Essais*.

M.A. Screech, *Montaigne's Copy of Lucretius*, Droz, Geneva, 1998.

J. Starobinski, *Montaigne en mouvement*, Gallimard, Paris, 1982. (This important study and *Montaigne and Melancholy* were both with their respective publishers at the same time and so neither alludes to the other.) Well translated into English under the title of *Montaigne in Motion* by A. Goldhammar for the Chicago University Press, Chicago and London, 1985.

Index